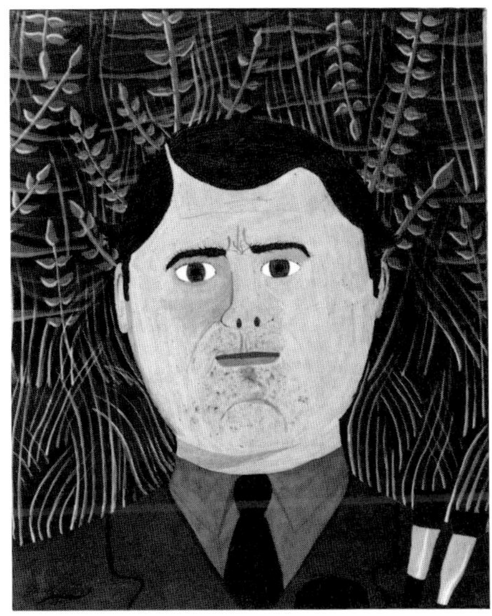

MY AMERICA

PAINTINGS AND COMMENTS BY OSCAR DE MEJ

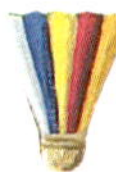

Introductory Text by Selden Rodman

Foreword by Gillo Dorfles

Harry N. Abrams, Inc., Publishers, New York

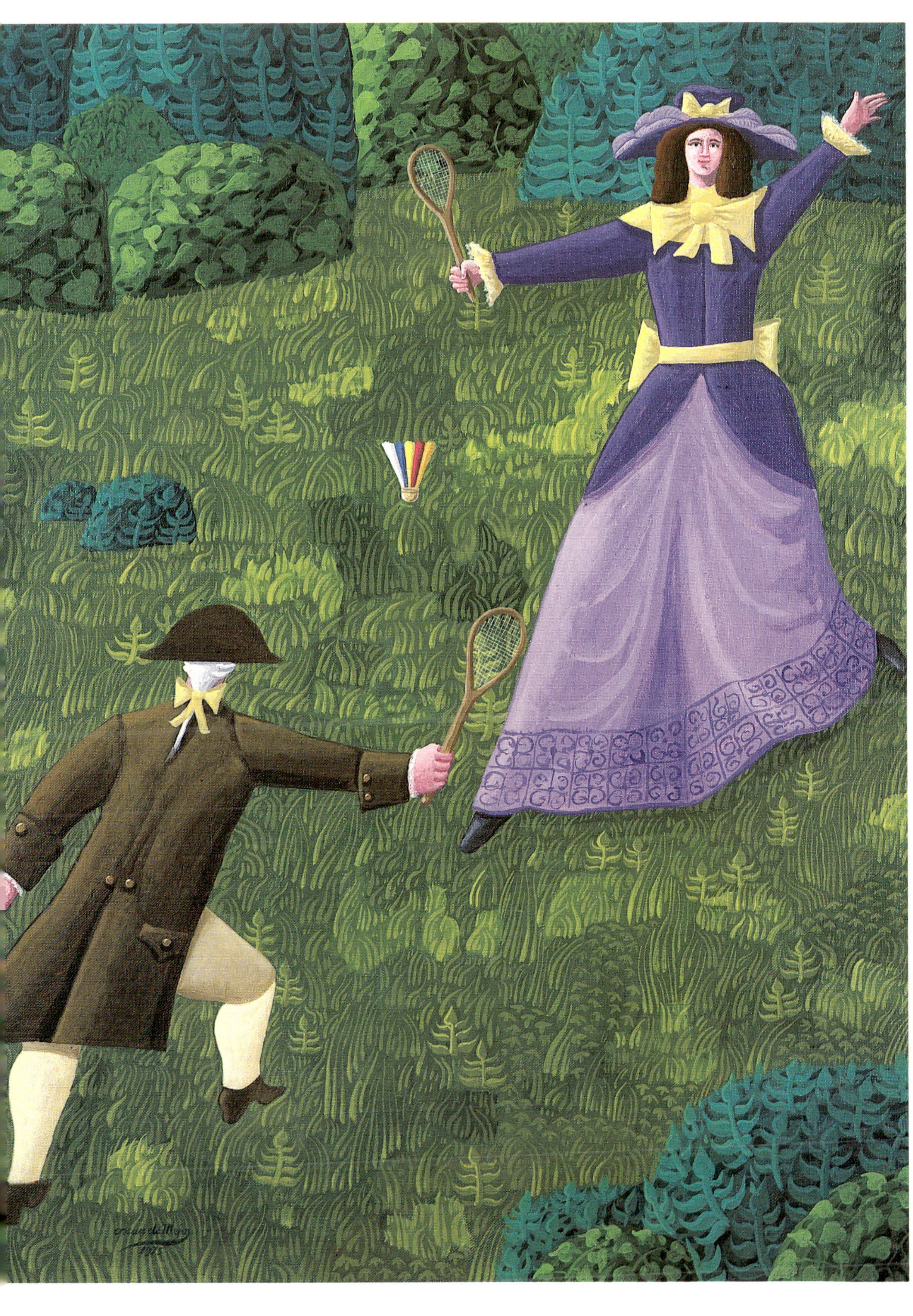

MY AMERICA

TO MY WIFE DOROTHY

Editor: Margaret L. Kaplan
Designer: Carol A. Robson

Library of Congress Cataloging in Publication Data
De Mejo, Oscar.
    My America.

    Bibliography: p.
    Includes index.
    1. De Mejo, Oscar.   2. United States in art.
I. Title.
ND237.D336A4   1983   759.13   82-22794
ISBN 0-8109-1804-8

Note: All works are painted in acrylic paints unless otherwise specified.

ON THE HALF-TITLE PAGE:
Self-Portrait as an Artist. 1949. Tempera on wood, 18 × 24″. Collection Ermanno Mori, Civitanova, Italy

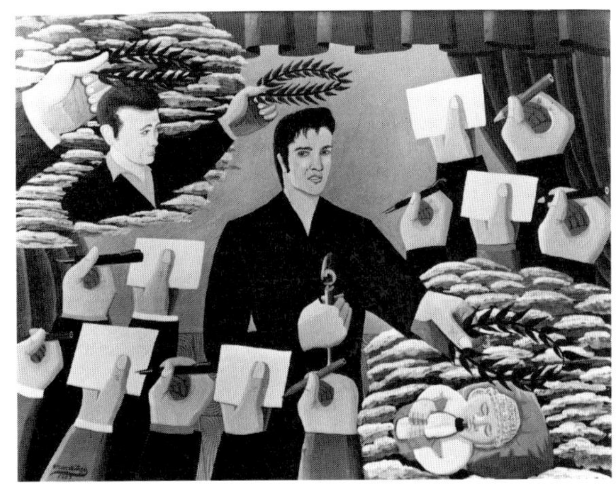

CONTENTS

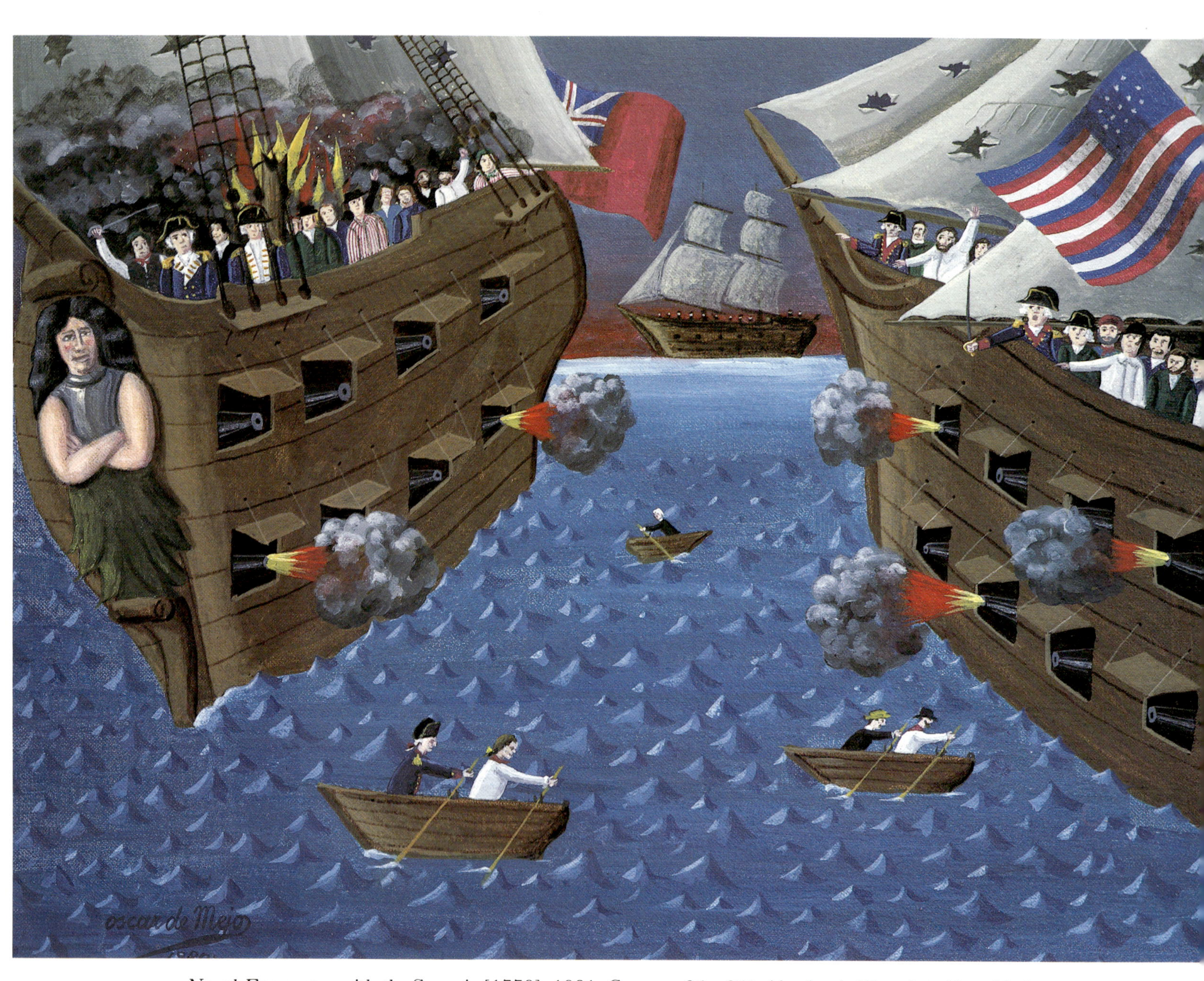

Naval Encounter with the Serapis [1779]. 1981. Canvas, 26 × 36″. Aberbach Fine Art, New York

6

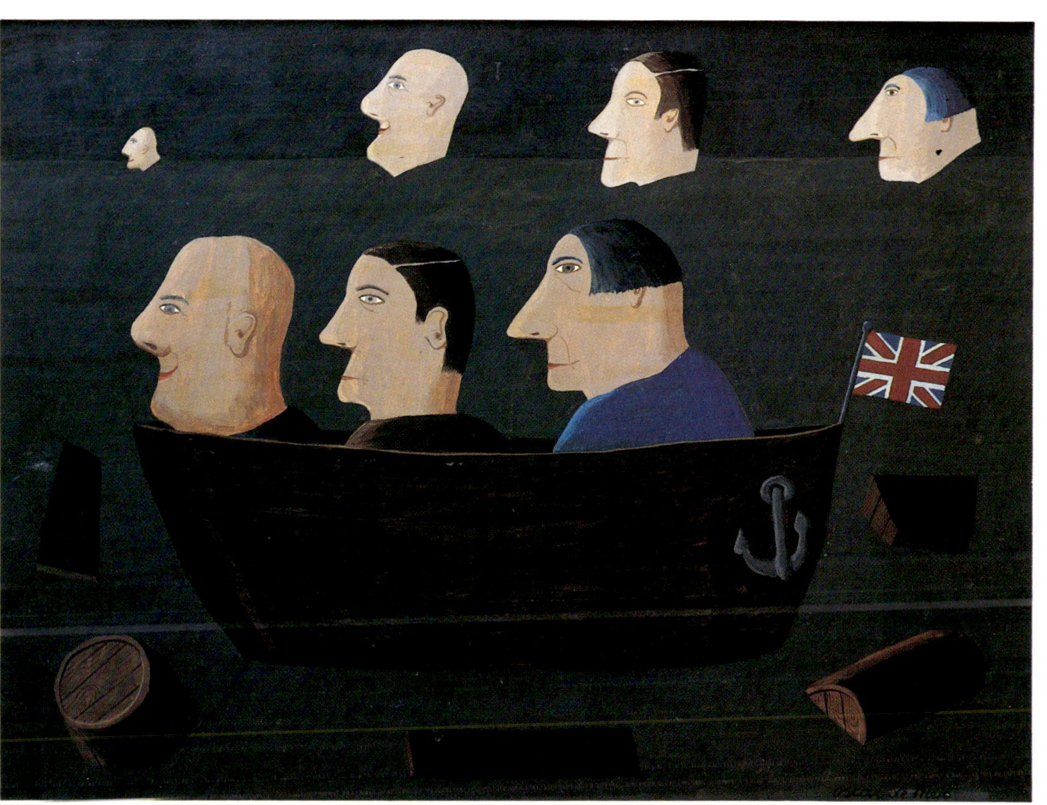

Disaster at Sea. 1952. Board, 15 × 20″. Private collection, New York

When John Paul Jones, at the head of the American fleet (four hardly seaworthy vessels), encounters the British ships Serapis *and* Countess of Scarborough *near the coast of England, he decides to engage the enemy.*

After a shipwreck, three sailors are still alive—their souls float above their bodies. A fourth sailor is dead and his soul is disappearing. The British flag is flying because most of the great sea disasters were British at a time when Britannia ruled the waves.

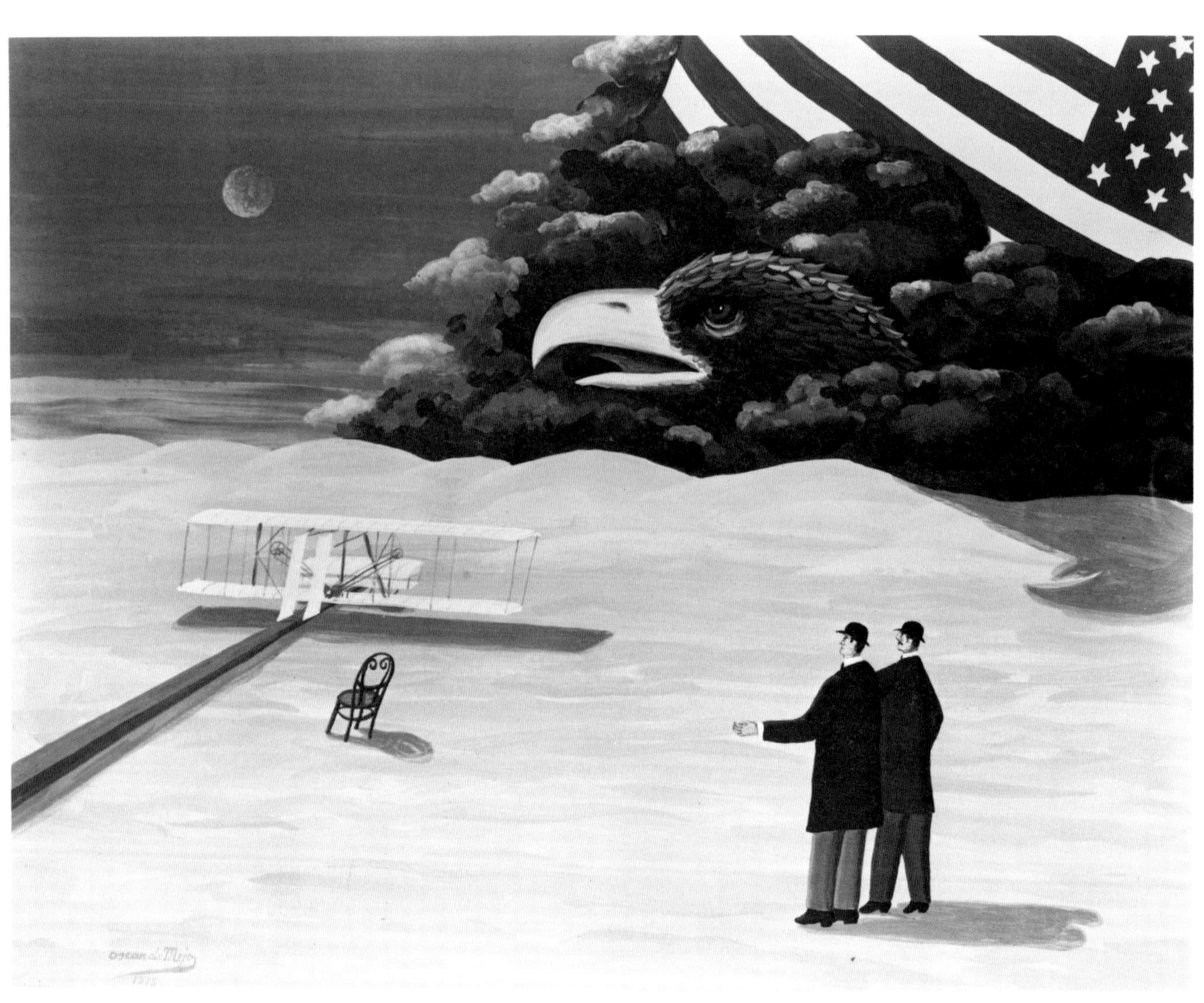

The Wright Brothers. 1975. Canvas, 20 × 26″. Collection Schenkers International, New York

FOREWORD
by Gillo Dorfles

Nowadays naturalistic representations that attempt to render the external world as "truthfully" as possible almost always seem tiresome. We admire certain distortions in the art of so-called "primitive" cultures—African, Polynesian—or in that of remote civilizations—Aztec, Maya—precisely because they violate commonplace naturalistic renderings that are all too often devoid of mystery and surprise.

This may be a subconscious reason for our interest in the work of modern primitive and "naive" artists. The distortions and absurdities—in perspective, in spatial relationships, in color—of their iconography offer us that magical, arcane element that allows us in our turn to imagine a world different from our own, an idyllic or barbaric world far from the mechanization, consumerism, and excessive rationality of our technological civilization.

But even with the best primitive painting, our satisfaction soon gives way to boredom. The repetitious forms, ingenuous pictorial rendering, and often banal "story" weary us and leave us finally indifferent.

This second phase, of disappointment and dissatisfaction, does not, however, take place with the work of that curious artist who is sometimes erroneously included in the great family of modern primitives: Oscar De Mejo.

De Mejo is *not* a primitive, nor is he an orthodox Surrealist, even though he often distorts reality. Rather, he is an ironic commentator on human and historical vicissitudes. His series of paintings devoted to the history of the American Revolution or to other pages of history probably owe their success to the ironic treatment of these Great Events, made playful and familiar by his brush. The artist strips these exploits of all true violence, looking on them with a benevolent and unconventional eye. The soldiers, officers, and bold knights with their caparisoned steeds, the swords and medals, the cannons, warships, and even airplanes are rendered in a style that makes them appear at the same time both believable and unbelievable, likely and absurd, historically unexceptionable (De Mejo studies every historical and technical detail with extreme care) but realistically improbable.

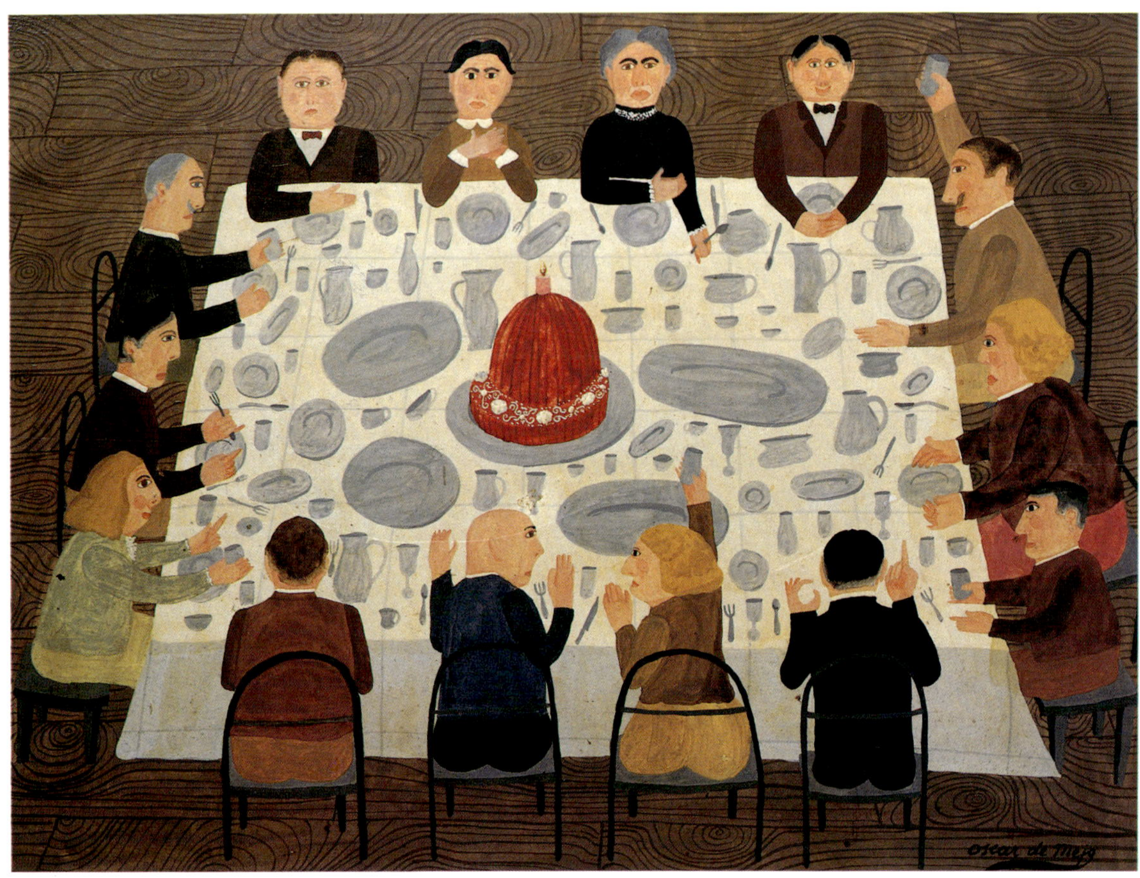

The Red Cake. 1952. Gouache on board, 14 × 18″. Collection Dorothy De Mejo, New York

This jovial gathering of gourmets has materialized thanks to the red cake, which is said to be one of the most precious American gourmet imports from Europe. Right now each guest is wondering whether he or she has been invited to avoid having thirteen at table.

The paintings celebrating the great episodes of war or revolution—and also the bourgeois and family scenes—indeed contain mockery and sarcasm. But it is a gentle sarcasm, incapable of wounding even admirers of those past exploits. Yet this alone is not the essence of De Mejo's originality. Its true source, I think, is something else and goes far back.

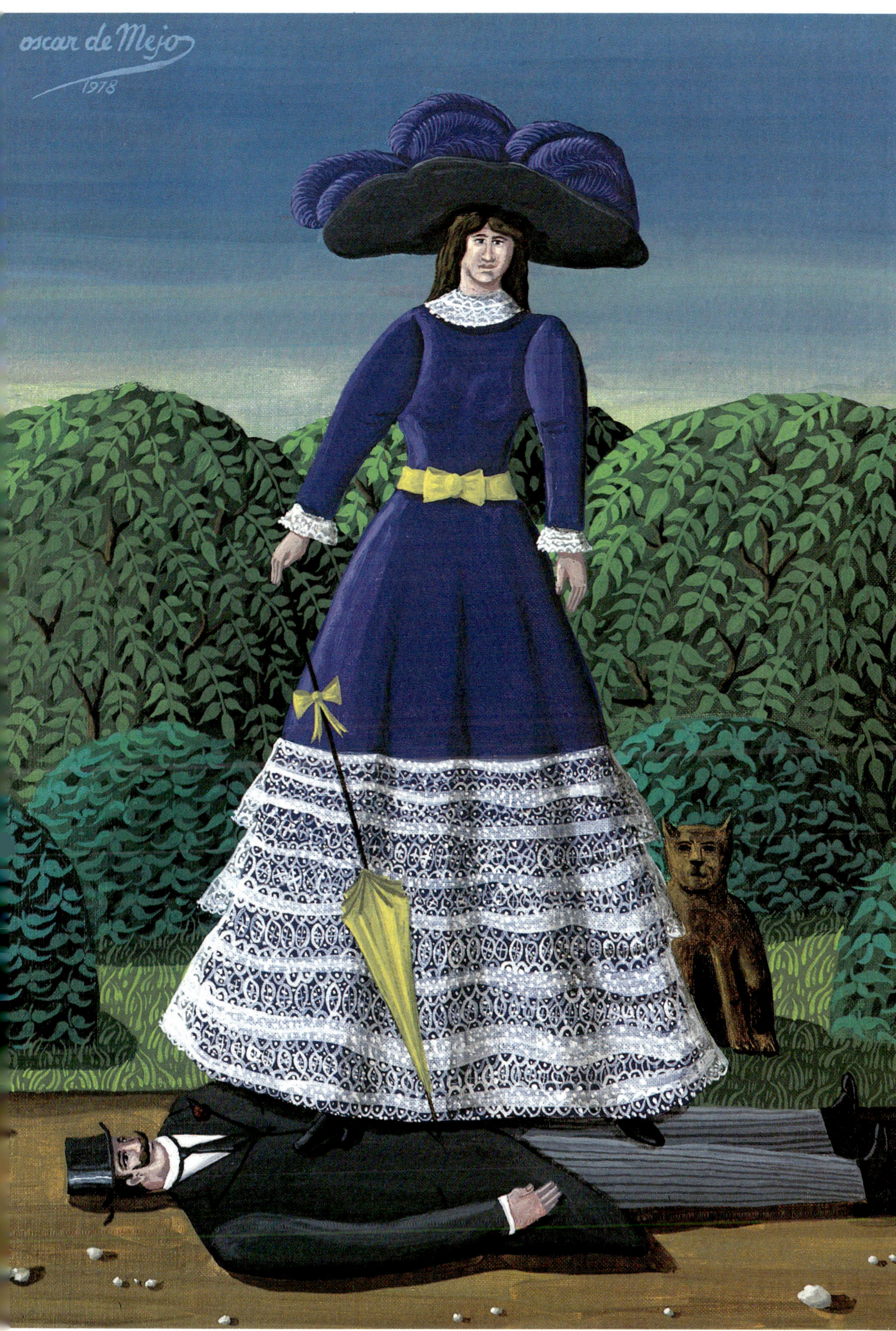

Lavinia Longfellow's favorite posture is the one here depicted. She loves her husband, but he has to yield.

A Domineering Woman. 1978. Canvas-board, 24 × 18″. Private collection, New York

Those who, like myself, have had the opportunity to follow not only Oscar's artistic progress but also his life, from his adolescent years on, know that the artist (who is from Trieste and was rather late in achieving fame) has lived and created since childhood and early youth in an atmosphere exactly corresponding to that of his paintings and drawings.

I remember, for instance, some of the drawings that Oscar enjoyed creating as a young boy. I say "enjoyed" because it was precisely through the creation of "narrative" drawings, illustrating "another" reality, that Oscar brought to life his state of mind, his view of the world. Already in those times his works were populated by familiar but comic characters—ladies or gentlemen rigid in their fossilized banality, petit-bourgeois figures clinging to a foolish but decorous way of life, malicious and garrulous old men, gossiping and vindictive old hags—often drawn in school notebooks or on scraps of paper and sometimes forming paradoxical yet familiar sequences, even complete stories.

This talent for rendering the absurdity of everyday life, unmasking conformity, making the paradoxical familiar allows De Mejo to "seem" at times a genuine primitive (to those who are unable to perceive the deeper and more hidden aspects). Yet it also allows him, as in some of his extraordinarily subtle illustrated stories for children, to confront certain apparently moralizing aspects from a viewpoint wholly detached from ordinary morality. Instead, he imbues them with naive and innocent sadism, the sadism of a child who pulls the tail off a lizard or enjoys teasing a rather deaf old aunt. Such elements of mischievous perversity still govern some of De Mejo's works today, from the notebooks devoted to childhood (but in reality more suitable for adults) to the large paintings filled with mock-heroic figures of American history—from Washington to Cornwallis, from the Battle of Cowpens to that of Yorktown—and finally (and these are the most magical and delightful of his works), such scenes of life, absurd rather than surreal, as *The Wright Brothers in Front of Their Famous Airplane* or the extraordinary nineteenth-century *Tennis Match*.

(Translated by John Shepley)

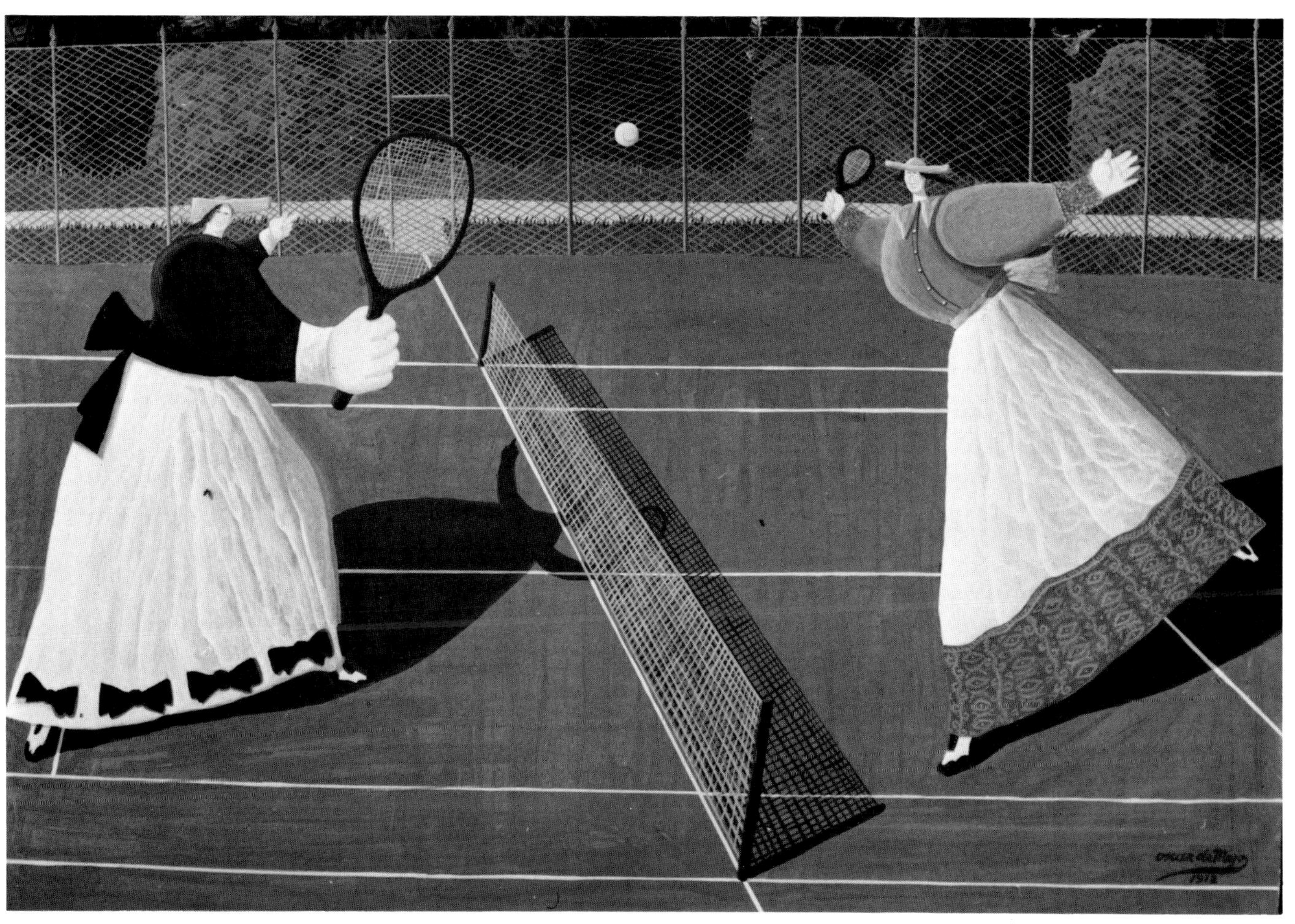

Tennis Match. 1972. Masonite, 32×46". Collection Dorothy De Mejo, New York

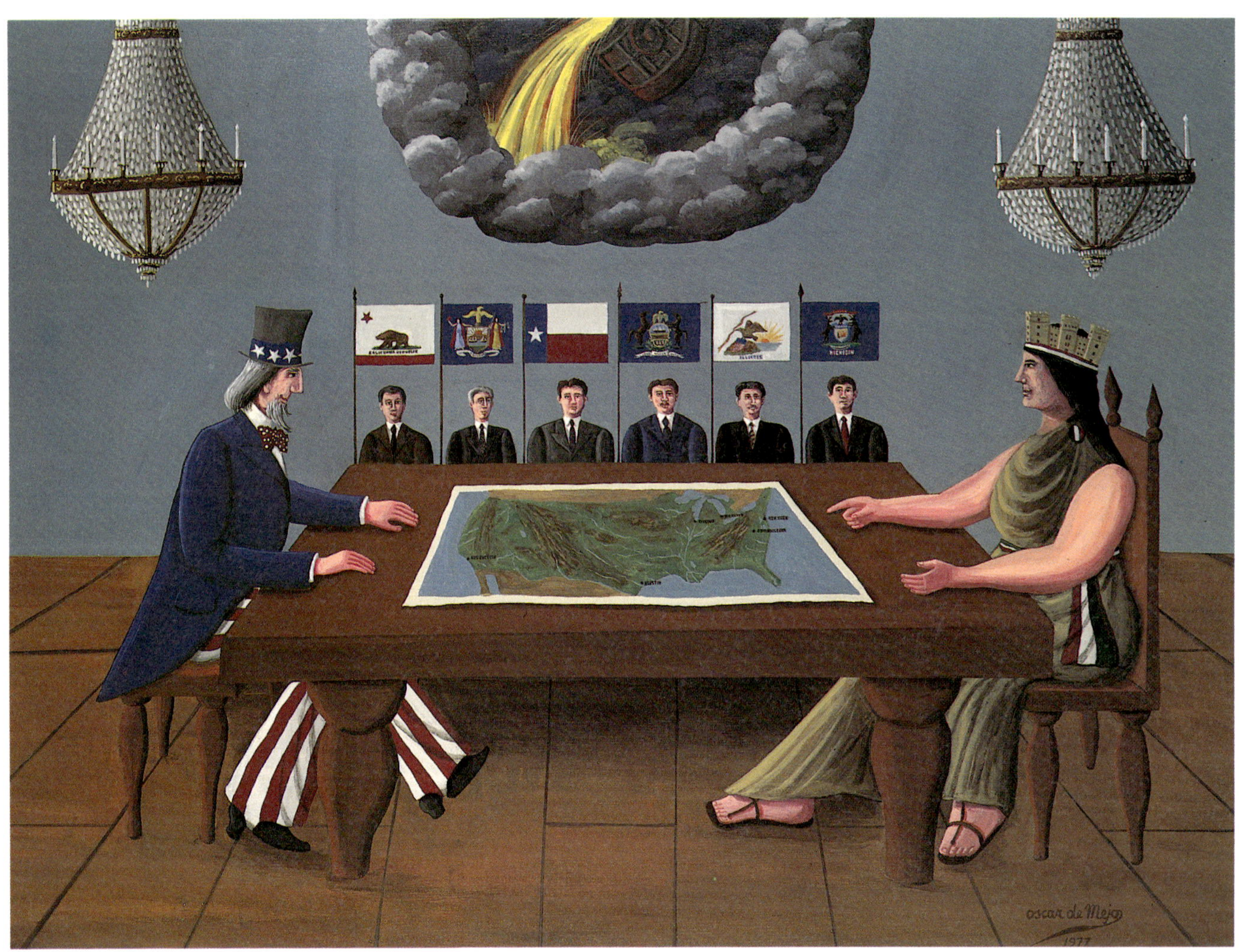

Uncle Sam and Mother Italy. 1977. Canvas, 36 × 50″. Siderexport, Genoa

THE ART OF OSCAR DE MEJO
by Selden Rodman

Oscar De Mejo's love affair with America began during his boyhood in Italy when he first heard American jazz. The only child of an Italian businessman and a Yugoslav *bel canto* singer, he spent his time drawing, composing music, and conjuring up the visions inspired by comic strips and horror movies. America was a fantasy, a beautiful never-never land, and it is that romance that he has continued to paint throughout the years he has lived here.

Untainted by the literal, his Founding Fathers, no matter how closely researched, are larger than life; his Revolutionary battles are disputes between gleefully arranged toy soldiers; his mysterious green vistas are greener than mere grass; and at least one benevolent spirit watches over almost every scene.

Indeed, the supernatural plays an important part in De Mejo's work, as it does in his life. The all-seeing Eye of God looks down, His hand appears in blessing, spirits float by on clouds, the departed return to watch a basketball game, a winged cherub bestows a laurel wreath on the head of the chosen. The spirits are painted as realistically as the people. For De Mejo they are as real. His entire *oeuvre* transcends mere historical and material "truth" and raises it to the level of legend.

It was not until 1947, after the war, that De Mejo actually came to the United States. By that time he had already had a life filled with excitement and incident. He had become a jazz pianist, had gone underground in Rome to escape the Fascist armies; he had even married a beautiful movie star and fathered a son. His life was sufficiently epic to reinforce his boyhood visions, and so when he began to paint seriously in Hollywood in 1949 he retained, as few adults do, that childlike sense of innocence, expectation, and joy that characterizes the best of self-taught painting.

Although he had filled notebooks with drawings while still very young, he had never taken any lessons in anatomy or gone to any art school. A well-educated, sophisticated man, he was well aware that he did not have the ability of a trained artist to produce works which were technically "correct." Yet he had seen the works of Early Renaissance masters like Sassetta and Giotto, modern naives like Henri ("Le Douanier") Rousseau, Camille Bombois, and Horace Pippin, and the Haitian school led by Philomé Obin and Hector Hyppolite. He was not, therefore, overly concerned by his lack of

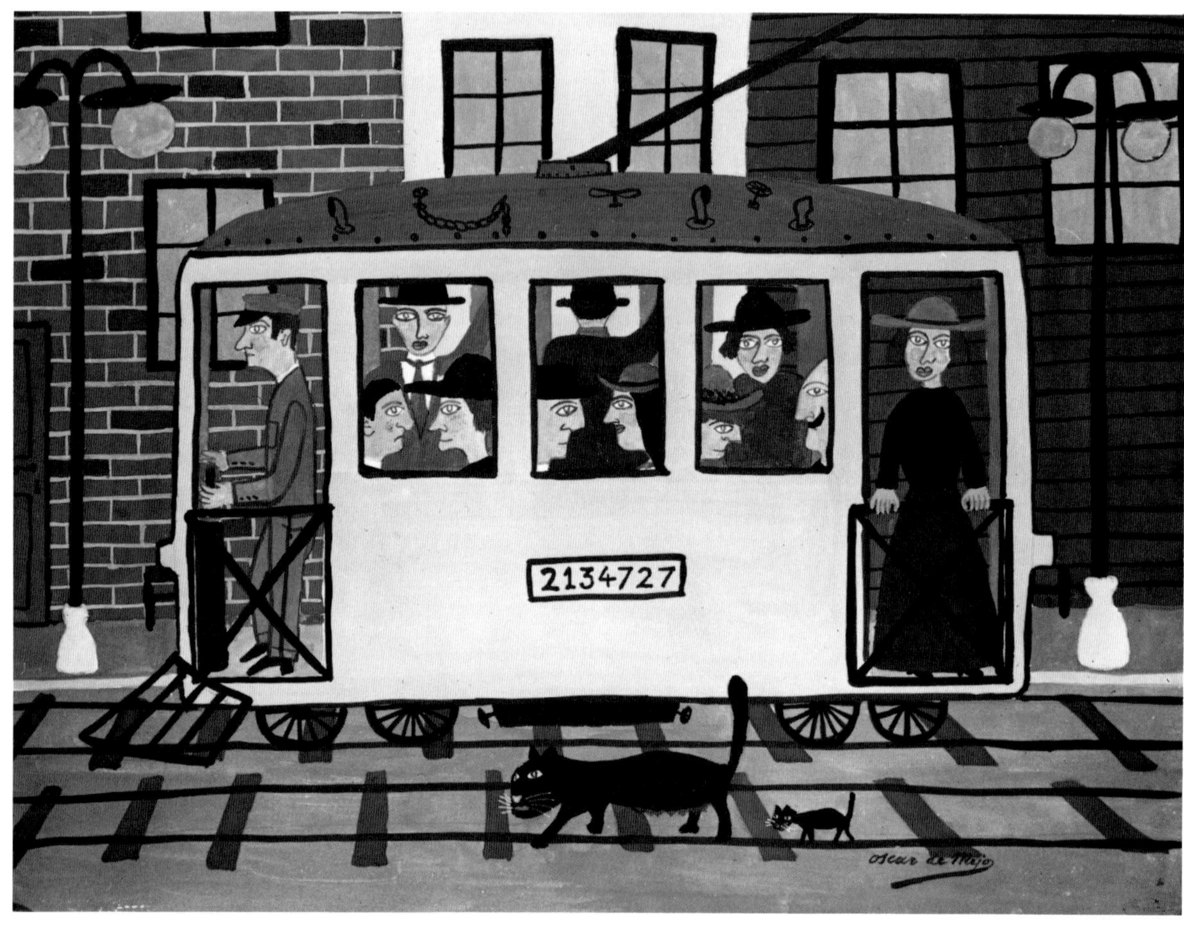

San Francisco Street Car. 1949. Tempera on board, 8 × 12″. Private collection, Los Angeles

skill in drawing the figure in correct proportion or landscapes in perfect perspective. His very clumsiness often helped him achieve the effects he desired.

His first works were small. His brush turns a San Francisco cable car into a crowded chariot peculiar to the New World. Engagingly gaudy Hollywood parties, absurd in their splendor, are embellished with bizarre detail. A harlequin, who may have been a psychological self-portrait, leaves the Old World behind and faces the

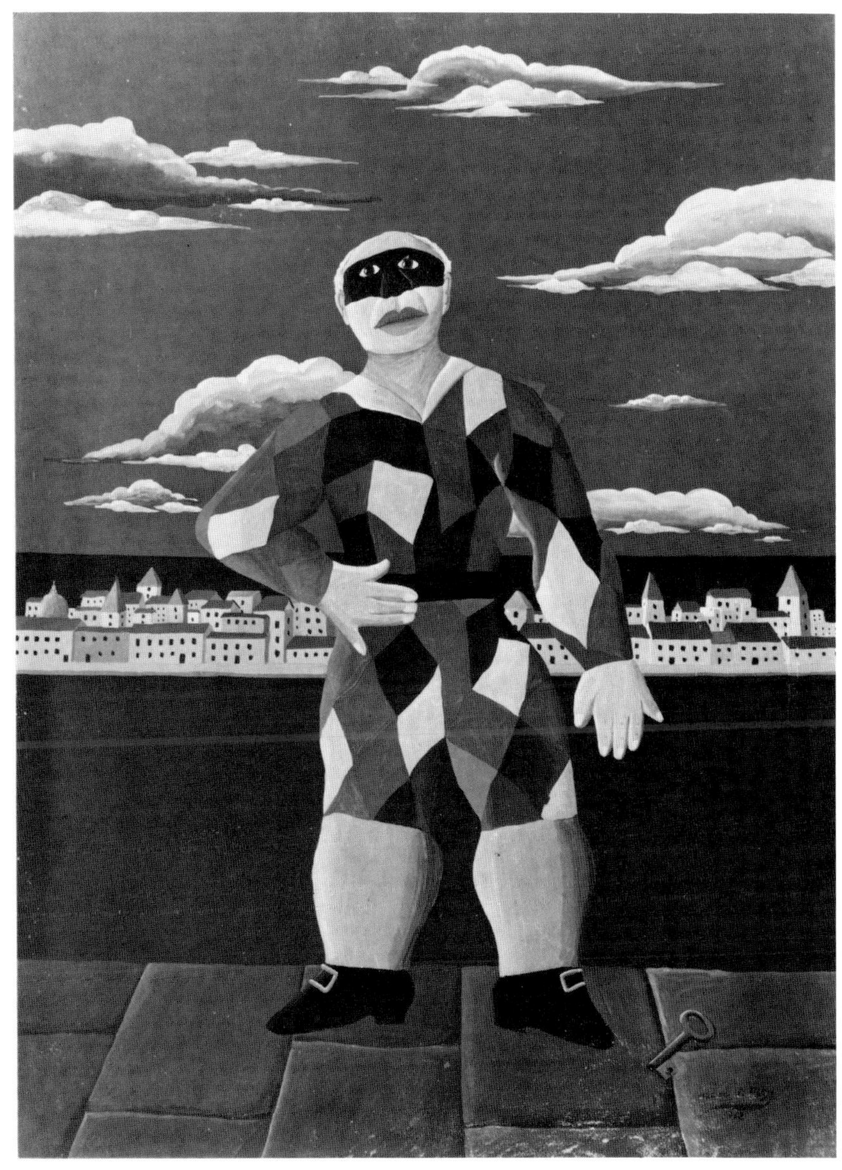

The Harlequin. 1952. Tempera on wood, 20×14″. Private collection

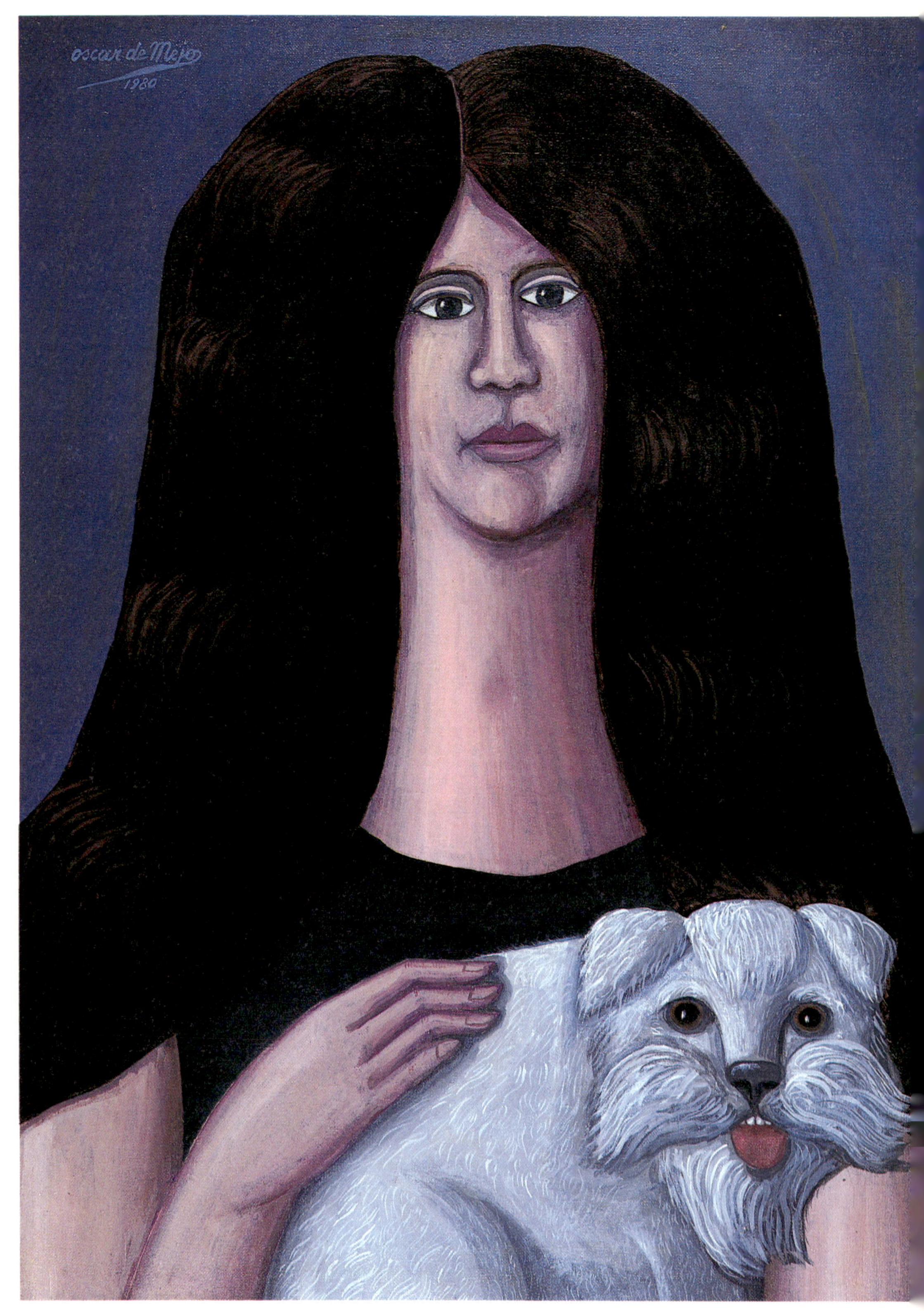

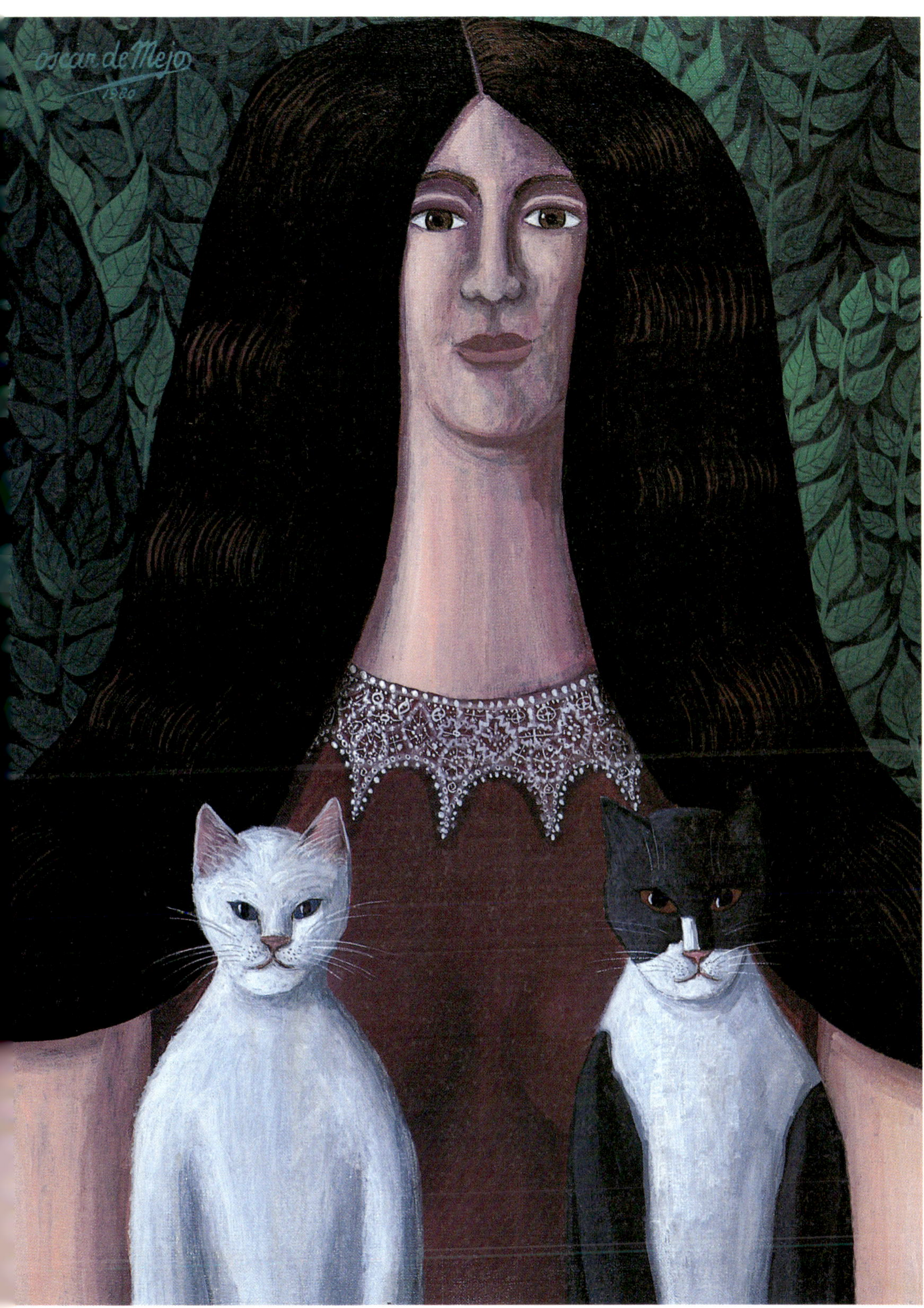

American Beauty I and *American Beauty II*. 1980. Canvas, 30×22″. Collection Dorothy De Mejo, New York

I observed these two American beauties at different windows of an ornate "palazzo" in Hollywood. The building was a faithful replica of some sixteenth-century Spanish royal castle. Were the two ladies replicas also?

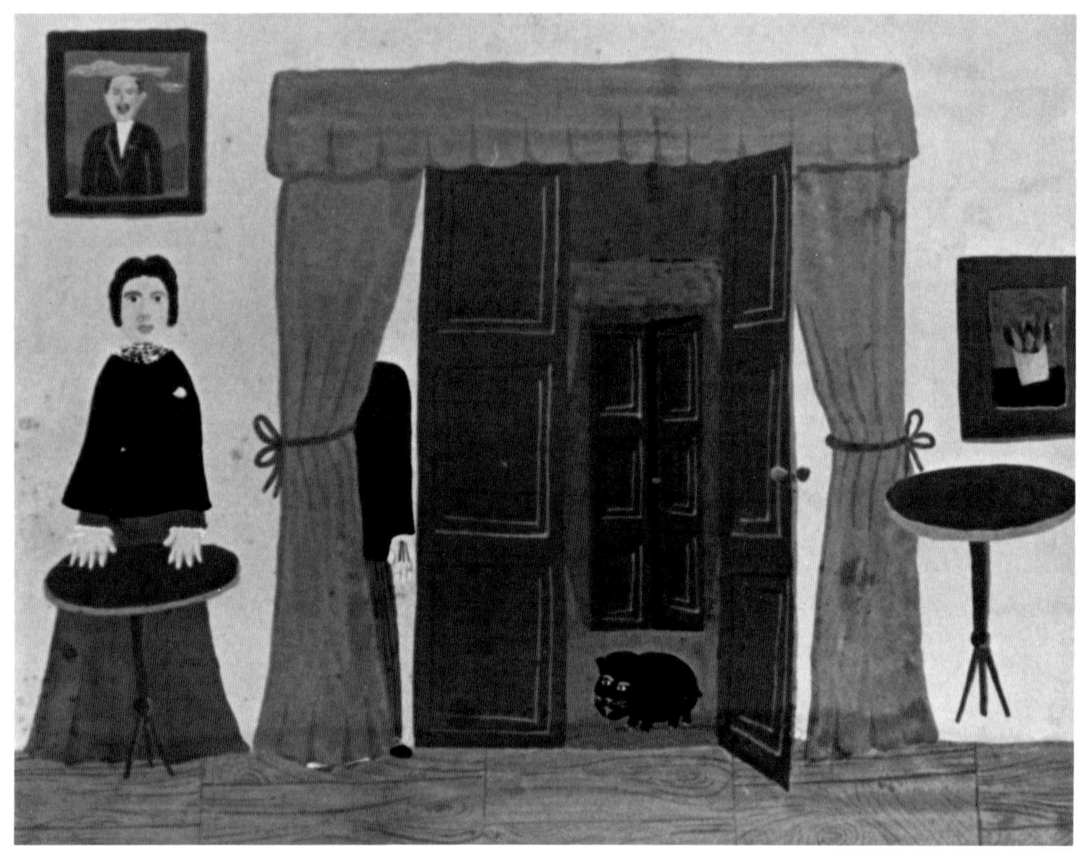

Eusapia Palladino. 1949. Tempera on wood, 9 × 12″. Private collection

New: masked, uncertain, but with a golden key at his feet. The famous Italian medium, Eusapia Palladino, is shown elevating a table while a man hides behind a curtain and a sinister dog blocks the doorway. A *Christ in Hollywood*, surrounded by reporters, eventually germinated the future series "Jesus Visits New York." Misunderstood by the public, the pictures were not meant to be satirical, sacrilegious, or even socially critical. They were simply De Mejo's sense of fantasy at work. "Now what would happen if"—if these two worlds, the material and the divine, were to meet? This first group of paintings pointed the way, helping the artist find his real métier: historical paintings *in series*. It would not be until the 1970s that all of his strengths—including his gift for costume, fantasy, narrative, humor, and the supernatural—were to come together to form the most successful body of his work.

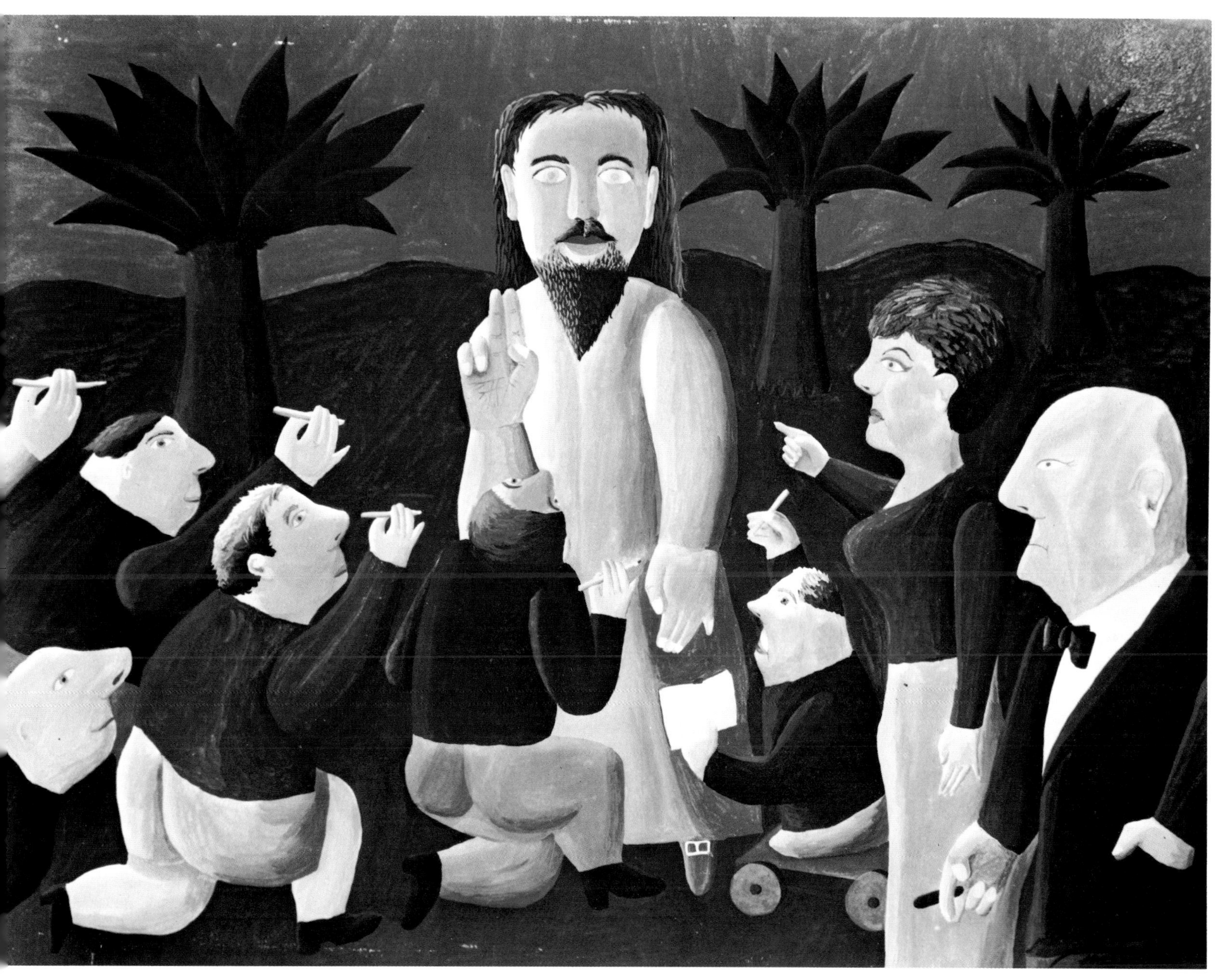

Christ in Hollywood. 1952. Tempera on board, 12 × 16″. Private collection, New York

Even though Oscar made drawings at a very early age (he is said to have drawn a train on the flyleaf of a *Brockhaus Lexikon* at the age of three), music was the initial passion of his life. But culture of any kind received little respect in the Trieste into which he was born in 1911. Not yet Italian, it was a tough commercial port of the Austro-Hungarian Empire. James Joyce was pointed out to Oscar as a rather eccentric teacher of English, while Italo Svevo, although hailed by the French as a second Proust, prided himself on being a banker.

Nevertheless, both of Oscar's parents were amateur singers who deeply loved opera. They took him often to performances of the great Italian melodramas by Rossini and Verdi, which were filled with the pageantry and elaborate costuming which turn up later in his historical paintings. But the scenes which his parents took so seriously seemed to him even then amusing if not downright absurd, and that same comic sense colors his historical paintings to this day.

His musical interests took a decided turn when in 1929 he saw Paul Whiteman's film *The King of Jazz*. George Gershwin immediately became his favorite composer. He secretly taught himself to play the piano while listening to the records of Fats Waller, Duke Ellington, and Mary Lou Williams—not musicians his parents would have appreciated. Later, at the universities in Siena and Padua where he studied law and political science to please his parents, he played piano in underground jazz clubs.

Finishing school, he found himself exiled to the accounting desk of an insurance firm in Trieste. From his desk he gazed wistfully at the harbor, where two great luxury liners, the *Saturnia* and the *Vulcania*, regularly set sail for America, capital of jazz.

At the beginning of World War II, when his firm moved him to Rome, Oscar finally got the opportunity for which he had been waiting. Almost immediately he quit his job for a much less secure one analyzing film scripts for a motion picture company. He was now composing songs which attracted the admiration of Vittorio De Sica, the leading Italian matinee idol, who was planning his first film.

As the Italian side of the war went from bad to worse, life for an anti-Fascist in Rome became dangerous. In the early days of the conflict he had joined an opposition group with his closest friend, an Italian of English-Jewish extraction named Paolo Rogers. When racial laws were enforced in Italy, De Mejo refused to give up his Jewish friends. After the Battle of Britain he wrote "The Adolf Hitler Blues" in English, and it became clandestinely popular. Some of the lyrics went:

> Adolf Hitler was his name
> His *Mein Kampf* he wrote in vain
> He was sure to win the War
> He was sure, now is no more

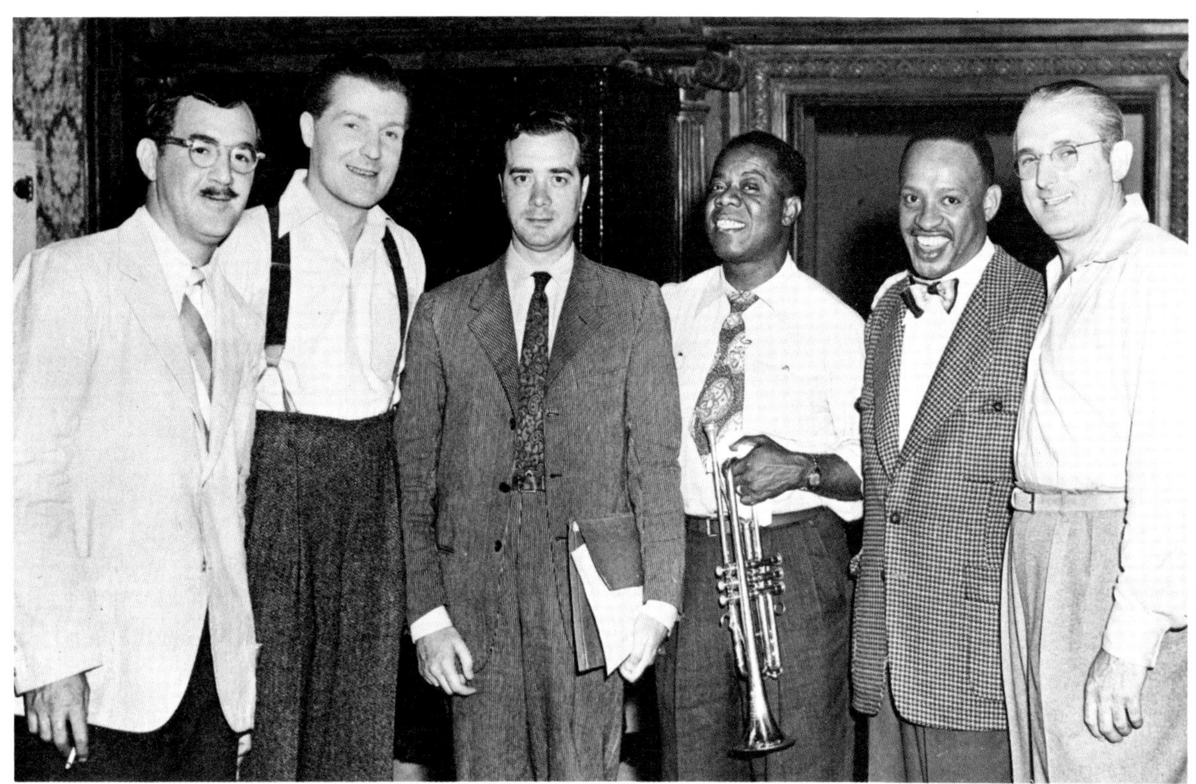

In 1950, at the Goldwyn Studio in Hollywood, with five of the greatest jazzmen. From the left, Benny Goodman, Charlie Barnet, the artist, Louis Armstrong, Lionel Hampton, and Tommy Dorsey.

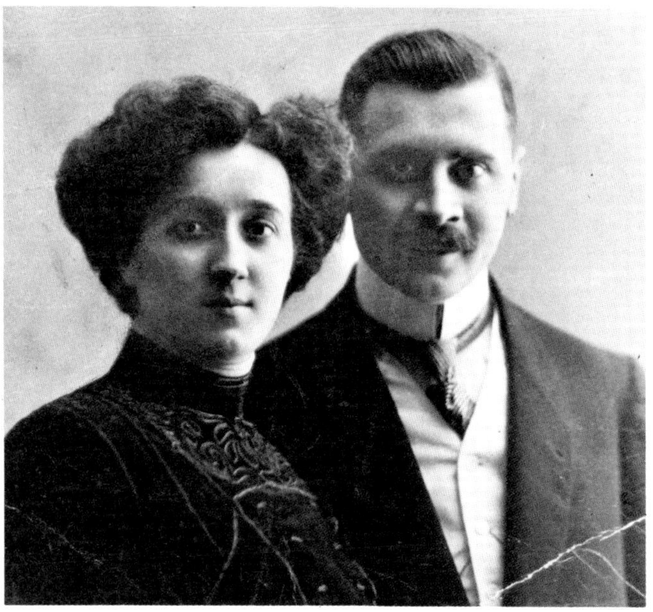

The artist's Mother and Father

In 1944, when the Germans were combing the streets for every able-bodied man to oppose the Americans, Oscar was forced to live from house to house and cellar to cellar. It was then that he met Alida Altenburger, herself in flight from the Nazis. Under the name Alida Valli, she was already the No. 1 Italian movie star. They fell in love, were soon married, and the first of their two sons was born in Rome shortly after the war ended. De Mejo's songs were being used in De Sica's films, and one American-style recording, "A Shopgirl's Song," became a Roman best seller. He also played piano in a fashionable nightclub, the Belisario, where the Tommies and the GIs covered the piano with money for his renditions of "Liza," "I Cried for You," and "Is You Is or Is You Ain't My Baby?"

All Oscar's dreams seemed to be coming true when Valli won a starring role in Alfred Hitchcock's *The Paradine Case* and she and Oscar took off together for Hollywood. For a time in 1947 their careers seemed to be orbiting together, and De Mejo was confident that he would conquer the musical world. One of his songs, "Bella Bimba," was launched by the Metropolitan Opera star Patrice Munsel on the RCA Victor label and by Dean Martin on Capitol Records. It was played and sung all over the world, but did not sell sufficiently to put Oscar in demand as a composer. It was a success performance-wise but never reached the top of the Hit Parade. The meshing of American music and Italian lyrics was proving a difficult hybrid. Oscar's English was not colloquial enough to produce mass market pop songs, and he refused to write the kind of Italian melodies which were considered "right" for his language. His musical career had reached its zenith—and its end.

Casting about for a new direction in which to grow, Oscar came increasingly under the influence of a force that had always affected him—the Supernatural. As a small boy he had been powerfully moved by horror films, especially *Nosferatu, der Vampyr*, an Austrian story set in nearby Transylvania. He was fascinated by the tales of Edgar Allan Poe, Gustav Meyrink, Hanns Heinz Ewers, and Camille Flammarion, studied the frightening photos of crime victims in Cesare Lombroso's *Medicina Legale*, the devilry in Meyrink's *The Golem*, and descriptions of what the mandragora root could accomplish when dug up at the foot of a gibbet in Ewers's *Alraune*.

His fascination with death and his subconscious fear of mortality and violence must have been greatly intensified when, at the age of seventeen, he watched his greatly loved mother die of cancer. Afterwards his grandmother took him to séances at which they tried to contact his mother. "They were not fake," he says today. "Many times we were able to reach her."

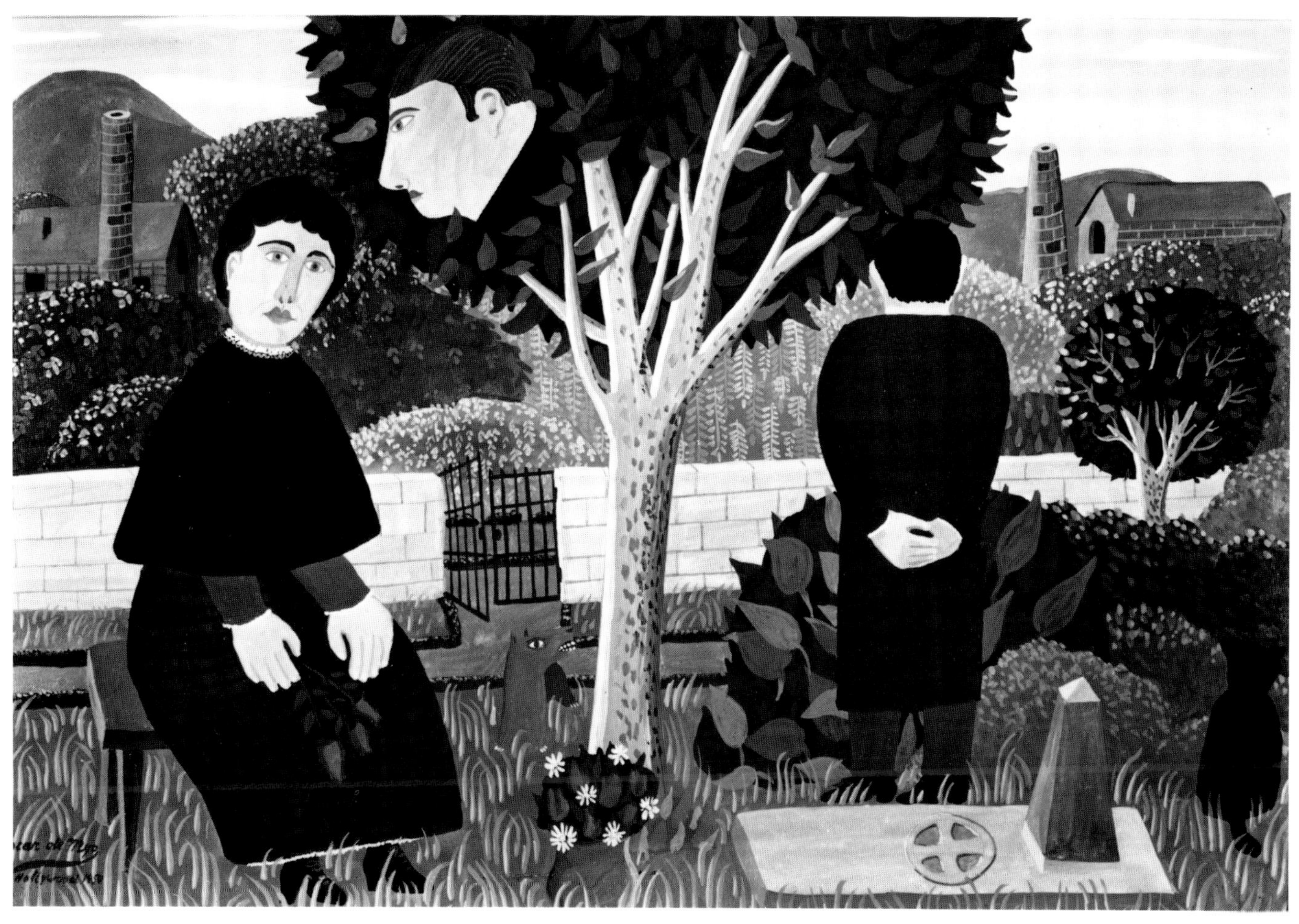

The Widow. 1950. Tempera on wood, 9 × 12″. Private collection

It was not strange that in Hollywood Oscar continued to attend séances. At one of these a wandering spirit suggested that he buy paints and brushes and begin to paint seriously. To this day Oscar feels guided by a mystic presence when he paints.

The Hollywood séance was by no means Oscar's last experience with the Supernatural. The most powerful phenomenon occurred twenty years later, when he and his second wife, Dorothy, were staying in an ancient farmhouse in Italy. The house had been lent them by Ermanno Mori, a Milanese industrialist who had purchased De

Mejo's entire "Jesus Visits New York" series. Elegant but neglected, the place was filled with turn-of-the-century furniture and the atmosphere was rather eerie.

One evening at exactly 7:12 they noticed a disgusting odor of rotting fish. The smell started in one spot and passed through the house room by room, like a presence. Soon it disappeared, but the next night and on many succeeding nights at 7:12 o'clock the same thing happened. Oscar said to his wife that it must be the ghost of some fisherman who had died at sea and was now stalking the house covered with seaweed. One night Dorothy awoke to the sound of strange music coming from the next room. It was like the clacking of a typewriter that hits notes instead of letters. She woke Oscar, and he too heard this unearthly music. Now he had no doubts: the house was haunted. Finally they realized that the phenomena had begun when they moved a chess table from one room to another. They returned the table to its original site and the odor and the music ceased. Later they were told that the original owner of the house had been murdered and his body dropped in a nearby well.

An important moment in De Mejo's career—and perhaps in his life as well—came in 1949, when he visited a show of Haitian popular art at the Haitian Art Center in New York. Up to that point his imagery had been satirical, a kind of humor not really sympathetic to his nature. Once exposed to the Haitians, De Mejo developed his style rapidly. In the Haitians' world the Supernatural is every bit as real as the events of everyday life. They treat it with no intellectualism or satire at all.

This was especially true of the two progenitors of Haitian art whose work De Mejo saw for the first time in New York. One of them was the late Hector Hyppolite. De Mejo's sense of poetry and religious illumination found confirmation in Hyppolite's work. Equally important was what he learned from the example of the other great early Haitian painter, Philomé Obin. From Obin he learned to put together an objective documentary or historical tableau without losing the sense of mystery. Perhaps the picture that made the most lasting impression on Oscar was Philomé's *Franklin D. Roosevelt Interceding in the Beyond for the Union of the Americas and World Peace.* In this little painting the president, draped in an American flag, is rising from the grave to commune with two descending angels. Above them, in a cloud, the Eye of God benignly looks on.

The scene, with variations, was to be echoed later in De Mejo's celebrations of the American Revolution. Philomé Obin's equally talented brother, Senêque, was a Mason, and often enclosed *his* all-seeing God's Eye in a triangle. In Oscar's pictures the watchful Divine Presence appears in both forms.

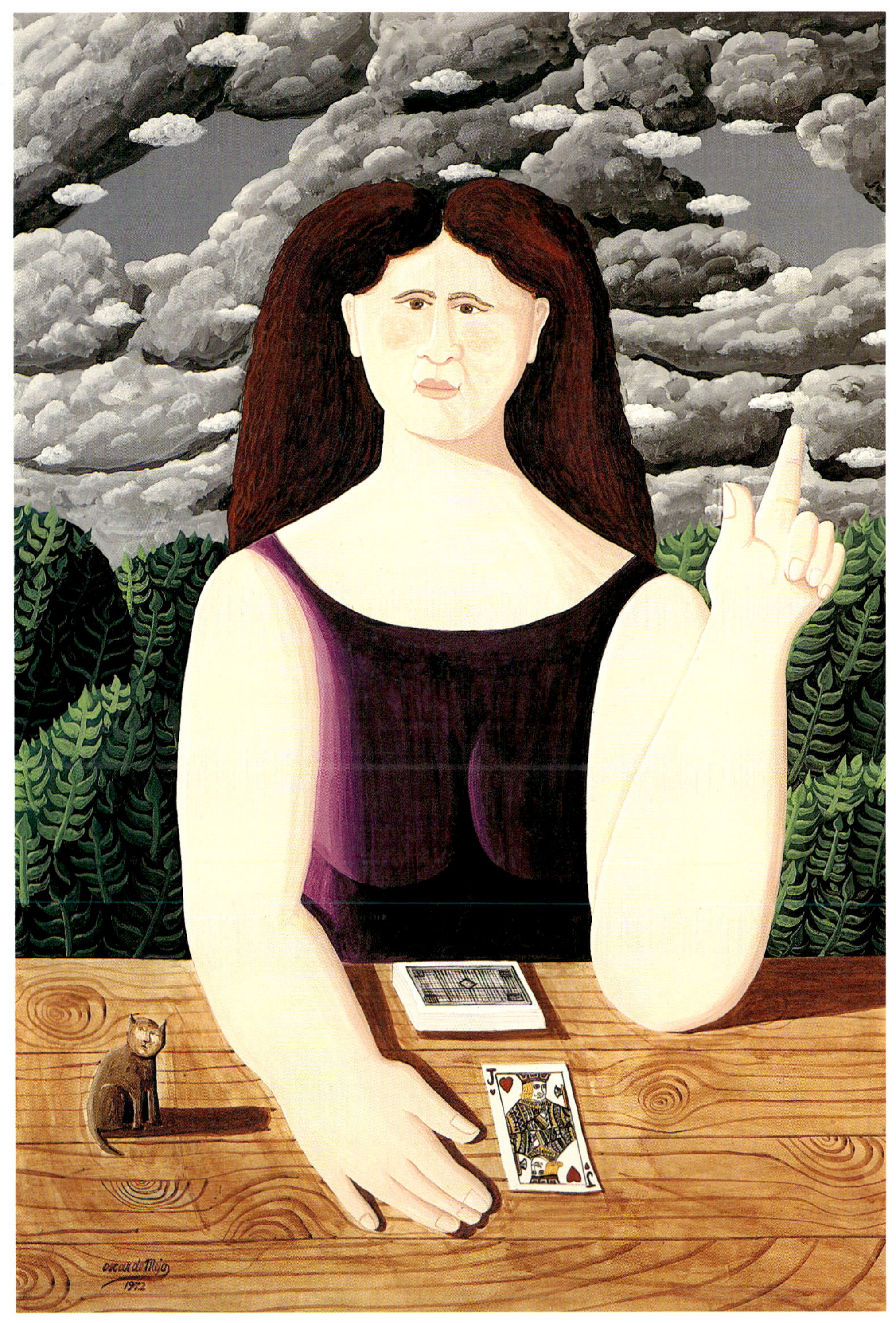

The Fortune Teller. 1972. Masonite, 46 × 32″. Collection Dorothy De Mejo, New York

The fortune teller is a California lady who claims to have supernatural powers. Most of the time her predictions are completely wrong. She does not care, however, as long as her clients pay. The little cat is perplexed —what will his mistress say about this Jack of Hearts?

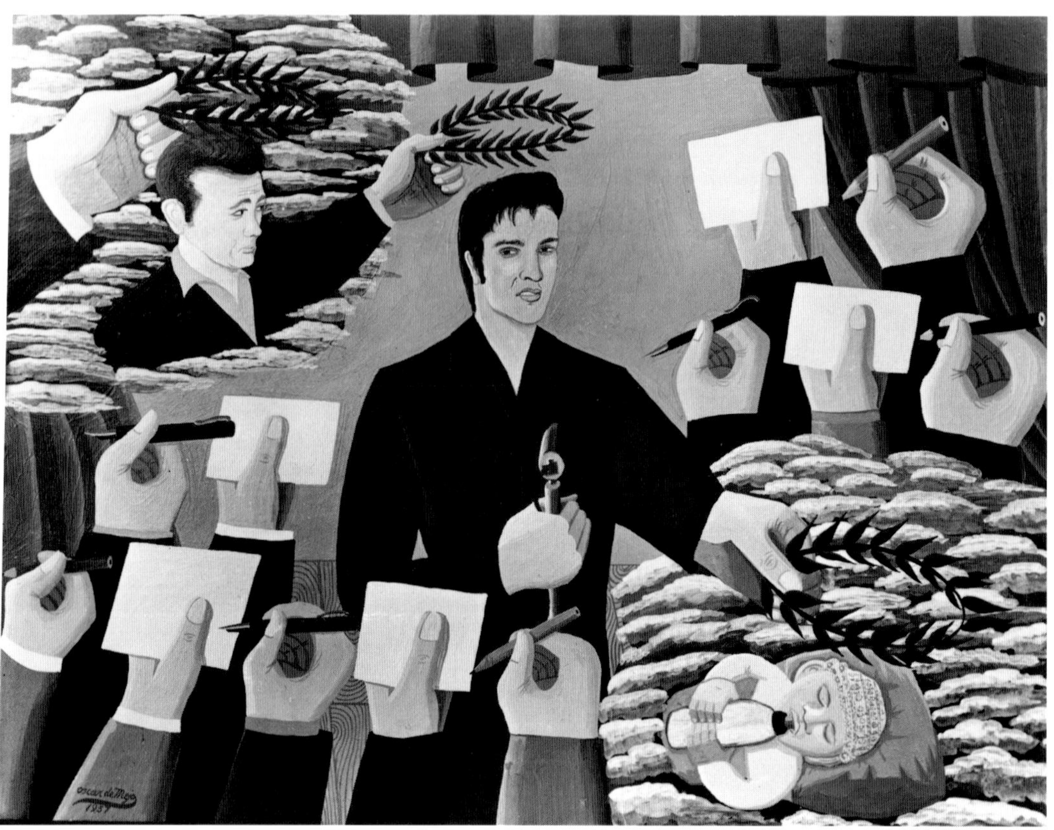

The Idols—of Yesterday, Today, and Tomorrow. 1957. Tempera on wood, 18×24".
Private collection

De Mejo found his style before he found his subject matter, and his best paintings came out of that conjunction. But until he had lived long enough in the United States to have the feel of what it was all about, there were experiments to be made, the Old World to be exorcized, the New to be appraised.

His first New York show, at the Haitian Art Center in 1949, was well received, though the American scene was presented still in his "Italian" style with caricature a strong component.

As his first marriage foundered—he and Valli were not divorced until 1967 but had lived apart since 1953—Oscar immersed himself in painting, developing a style in which he could express his growing passion for America. The key to his success in this endeavor, and to his worldly success as well, was always the series. But to paint serially, a patron, private or corporate, was required, and for many years such patrons were hard to come by. Once again the artist was forced to work in an office from 9 to 5,

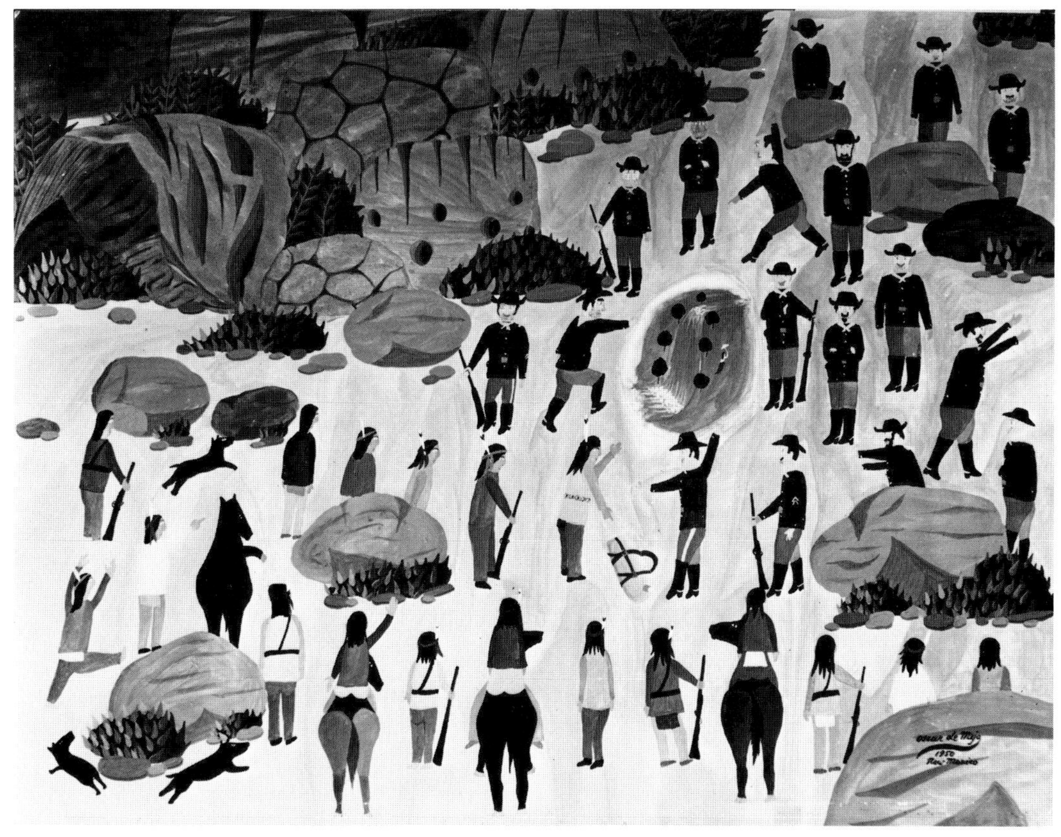

One of the paintings created for the film *New Mexico*. 1950. Tempera on wood, 10 × 14″. Private collection

this time as a publicity man. He had now indeed become a "Sunday painter." Still, one opportunity had materialized during the Hollywood days when the producer of a film titled *New Mexico* asked De Mejo to paint six small paintings of Indians for publicity purposes while "on location." One depicts the cave dwellings and stone "skyscrapers" of those master builders, the Hopi Indians. Spirited battle scenes are prototypes of the more brilliantly painted pictures of the American Revolution to come.

The first real break came in 1970 when two Milanese industrialists, David Colombo and Elio Mottura, sponsored him to return to Milan for a year, all expenses paid, to paint. By this time his life had stabilized with his marriage to modern jazz dancer Dorothy Graham, of British West Indian parentage. He sold many pictures to European galleries and collectors and, best of all, he began to receive feelers about commissions that would enable him to return to the United States.

In the 1970s he struck a distinctive American note in paintings inspired by F. Scott Fitzgerald's *The Great Gatsby*, capturing characters quintessentially American.

More remarkable still are De Mejo's paintings of American sports events. He exhibits, though not a sportsman or fan himself, an uncanny perception of what goes on in baseball, basketball, and boxing, and he delights in the charming absurdities of lawn tennis, badminton, boating, and horsemanship as practiced in the nineteenth century. His most faithful patrons in the 1960s and 1970s were Nathan and Gwen Alexander of Gladwyne, Pennsylvania. Nathan, himself a formidable tennis player and at one time Travelling Secretary of the Philadelphia Phillies baseball team, undoubtedly quickened Oscar's interest in sports, and Oscar's work ended the Alexanders' search for an artist who could combine human feelings with the facts of everyday life, humor with the sort of vision every child has but few retain into adulthood. They recognized these capacities in De Mejo, and respected him for painting what he felt instead of what might have made him acceptable to the dominant critics. The Alexanders and a few other collectors like them made it possible for Oscar to survive a period riddled with disappointments.

In December 1972 Paul Foley, board chairman and president of the largest advertising firm in the world, the Interpublic Group, commissioned him to paint a series of sixteen pictures illustrating the history of the American Revolution. In terms of subject matter the choice could not have been more felicitous. The Revolution, so dehydrated by the researches of partisans and debunkers, fell into his lap, and Oscar saw it, or chose to see it, as legend pure and simple. The strategies and military tactics of that faraway war had indeed been puerile—"primitive" if you like. What held the rebel army together against the greater quantity and quality of British arms had been one factor alone: the indomitable character of George Washington. Because Washington refused to acknowledge adversity or accept a succession of defeats, he gave the wavering Americans a symbol to rally about.

De Mejo depicts the famous battles as confrontations of toy soldiers firing at one another with explosive feather dusters. There are no fallen heroes or villains in his battles, no dead at all—and this too enhances the legendary view of events.

In 1976 Foley wrote a book devoted to the series. It was very well reviewed, and helped De Mejo renew old ties with the New York art world.

His work for the Bicentennial brought him more recognition. His career began to flourish. The Yorktown Victory Center in West Virginia showed the "American Revolution Series," as did the Botetourt Gallery at the College of William and Mary in Williamsburg, Virginia, and at the New World Pavilion in nearby Jamestown.

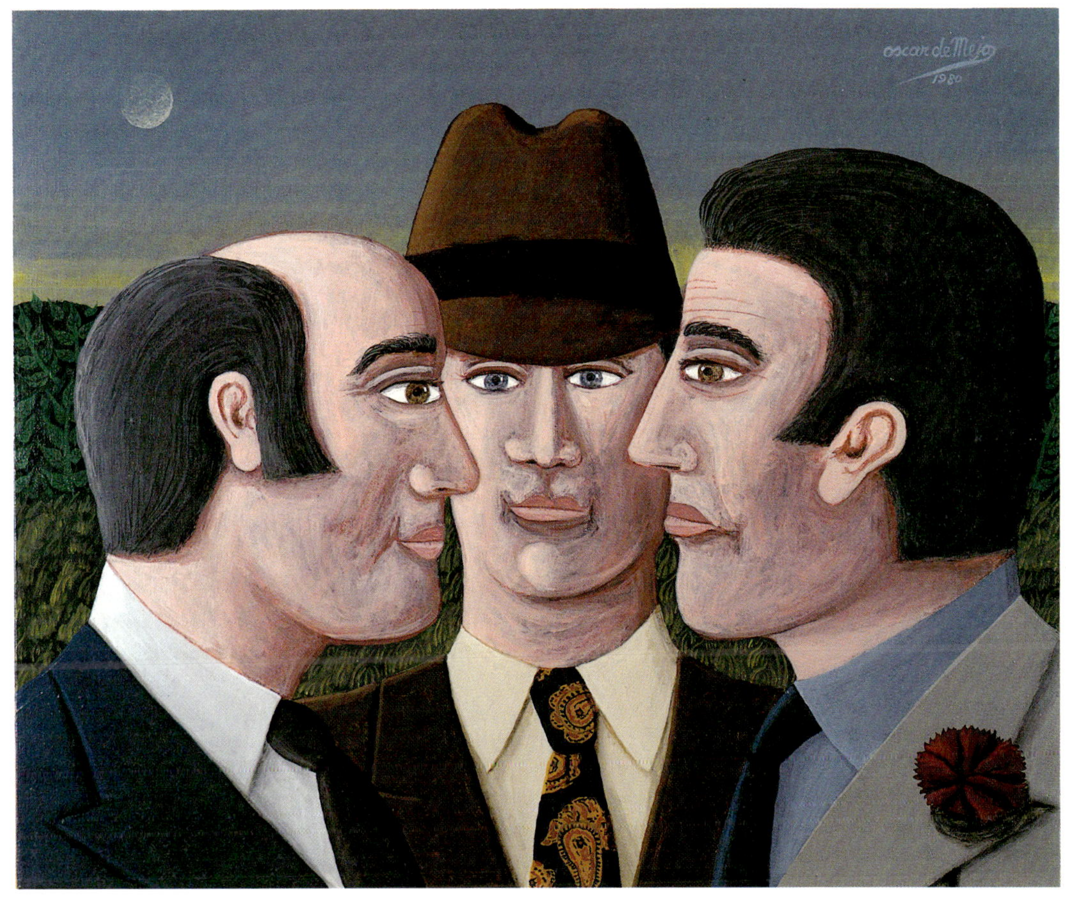

Gatsby and His Friends III. 1980. Canvas, 20 × 24″. Private collection, New York

Gatsby, on the right, is meeting two friends.
The meeting is extremely secret, so noth-
ing can be revealed about it.

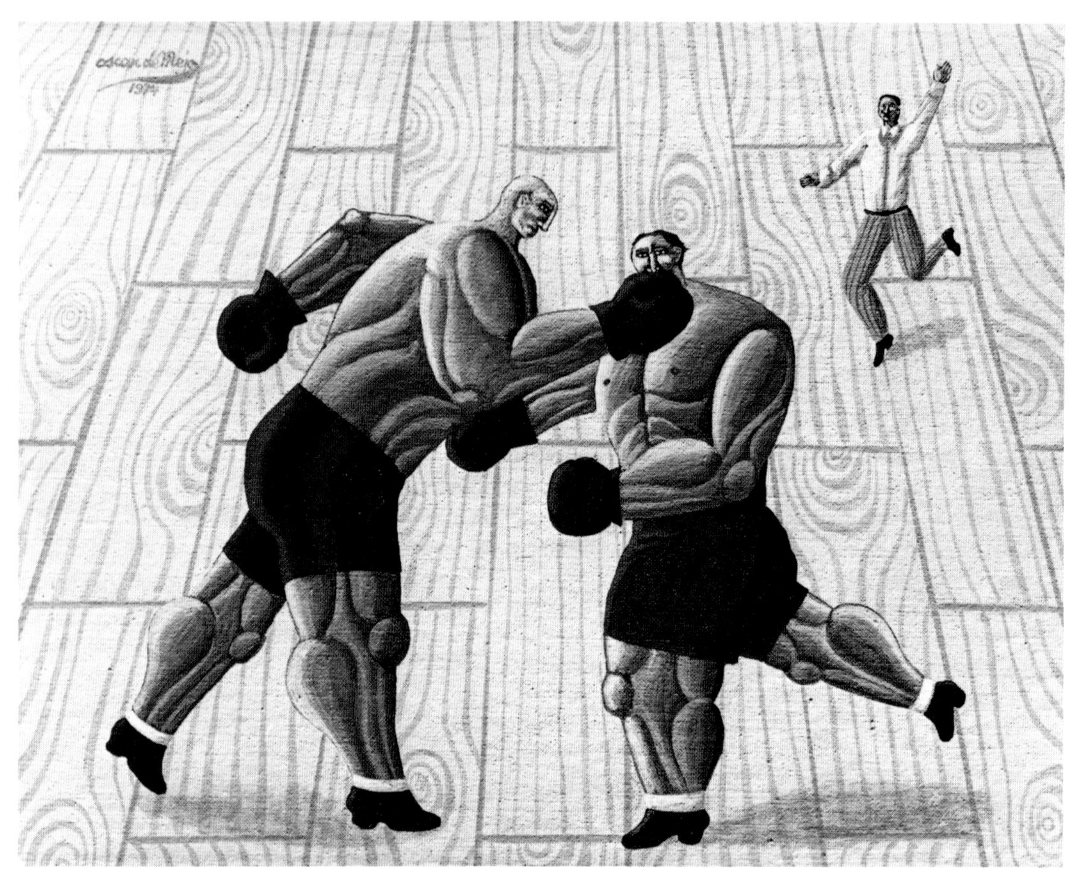

Boxing Match. 1974. Masonite, 14×18″. Private collection

He was commissioned by art collector Bob Guccione to paint twenty-five scenes from the history of America, and by John Kluge, chairman of Metromedia, to do a series on the Harlem Globetrotters basketball team. The magazine *Sports Illustrated* commissioned two series, one on sports during the American Revolution and the other on the Kentucky Derby. Paintings are in the permanent collection of the Musée International d'Art Naïf Anatole Jakovsky in Nice and the Musée d'Art Naïf de l'Ile de France at Vicq, near Paris.

Like the work of painters we admire from so-called primitive societies, De Mejo's is alive with mystery and surprise. And it rises—as in the great picture of the demon on the beach scattering offal from a garbage can while an angel pours purity from a

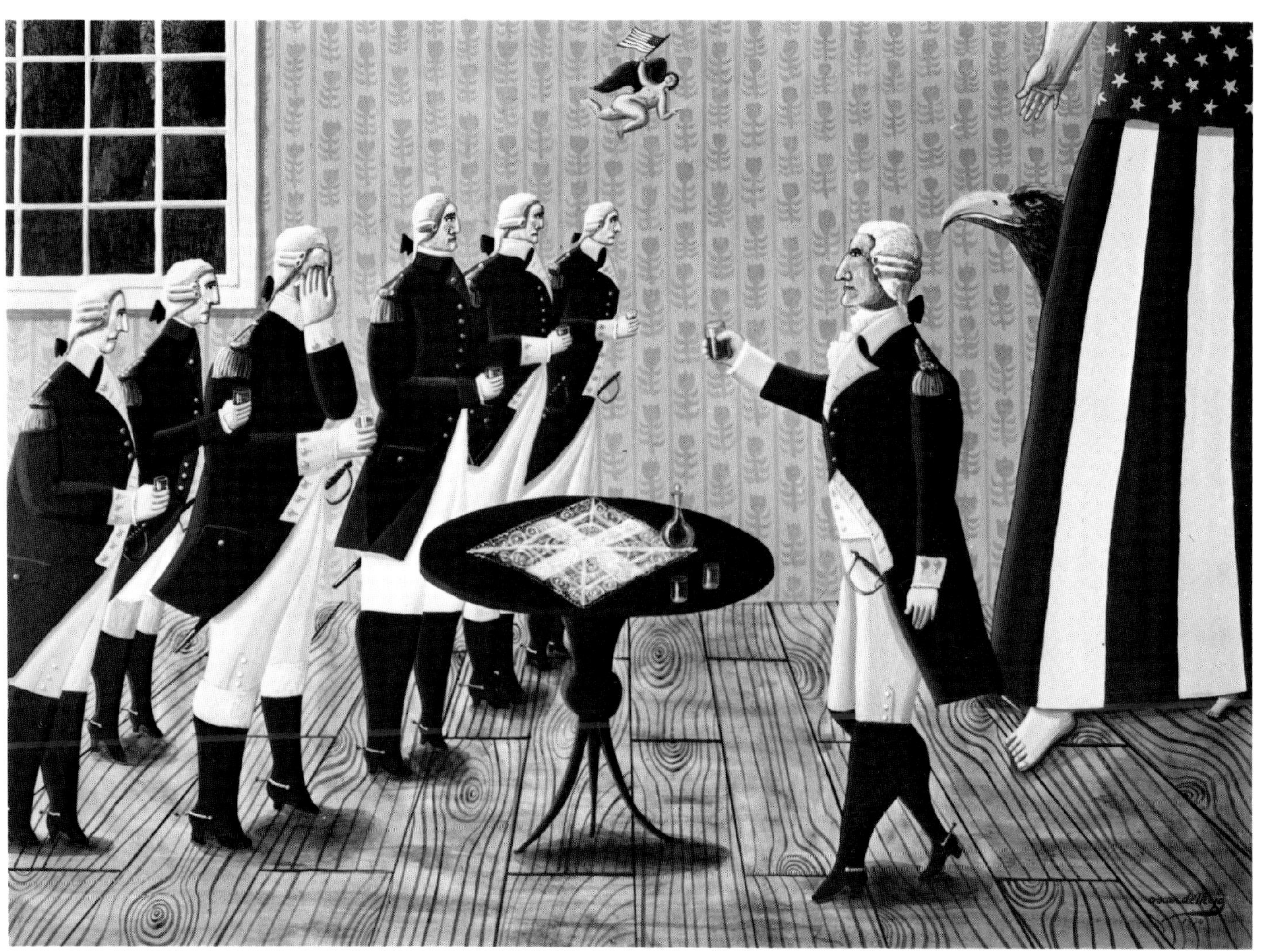

Washington's Farewell at Fraunces Tavern. 1974. Masonite, 26 × 36". Collection Paul Foley

cornucopia into the threatened ocean—beyond any specific product or commission. The artist's magical ability to distort reality in the service of an idea offers an antidote to the tiresome or banal. Though his treatment of historical events may be ironic from time to time, the artist never loses his simplicity and directness nor his sense of humor and his faith in mankind. He retains that rare ability to capture scenes from everyday

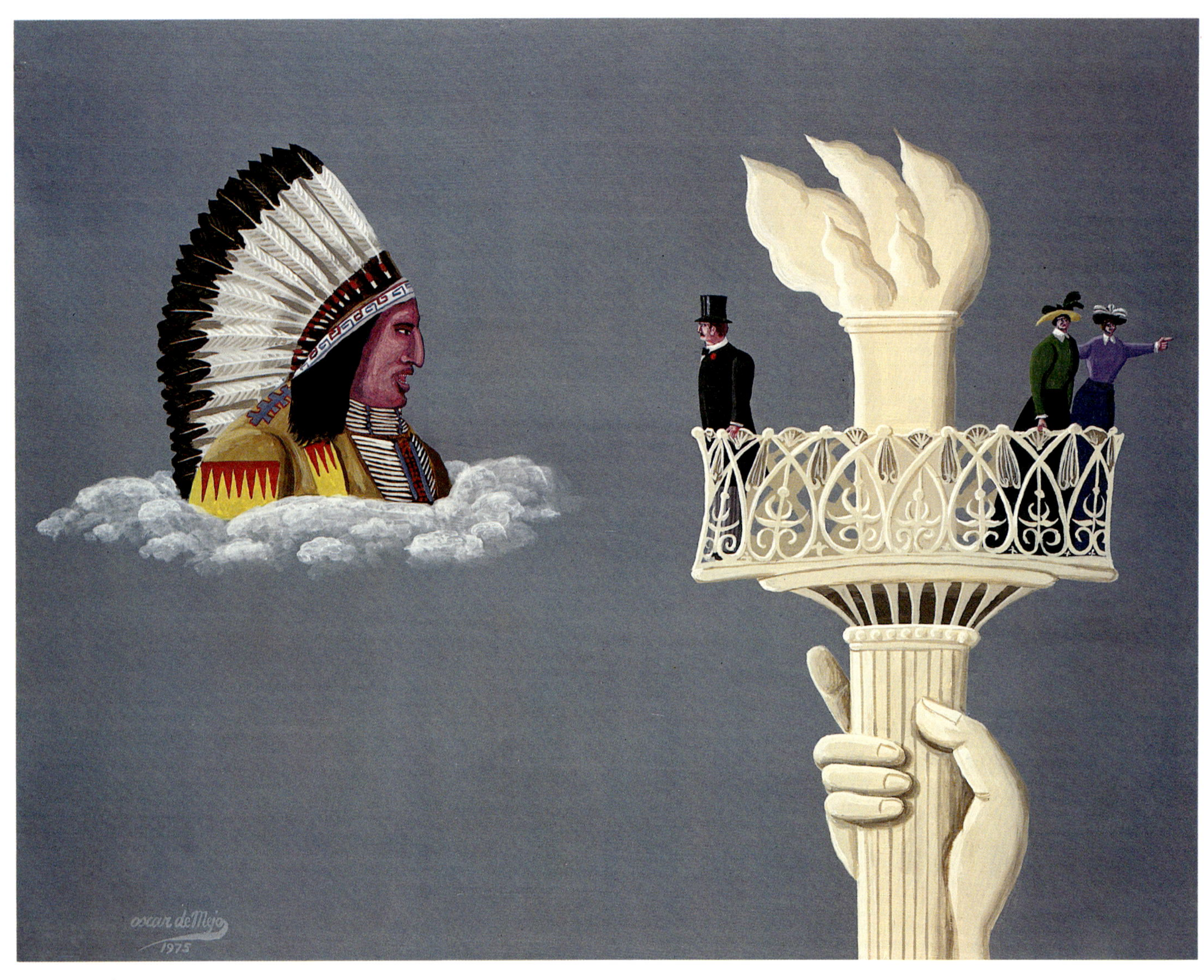

Dr. Merck Visits New York. 1975. Masonite, 20 × 26″. Merck Sharp & Dohme, Belgium

On a fanciful excursion to the top of the
Statue of Liberty, George Merck is greeted
by a fellow man of medicine, Heammwi-
hio, "The Wise One Above," a supreme
deity of the Cheyenne Indians.

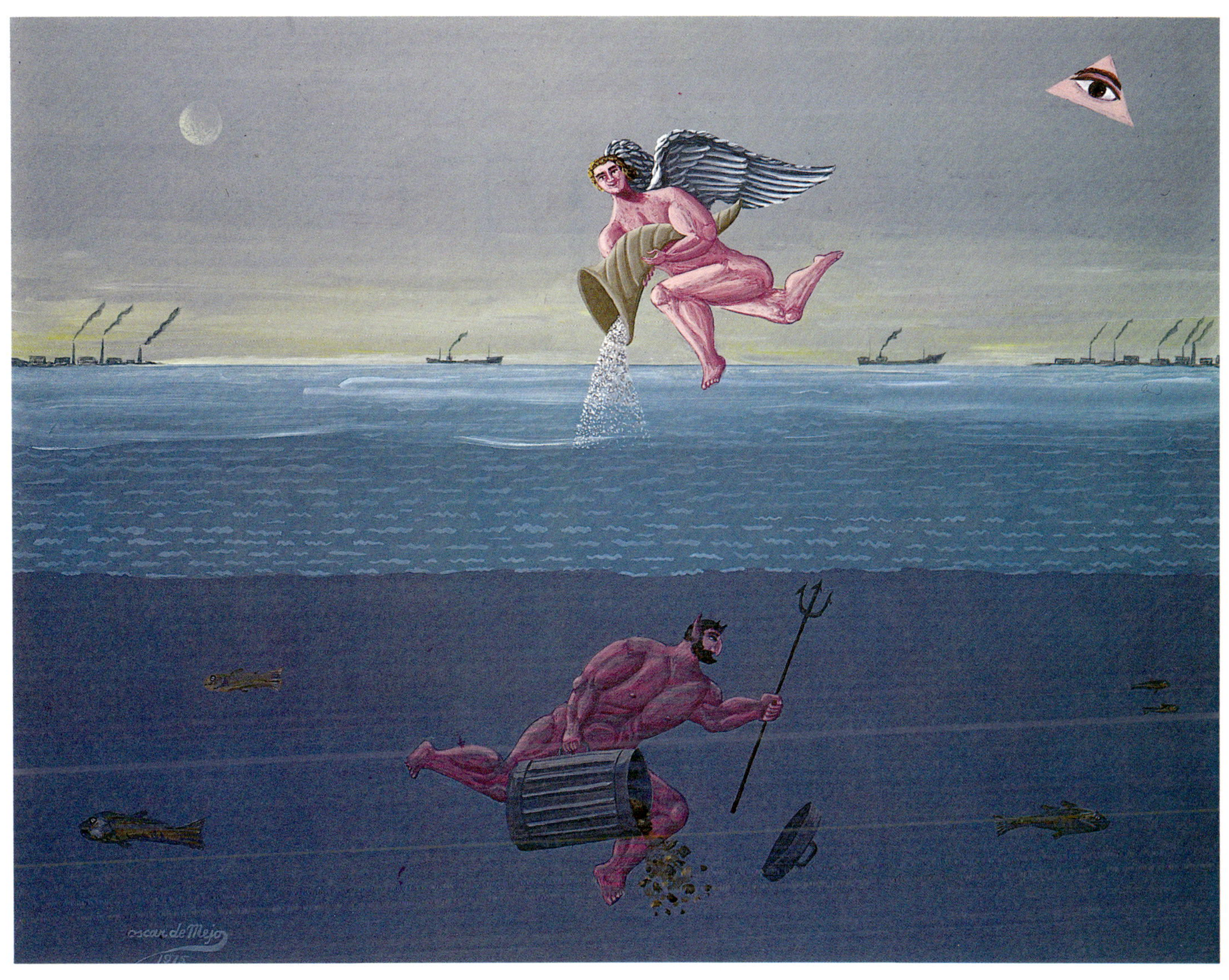

The Pollution Problem. 1975. Masonite, 20 × 26″. Merck Sharp & Dohme, Belgium

This painting was commissioned by Merck Sharp & Dohme to show the "miracle" of Calgon purifiers. A devil is polluting the water while an angel successfully neutralizes the effects of pollution and poison with the celebrated product.

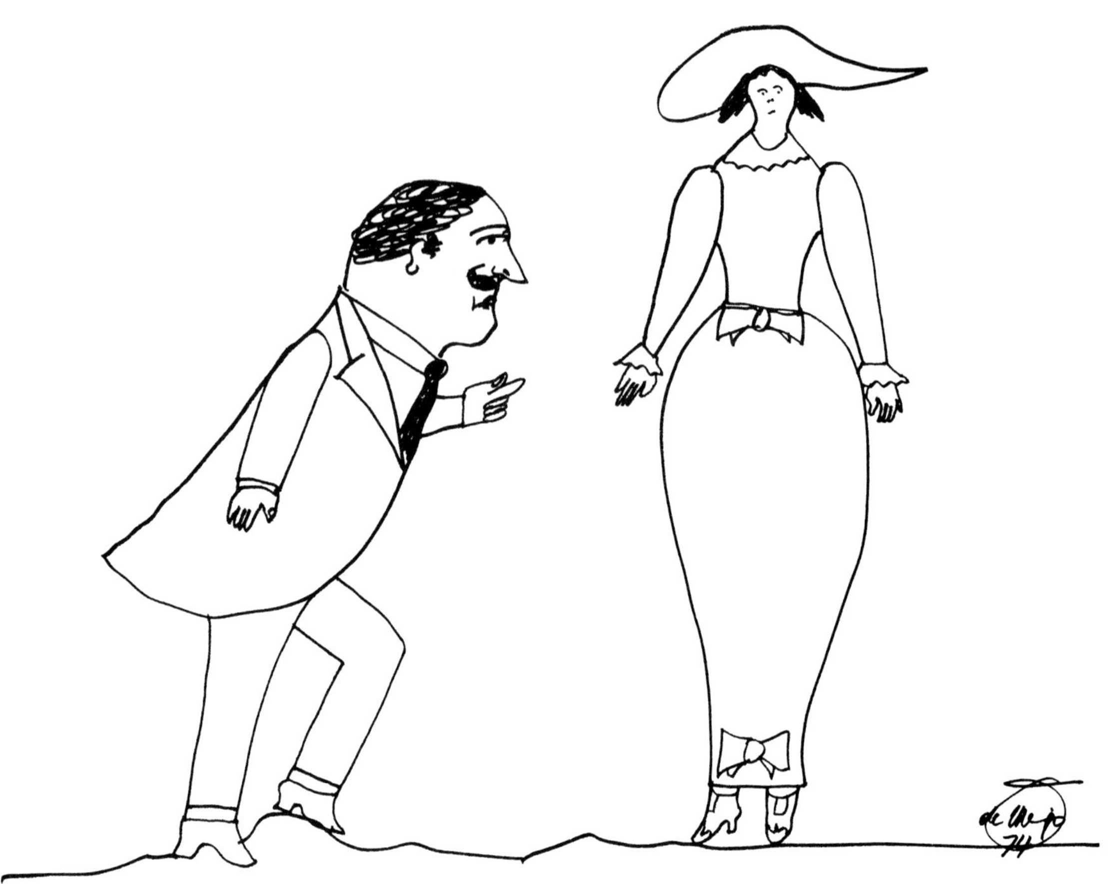

The Complaining Husband. 1974. Ink on paper, 8½ × 11″. Private collection

life because of his feeling of wonder that something unique is happening every moment. He deals subtly with moral dilemmas that have plagued the human race throughout history, but never descends to a political or partisan level. Movements come and go in the art world, but Oscar De Mejo quietly offers a fresh alternative—his own.

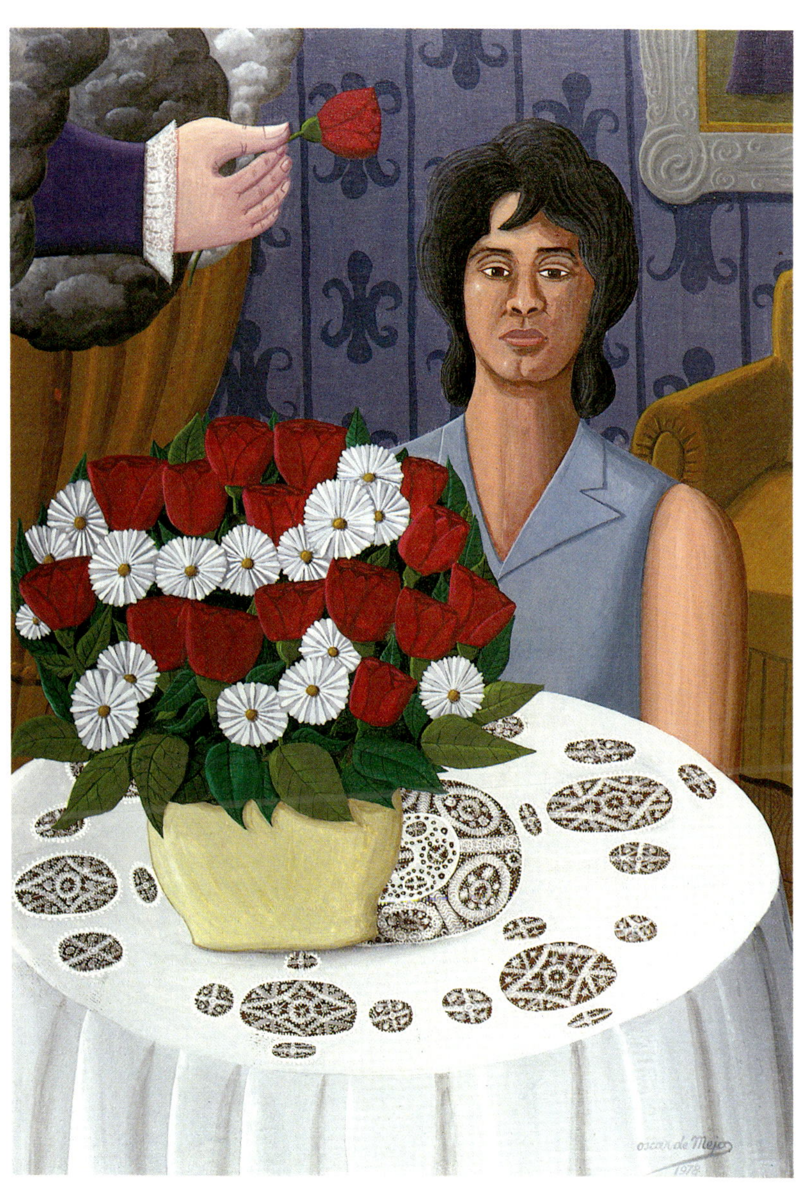

LOVE

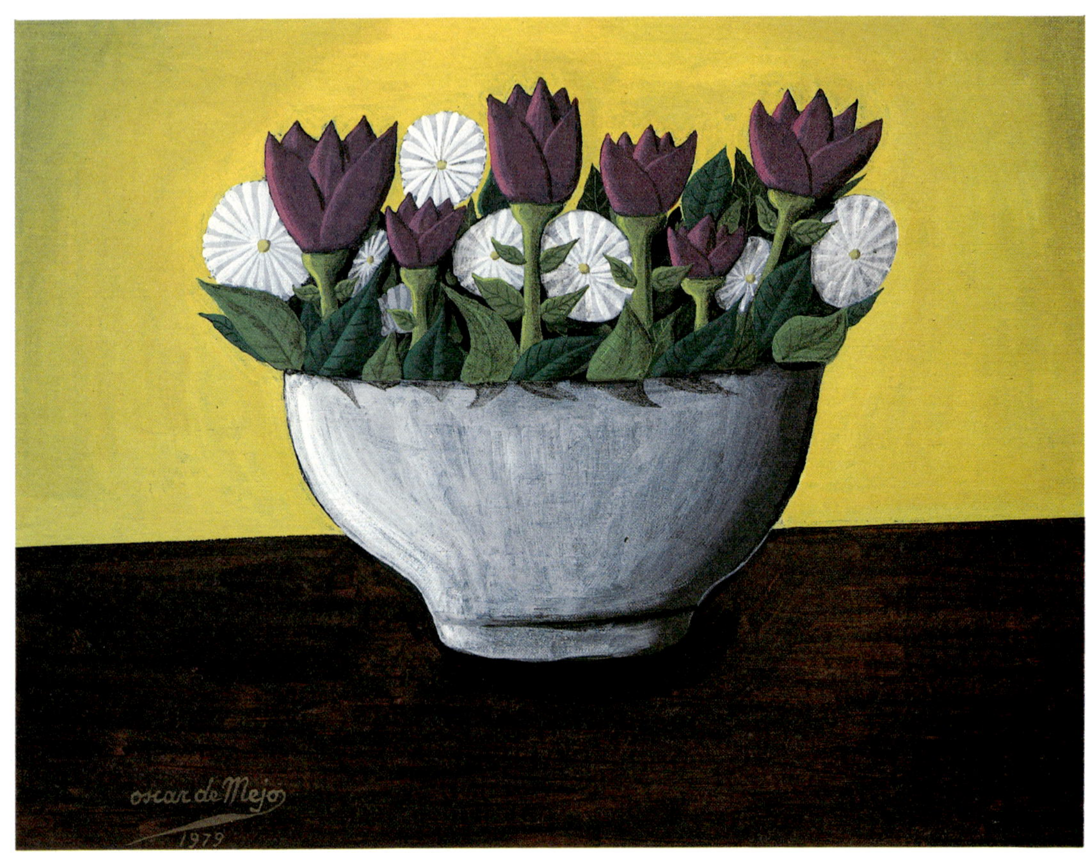

Flowers. 1979. Canvas-board, 18 × 24″. Aberbach Fine Art, New York

*These flowers have just been purchased by
Rollo FitzJames for his beloved Laura
McClintock. Shall I say more?*

PRECEDING PAGE:
My Wife Dorothy. 1978. Canvas, 50 ×
36″. Collection Dorothy De Mejo,
New York

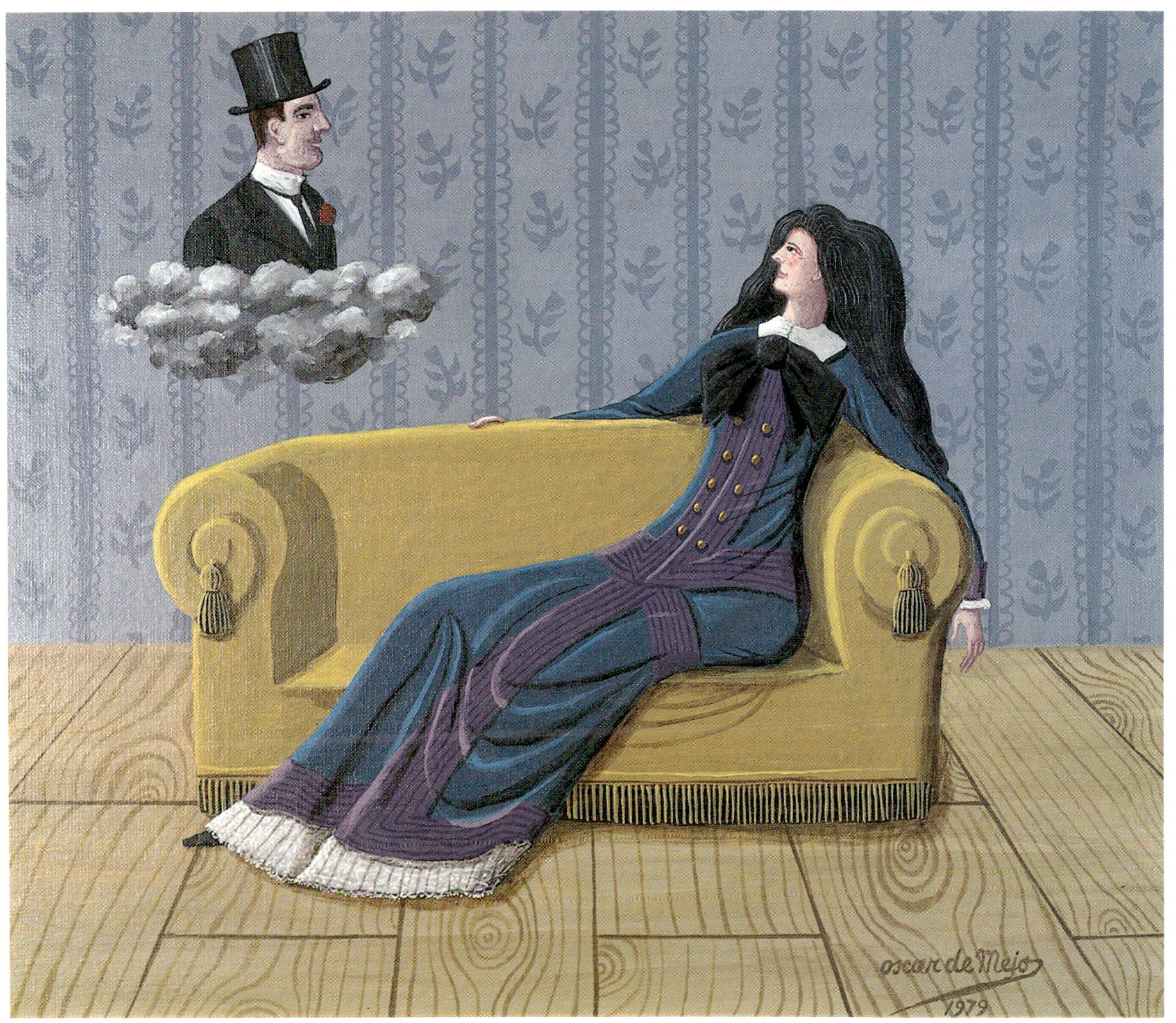

The Romantic Lady. 1979. Canvas, 20 × 24″. Private collection, New York

The romantic lady is thinking so hard
about her faraway beau that he has mate-
rialized in a little cloud above the sofa.

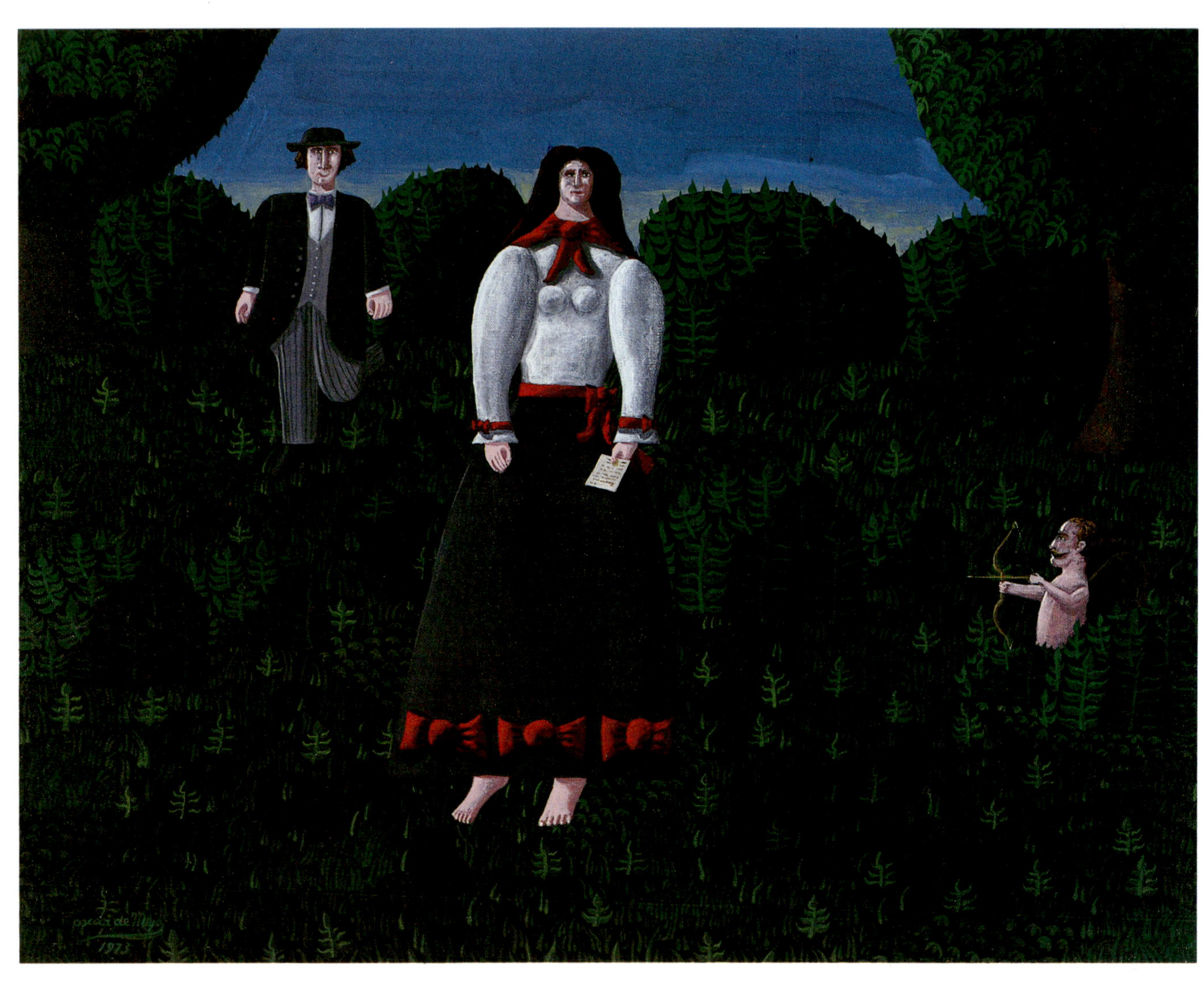

Love in the Country. 1973. Canvas, 20×23″. Collection Dorothy De Mejo, New York

The young country girl has just received a letter from her lover (left) in which he proposes. Cupid is naturally there, ready to shoot his arrow. Why Cupid's mustache? Well, the year is 1907, and Cupid's grooming must be up-to-date.

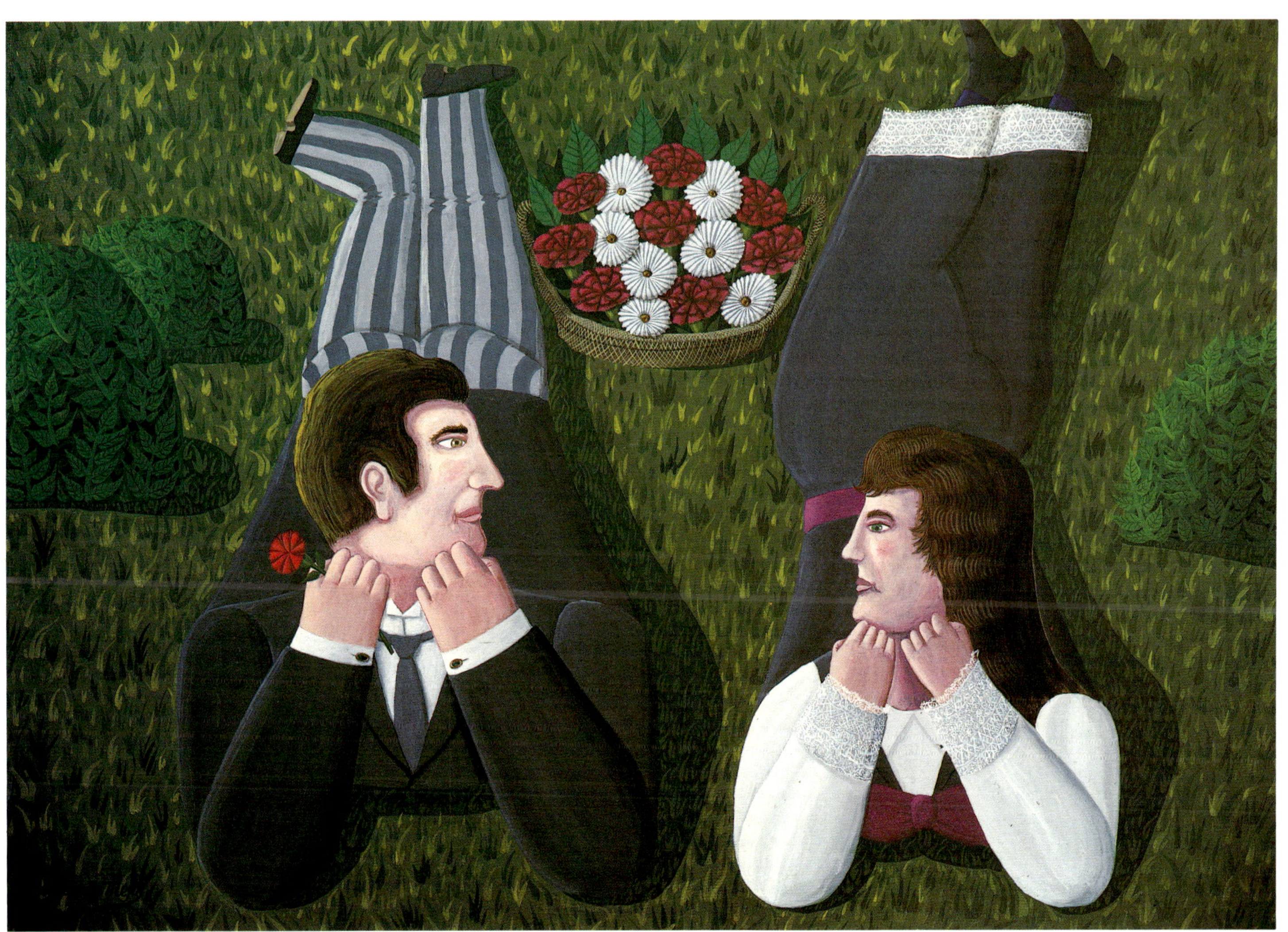

The Affianced. 1981. Canvas, 46 × 66″. Aberbach Fine Art, New York

The affianced are very much in love
(otherwise they would not be affianced).
He is quite sophisticated and slightly
intellectual. When he speaks about royal-
ty in Europe, she hangs on his every word.

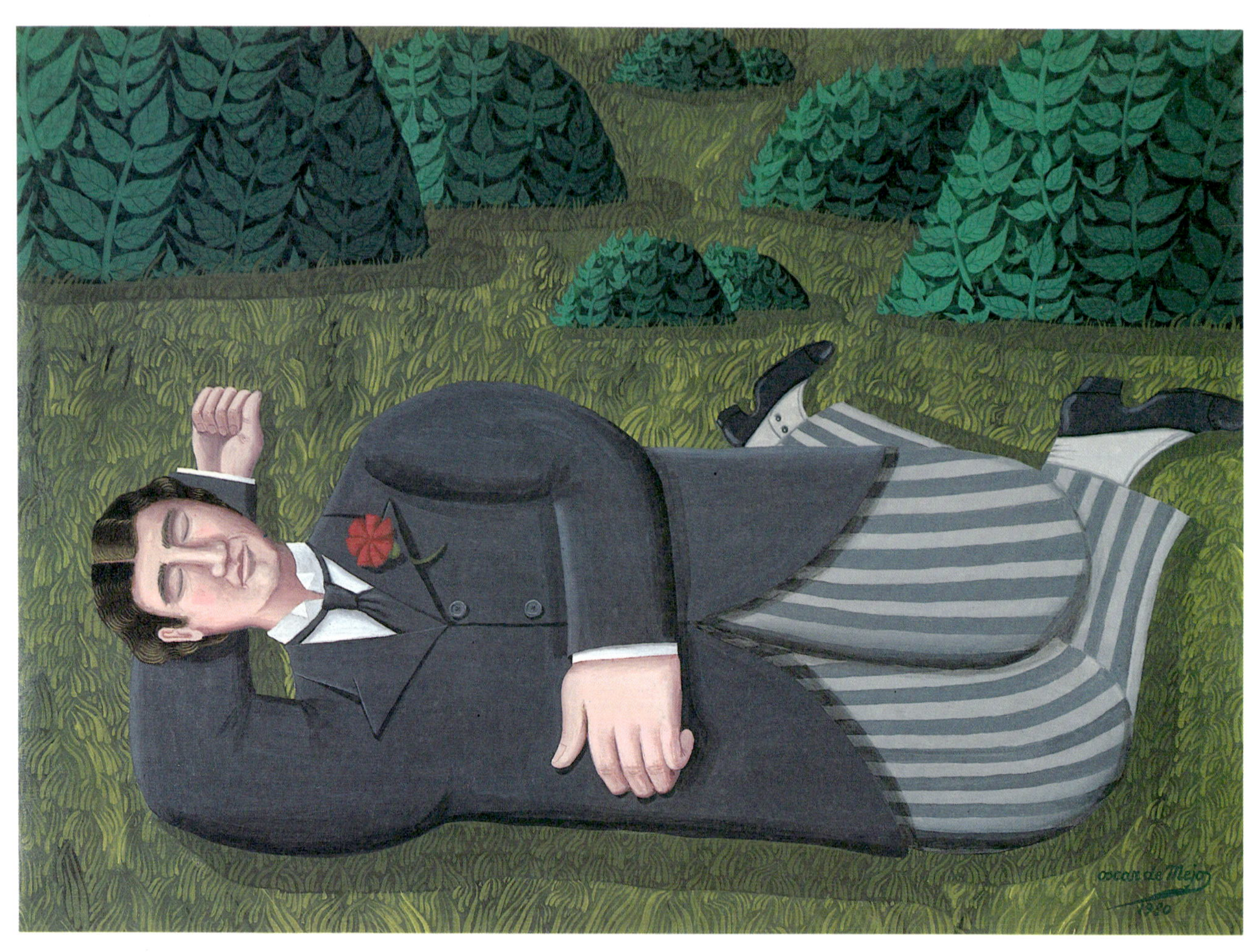

The Siesta. 1980. Canvas, 36×50″. Collection Dorothy De Mejo, New York

This painting is also called The Dreamer *because the handsome man enjoying the siesta is dreaming. He sees himself as an aspiring young actor touched by Lady Luck. At this very instant he is being interviewed by actress Ellen Terry, and she wants him for the lead in* Cymbeline, *which opens next week at the Lyceum in London. The pay—200 pounds a week!*

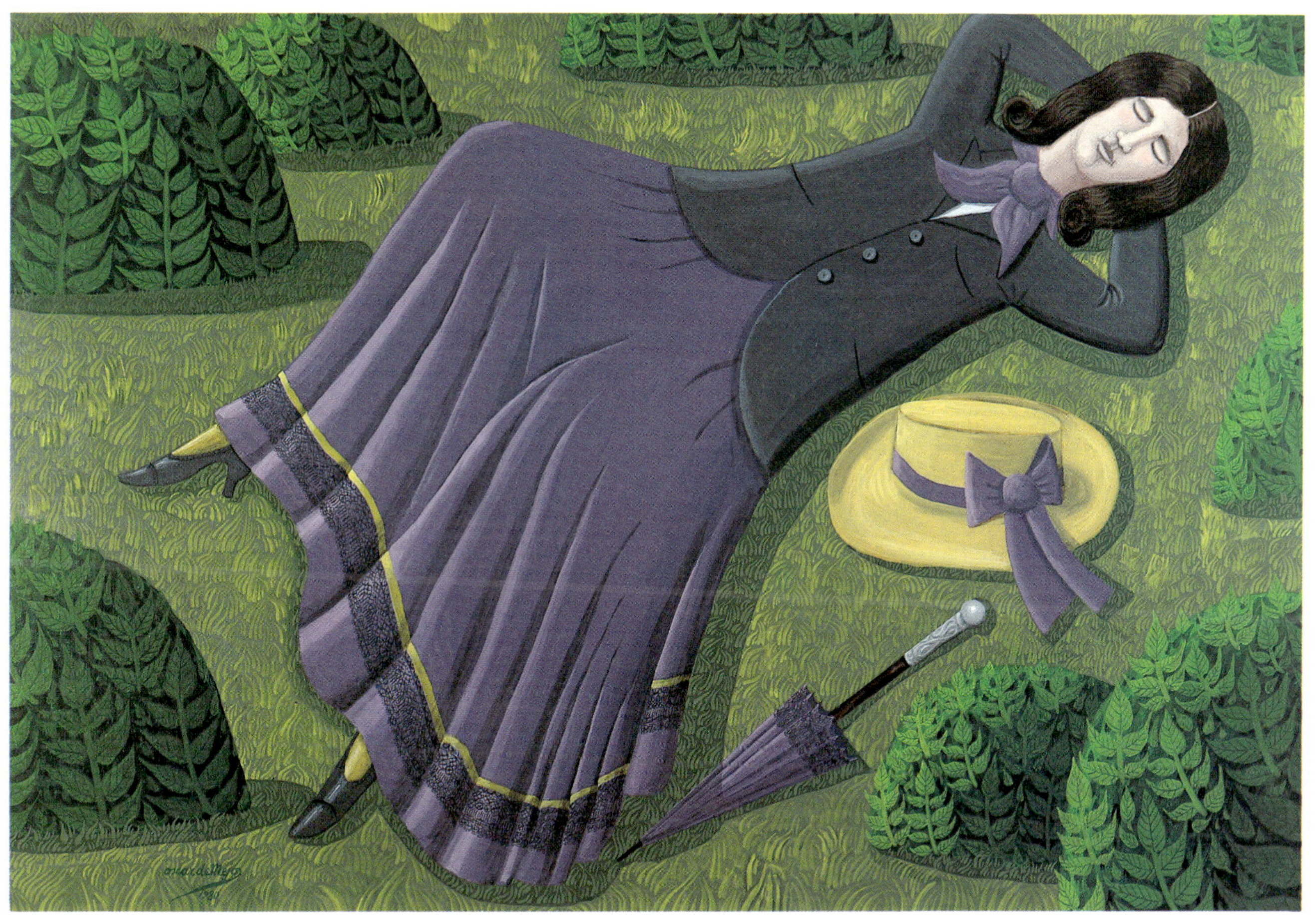

Girl in Purple. 1980. Canvas, 46×66″. Private collection, New York

The girl's name is Victoria and she works as a seamstress in one of the major department stores in the city. Her ambitions are high. She expects to be discovered, and subsequently married, by the most handsome and richest bachelor in town. True that five years have gone by without success —but she can wait.

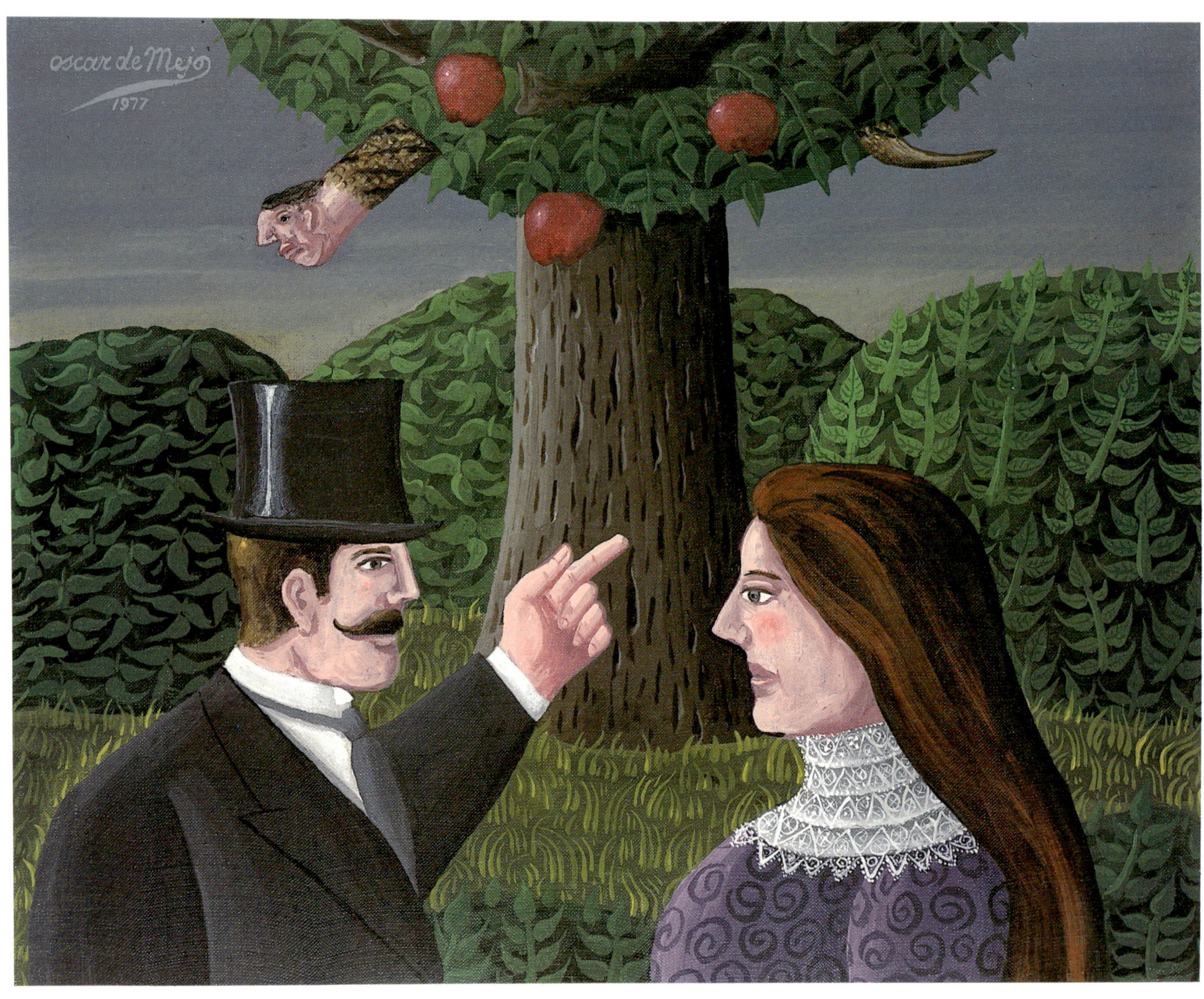

Adam and Eve. 1977. Canvas, 16×20″. Collection Dorothy De Mejo, New York

Adam and Eve are discussing the apple.
They find the snake rather odd-looking
and are uncertain whether to eat the fruit.

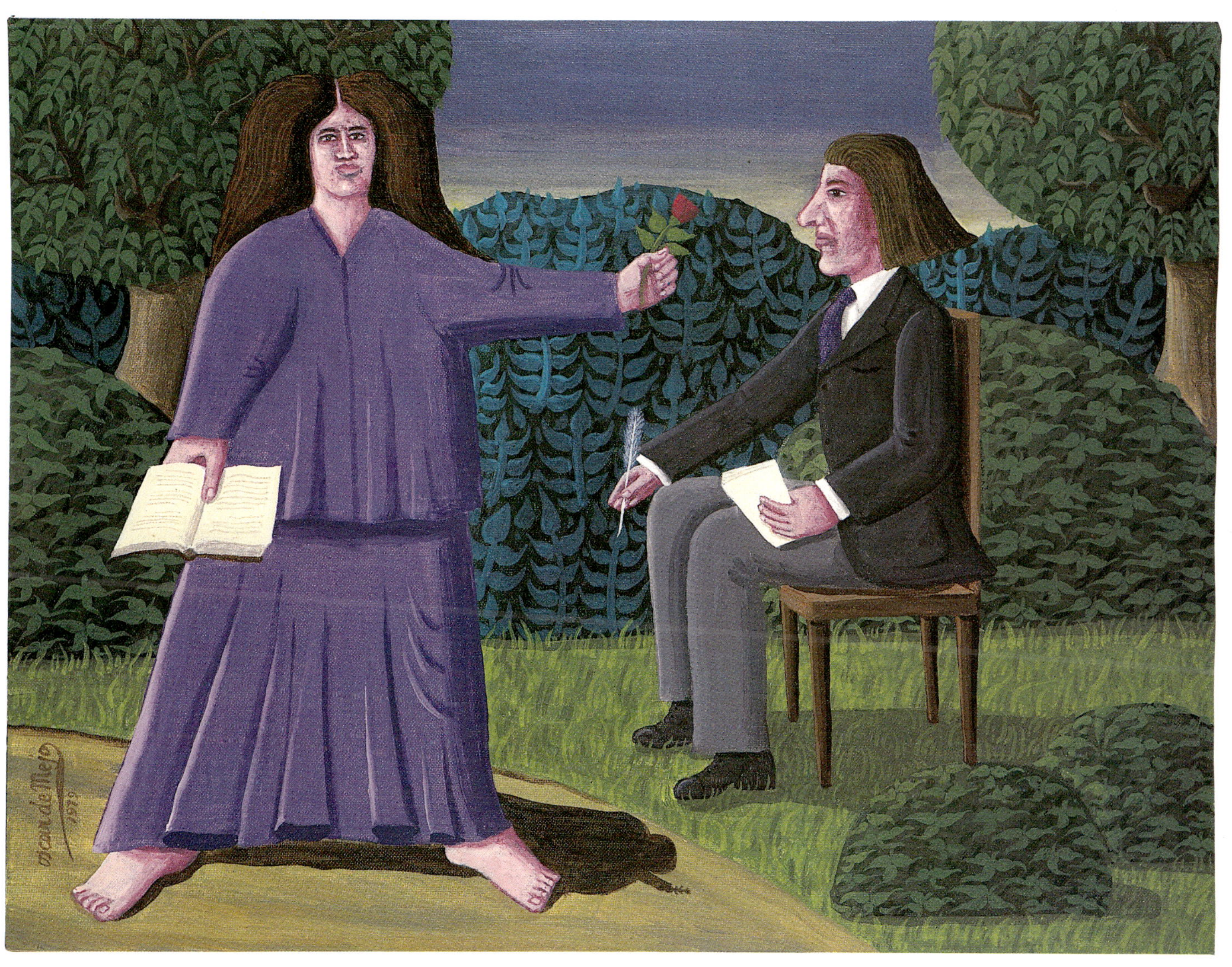

The Two Poets. 1979. Canvas-board, 18×24″. Private collection, New York

The two poets keep writing each other love poems day after day. They never tire. Sometimes they stop for a small sandwich, then resume writing. Per aspera ad astra.

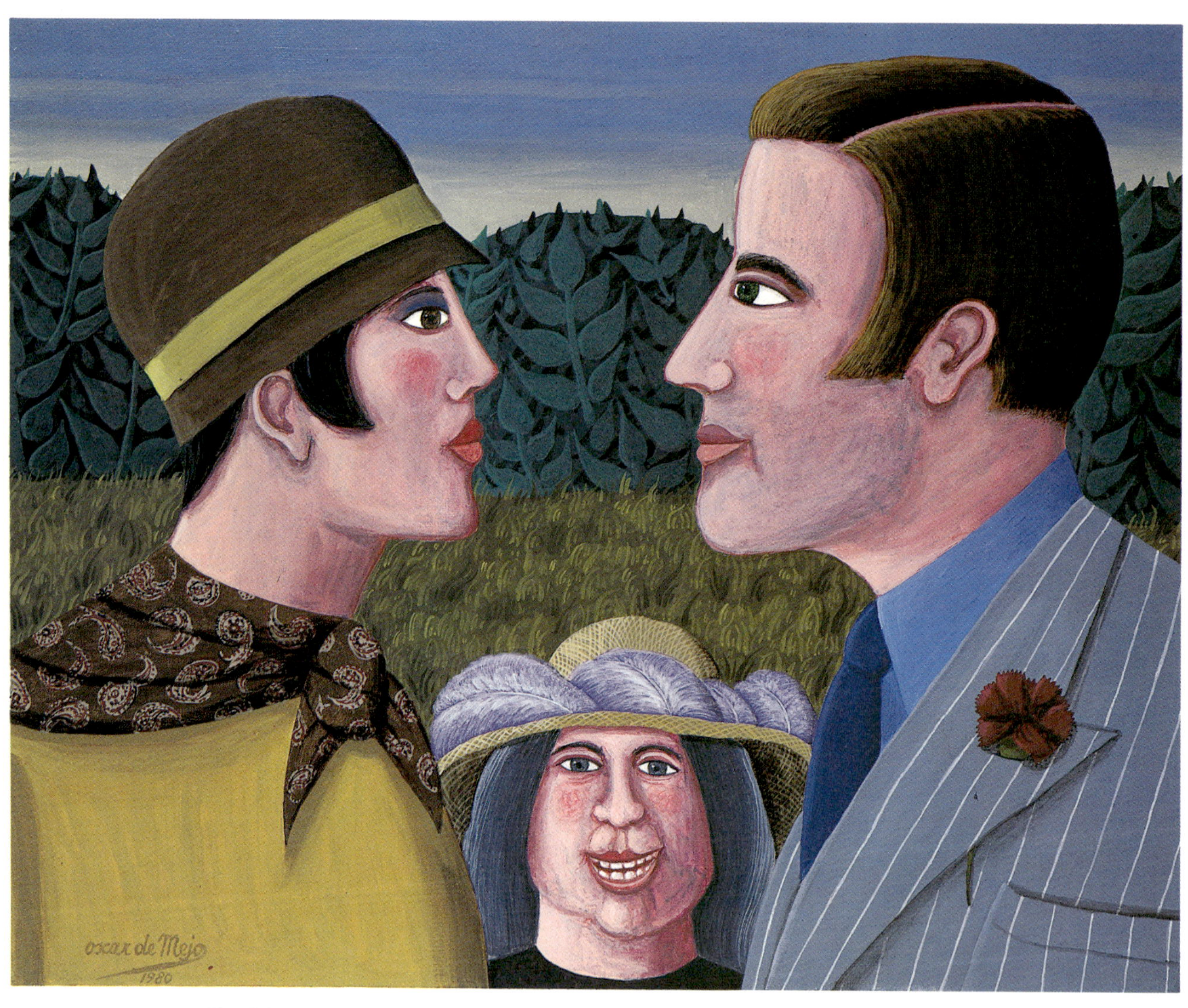

The Matchmaker. 1980. Canvas, 24 × 30″. Private collection, New York

Mirabella Lovelace (left) has an aunt (center) with a special talent for finding husbands for her nieces (she has found twenty-nine so far). She chose Count Johann von Volkenstein for Mirabella, and he has just proposed.

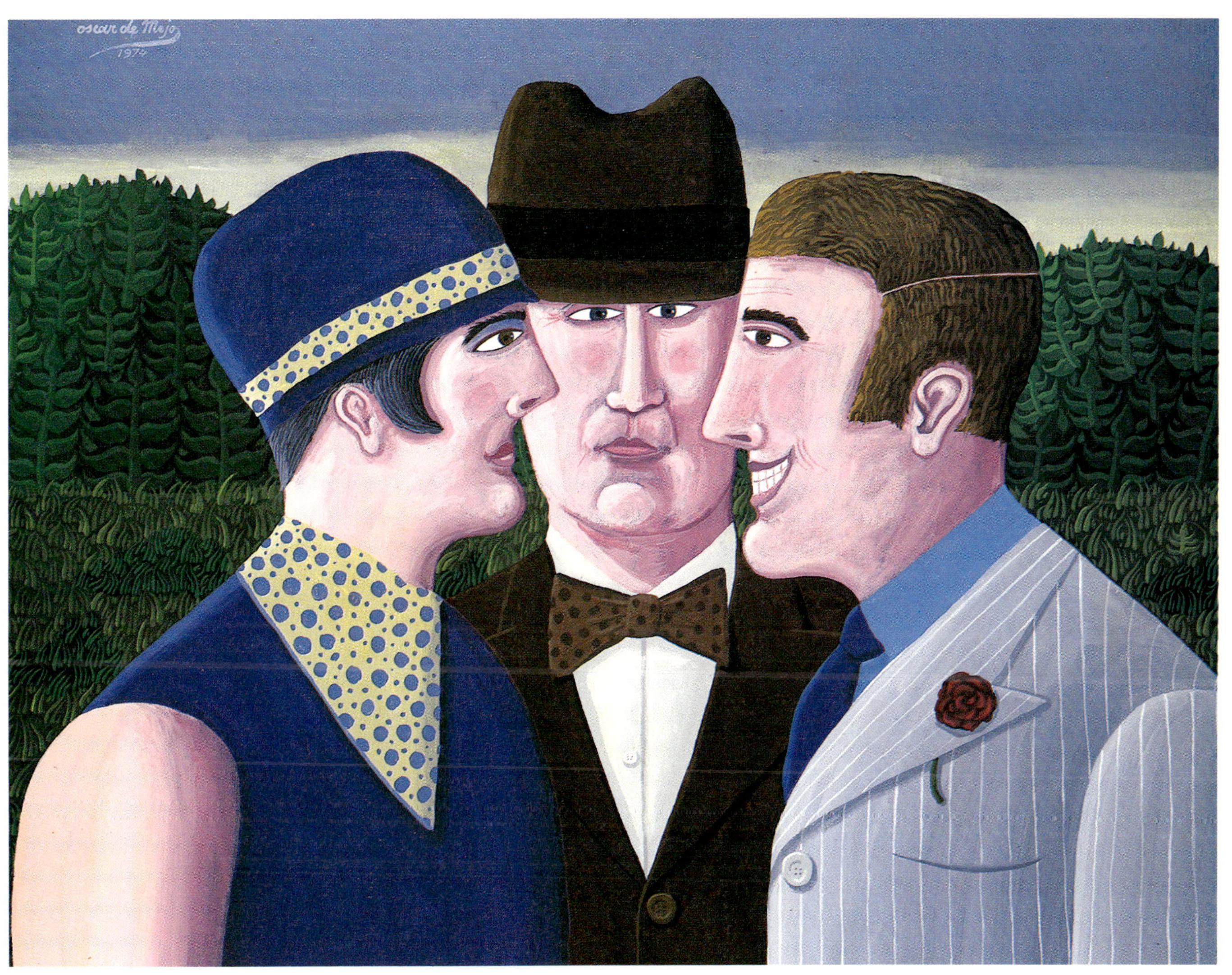

Gatsby's Friends. 1974. Canvas, 22 × 28″. Private collection, New York

Gatsby's friends are undoubtedly plotting something—not all matchmakers are women, you know. Jim Farrow McAdoo (center) wears a hat for a specific reason —he's bald.

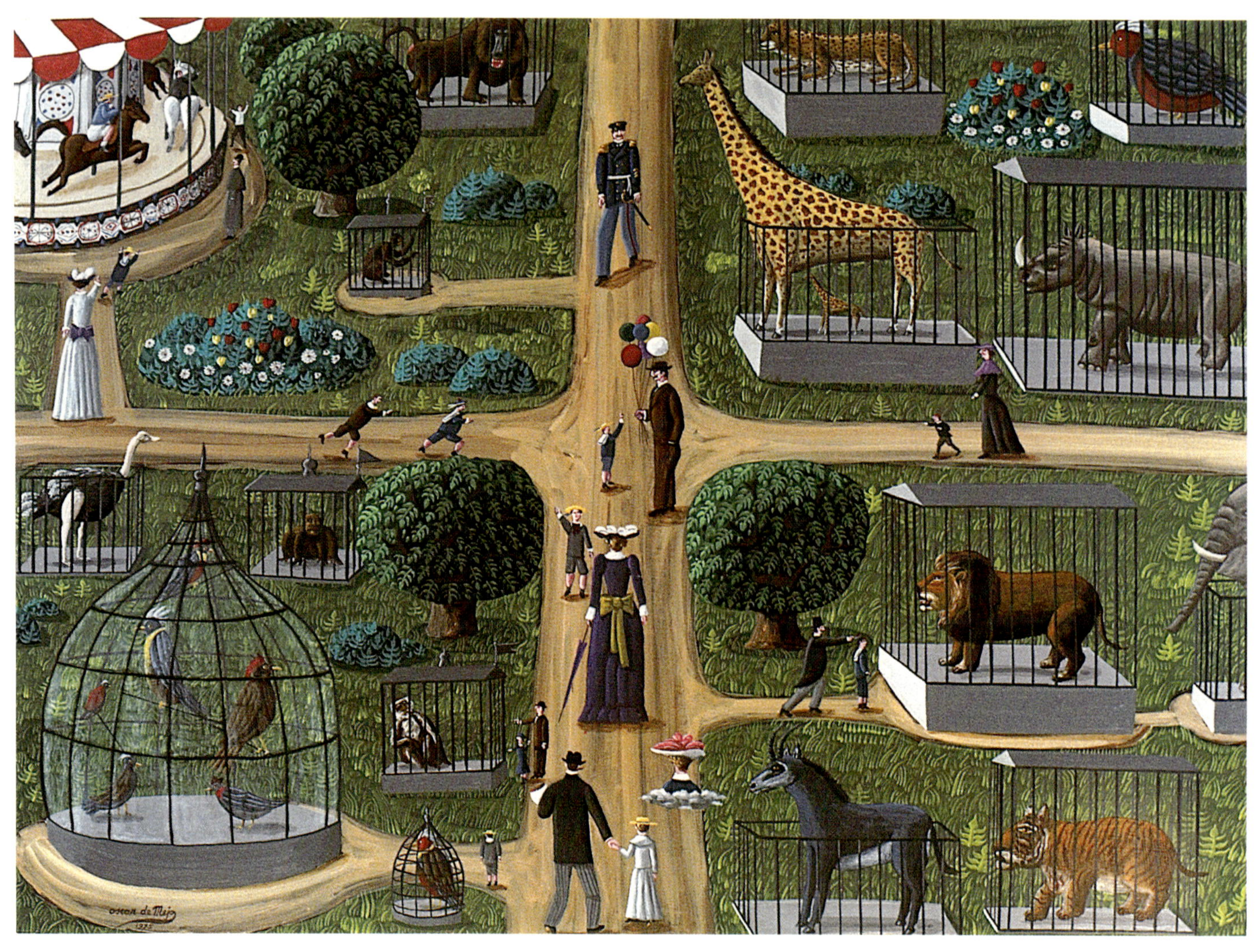

Animals in Captivity. 1975. Masonite, 26×36″. Private collection, New York

The zoo is a happy place for children, with a touch of sadness because the animals are in captivity. The father takes his little girl to the zoo. The mother could not come because of a previous engagement with the hairdresser, but she is near them in spirit.

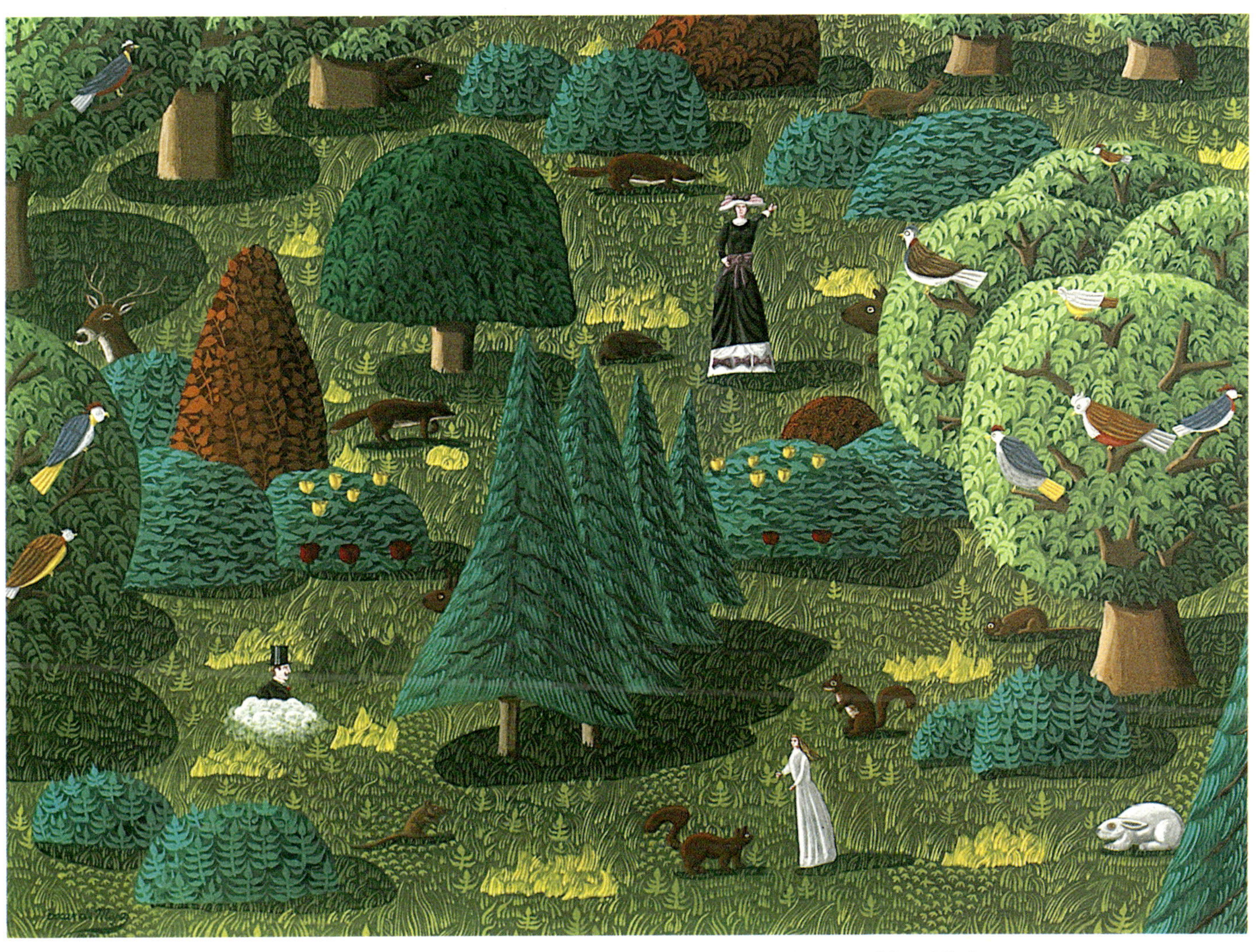

The Forest. 1975. Masonite, 26 × 36″. Private collection, New York

What happier place for the animals than a deep forest in wooded country. The animals are free—they can go where they want, when they want. One exception is the partridge in the center of the tree on the right. She has always longed to be in a zoo, but to her sorrow she has not succeeded. The mother takes her little daughter to the forest. "Too bad father could not come," says the girl. "Yes," says the mother.

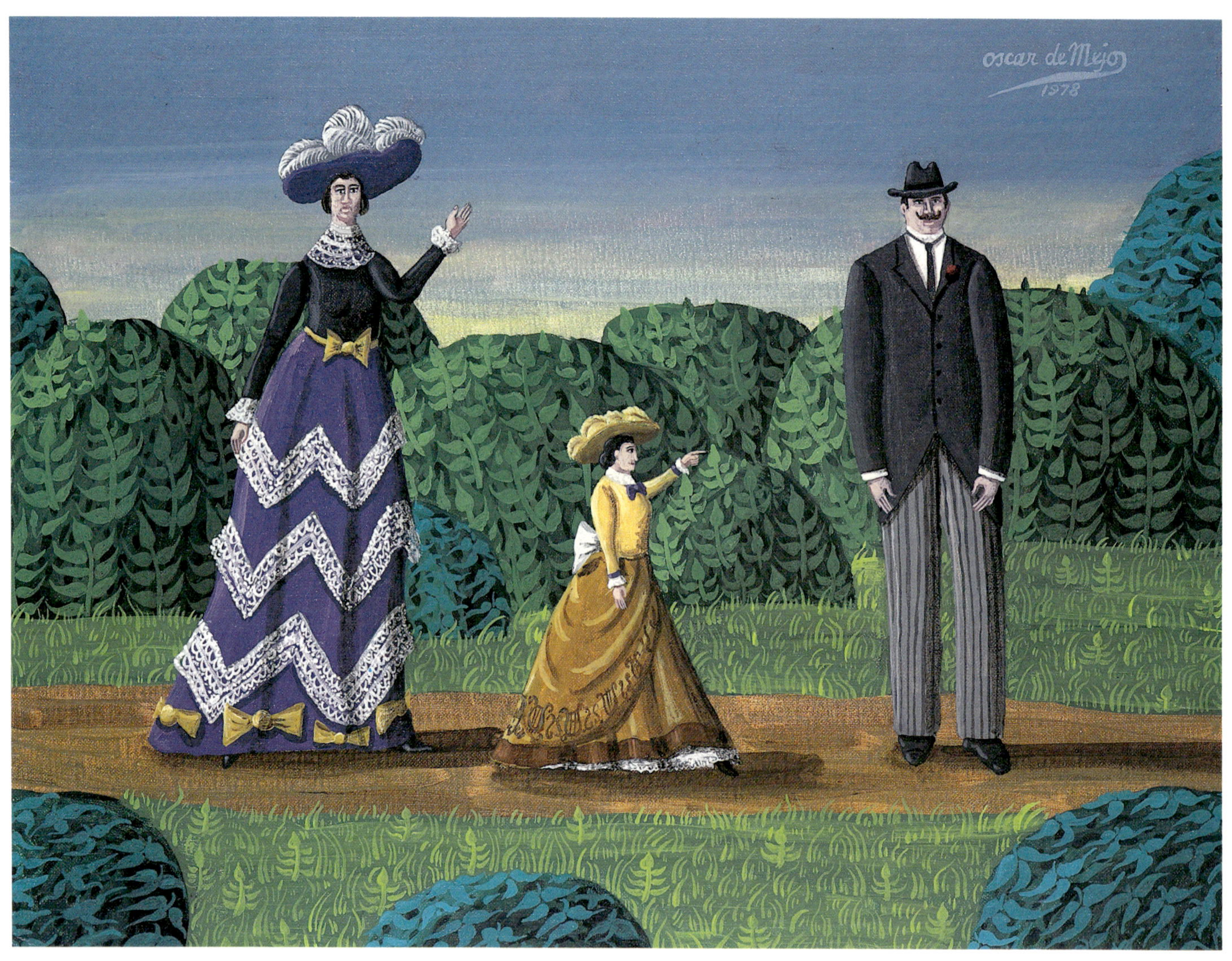

The Little Mother-in-Law. 1978. Canvas, 18 × 24″. Private collection, New York

*The little mother-in-law (center) is from
Kansas City. Despite her size, in the quar-
rels between her daughter (left) and her
son-in-law she becomes very vocal. He is
usually terrified.*

50

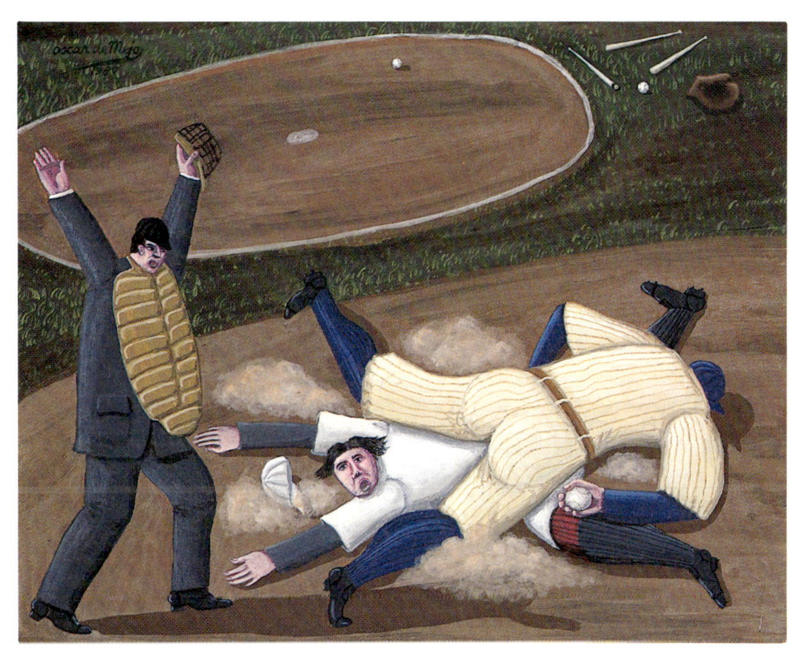

SPORTS

Horse Racing [1776]. 1975. Masonite, 26 × 20″. Collection Mr. and Mrs. Vincent Cassanetti, Greenwich, Connecticut

These brave men have just returned from the war and are competing in a horse race on the main highway. Citizens look on admiringly; a child is scared; a dog follows the horses, barking festively; another dog thinks the world is coming to an end—but the little man on the left faces the galloping horsemen with utmost nonchalance. He is a racer himself, naturally, but nobody knows.

PRECEDING PAGE:
Tagged. 1980. Masonite, 16 × 20″. Private collection, New York

This painting was commissioned by Sports Illustrated. *It was never used by the magazine. Did I feel bad about it? Yes, I did.*

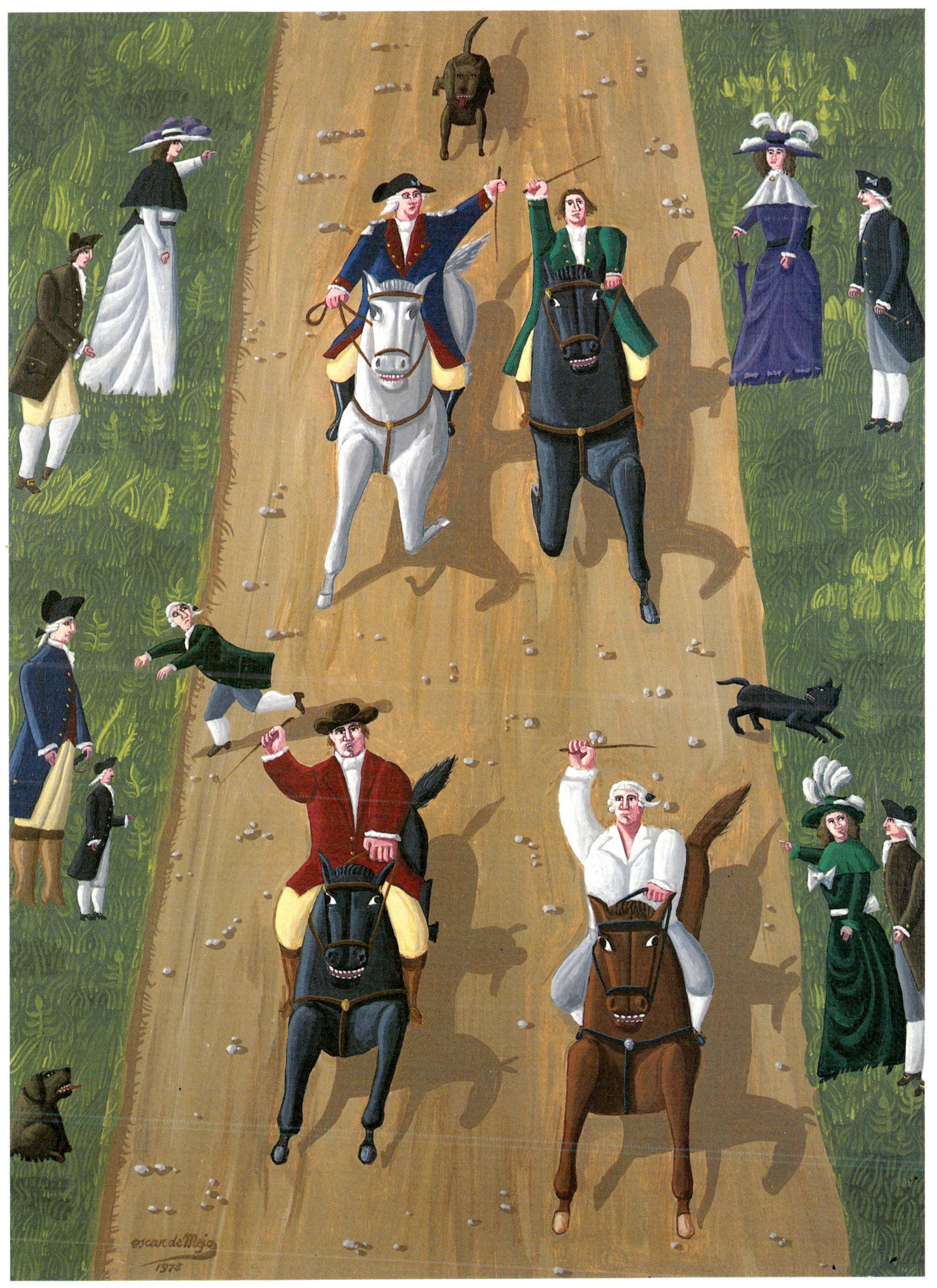

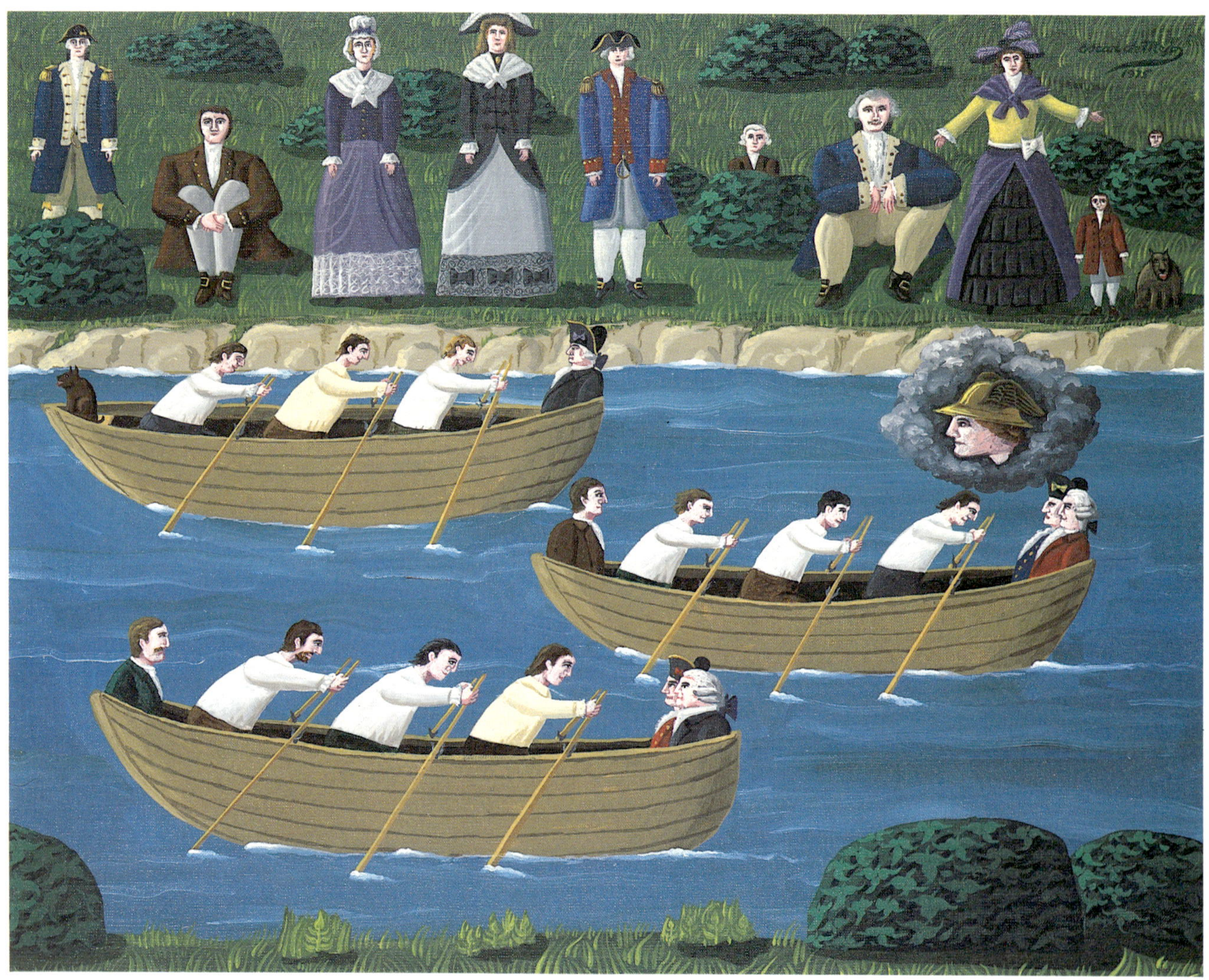

Rowing Contest [1776]. 1975. Canvas, 22 × 28″. Private collection, New York

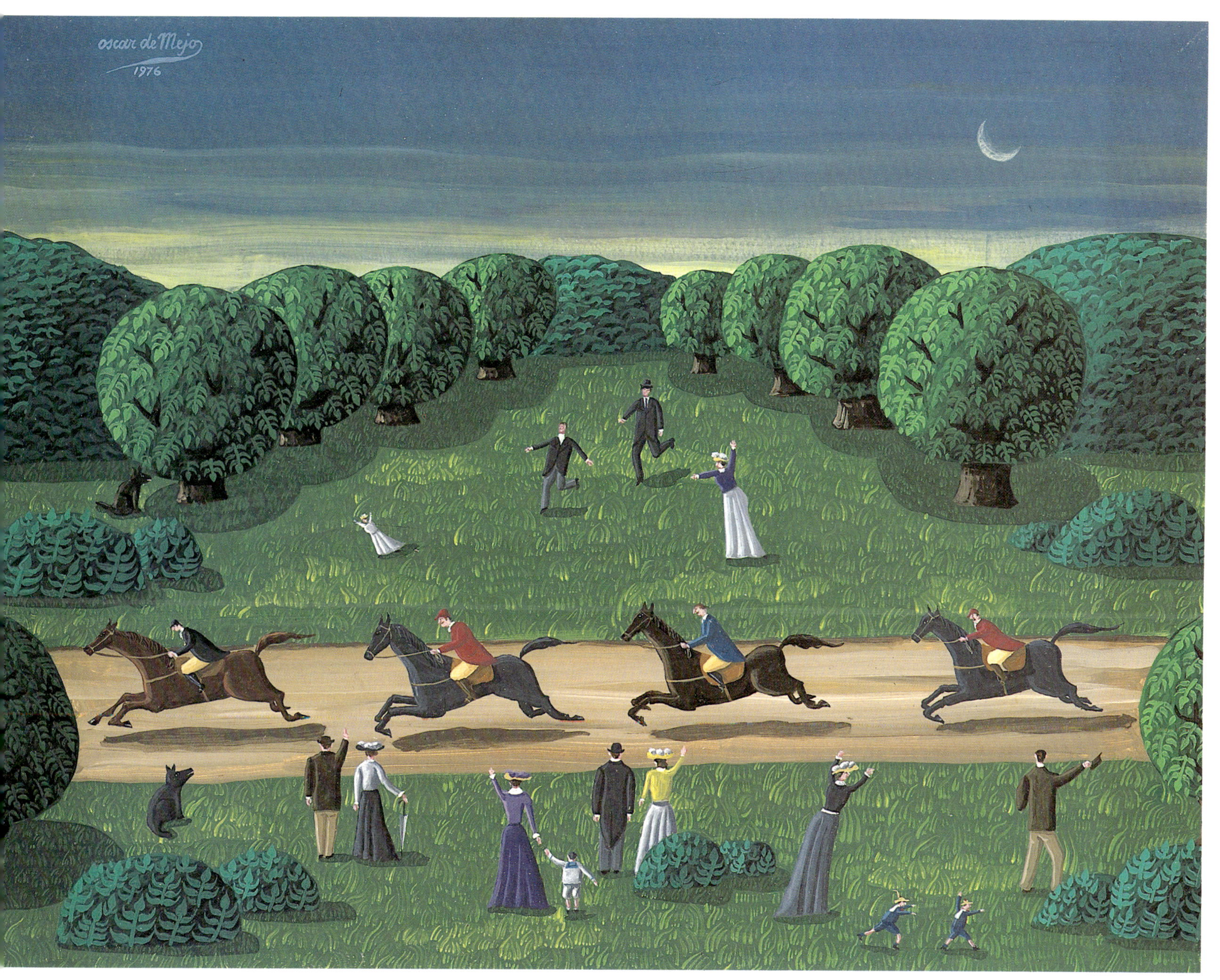

Horse Racing [1900]. 1976. Masonite, 20 × 26″. Private collection, New York

The four horsemen proudly *galloping*
along one of the park's main avenues
arouse a most flattering excitement among
strollers. Only the twins, Michael and
Timothy (foreground right), ignore them
with total disrespect.

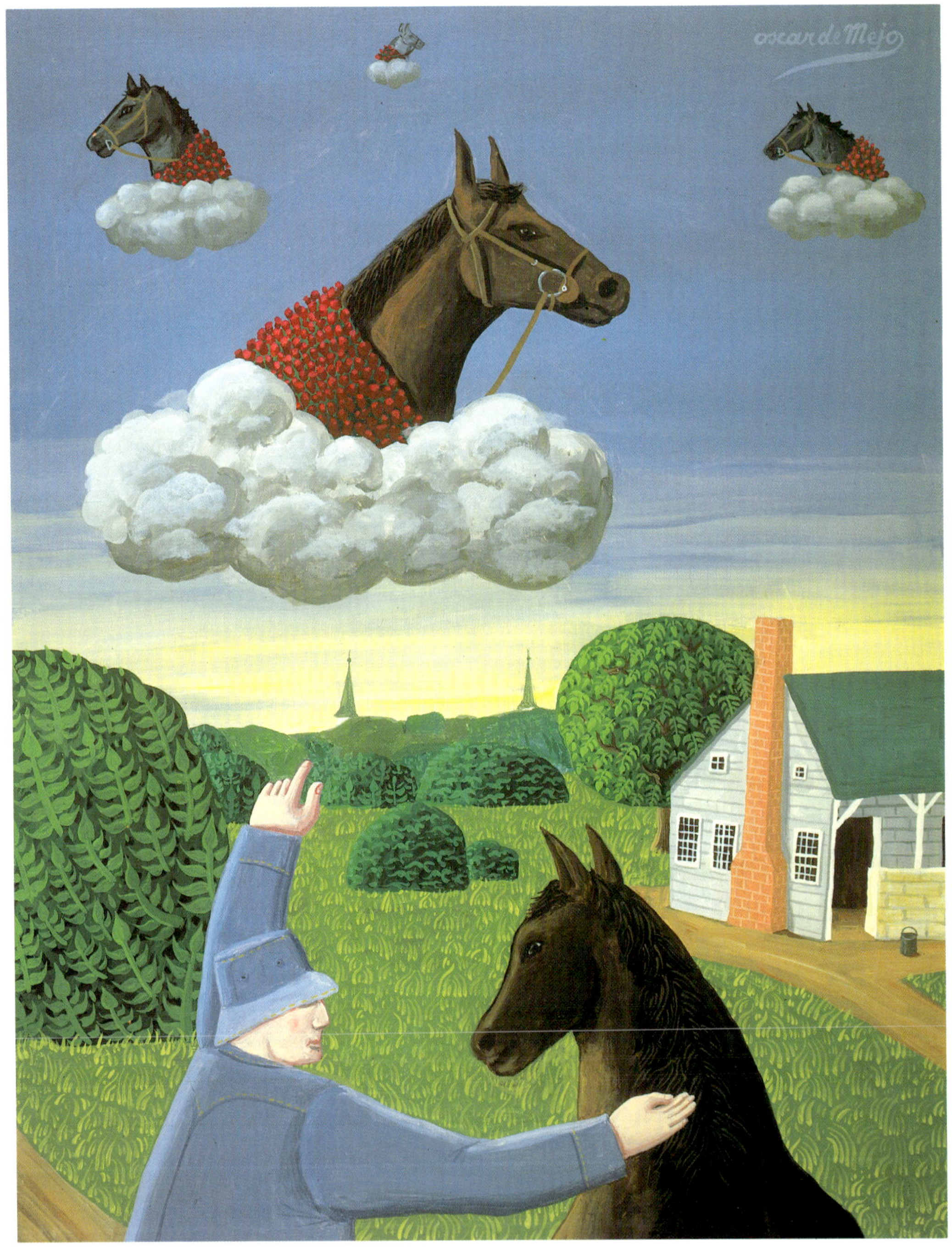

Kentucky Derby I [1977]. 1977. Masonite, 26 × 20″. Private collection, New York

On the night before the race, horse and trainer take a little walk. "See up there," says the trainer, "you too can be there tomorrow." "I know, I know," says the horse, "you want me to run a little faster." "No!" says the trainer, "I want you to fly! And without wings!"

OPPOSITE:
Looking at the binoculars of the spectators is like looking into their heads with a CAT scanner. When the race is on, they think only of their favorite horse and jockey. Incidentally, this particular gentleman is very lucky: he is not only looking at his favorite horse and jockey, he is looking at the Winner.

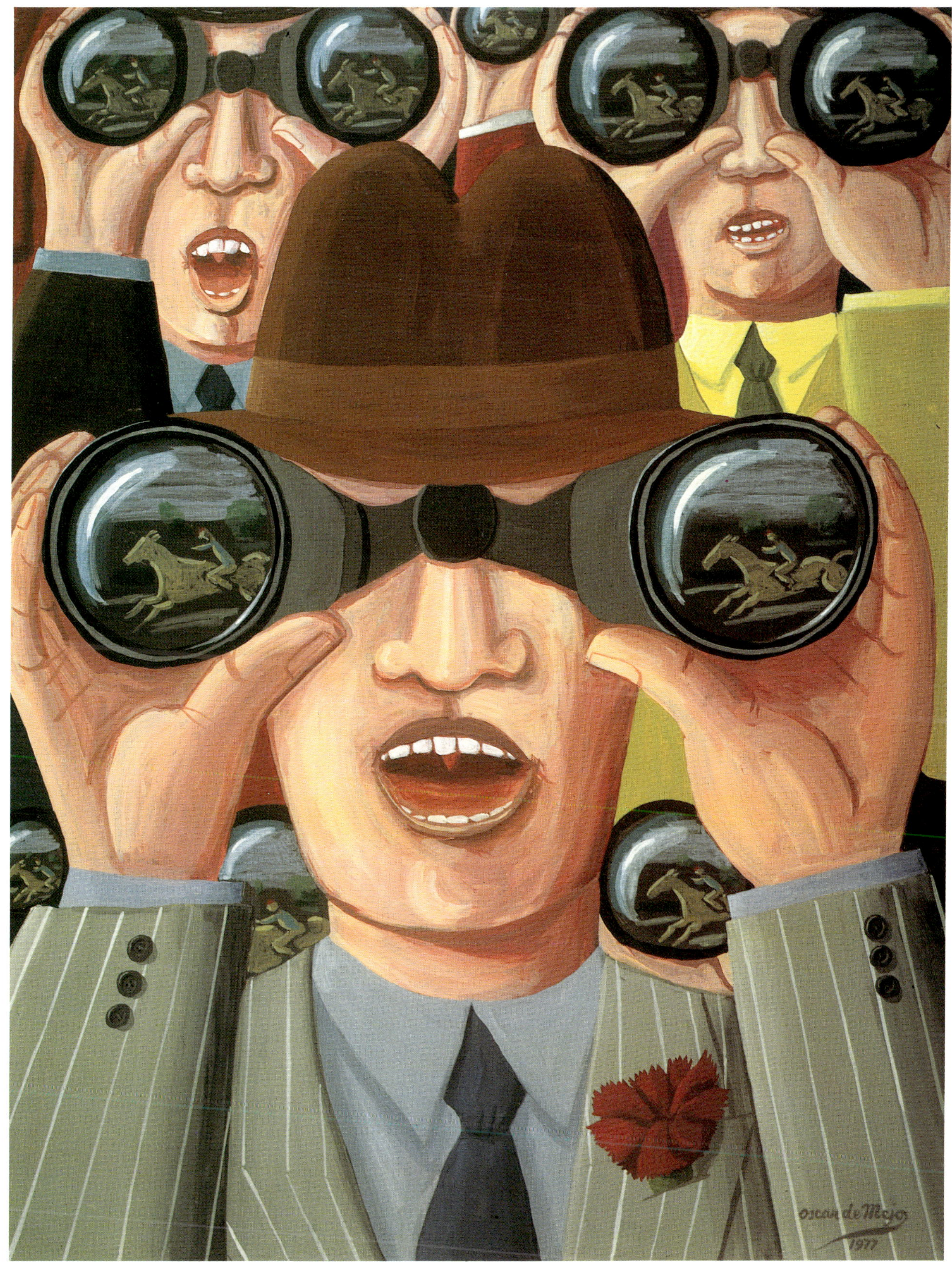

Kentucky Derby II [1977]. 1977. Masonite, 26 × 20″. Collection Carl Palmstierna, Stockholm

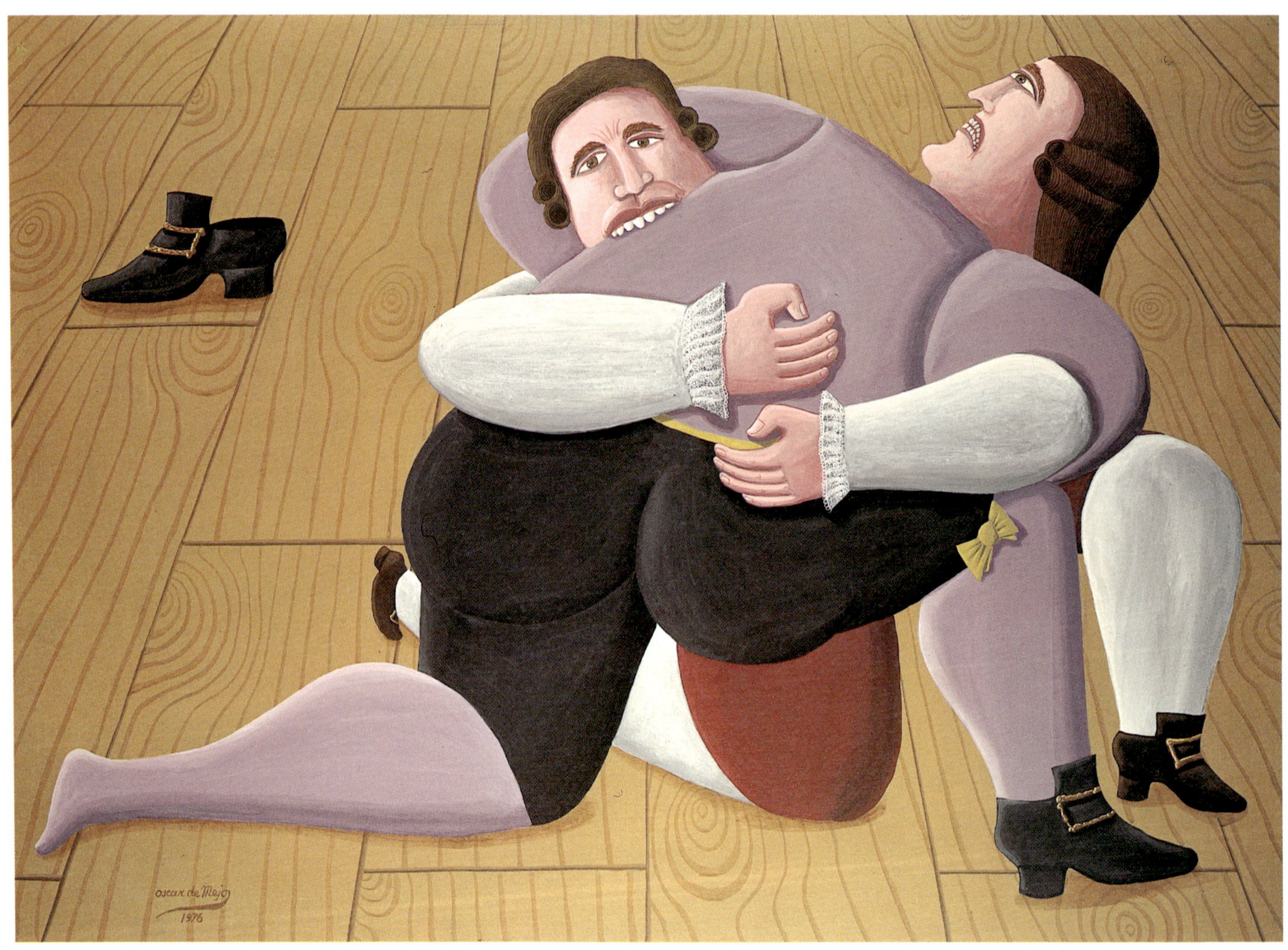

Champions of Gouging [1776]. 1976. Canvas, 48×68″. Private collection, New York

One of the most violent sports in America in Colonial times was gouging, if one considers that the rules permitted the gouging of an eye from the adversary's face. Biting was one of the mildest forms of behavior in these fights, and our champion (above), whose name is Ladislaus Dickson Mc-Nulty, plants his teeth with gusto in his adversary's body.

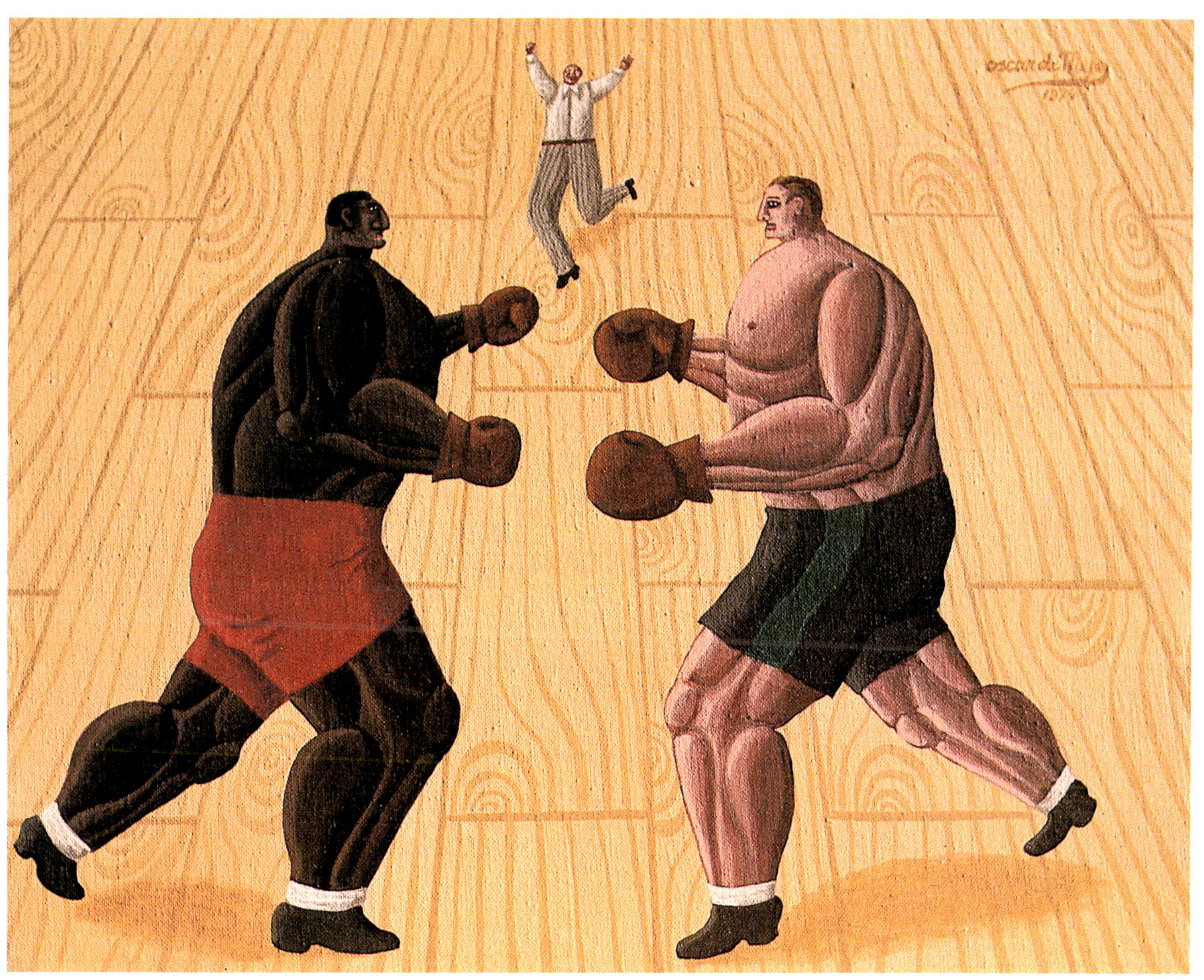

The Boxers II. 1974. Masonite, 14 × 18″. Private collection, New York

Need I mention that these are heavy-weights? Actually, they are heavy heavy-weights. The brutality of the sport is em-phasized by the big bodies and the bulging muscles. But don't get me wrong, I love boxing.

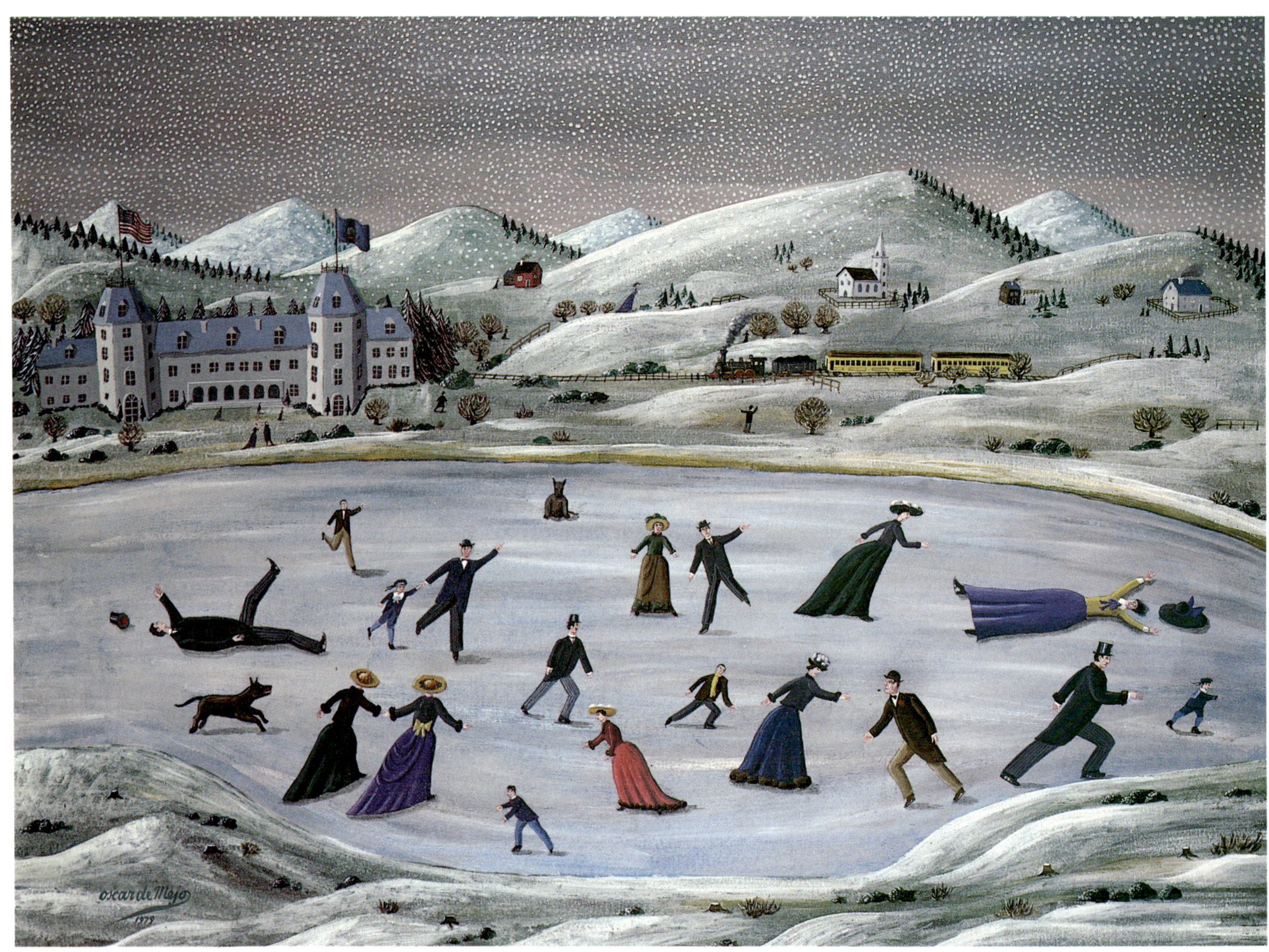

Vermont Skating [1900]. 1979. Canvas, 36 × 50″. Private collection, New York

The harder they fall, the happier they feel. This seems to be the motto of the happy skaters who practice their favorite sport from morning to night in front of this plush Vermont hotel. Not taking part in the fun is a mysterious lady who appears to be at least eight to ten feet tall (center above train engine). Is she an effect of light refraction, a Fata Morgana, or the real thing?

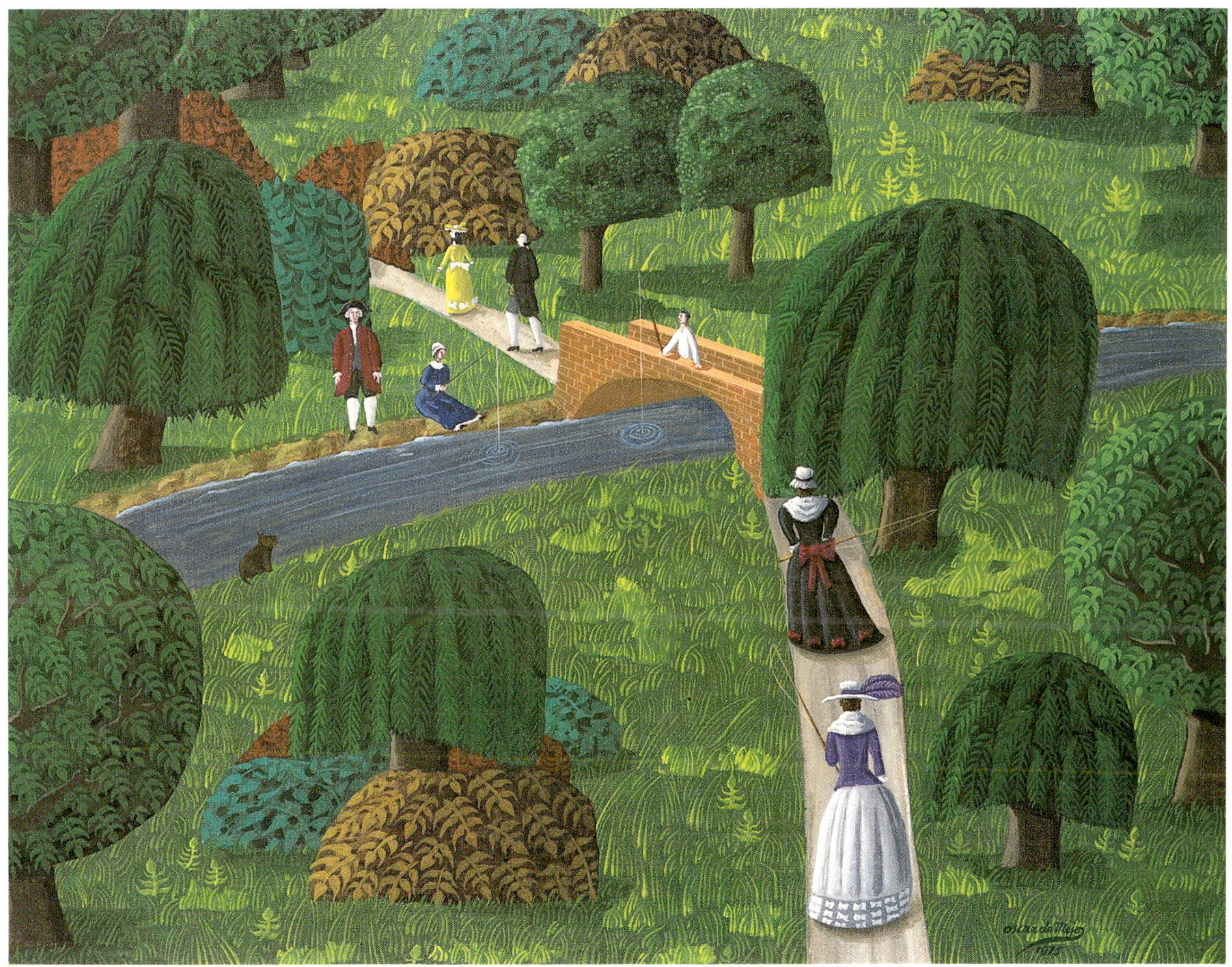

Philadelphia Fishing Club [1776]. 1975. Canvas, 20 × 26″. Aberbach Fine Art, New York

In this painting commissioned by Sports Illustrated *for the Bicentennial, we see one of the favorite sports of that time —fishing. While cannon and musket fire are disrupting the peace only a few miles away, here in this bucolic landscape unharassed ladies and gentlemen dedicate their time to the total destruction of the fish in the little brook.*

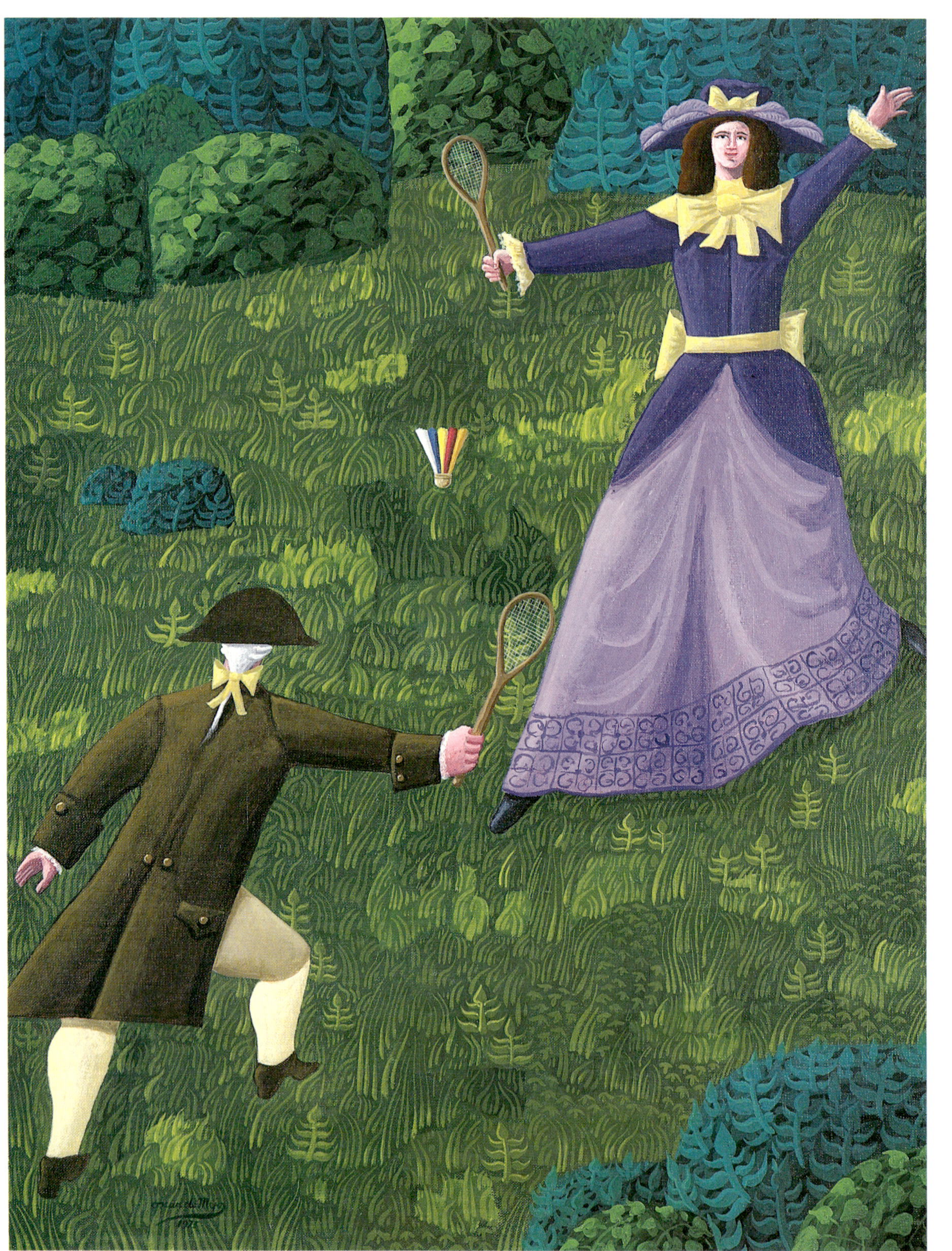

Badminton [1775]. 1975. Canvas, 2
22". Aberbach Fine Arts, New Yor

*He fought at Breed's Hill and is now
leave. With his Linda he plays badmir
in the municipal park, never suspec
that her heart belongs to somebody ɔ
After the game, Linda takes a little res
the grass while he romantically pulls
feathers from the badminton ball: "...
loves me, she loves me not, she lɔ
me..."*

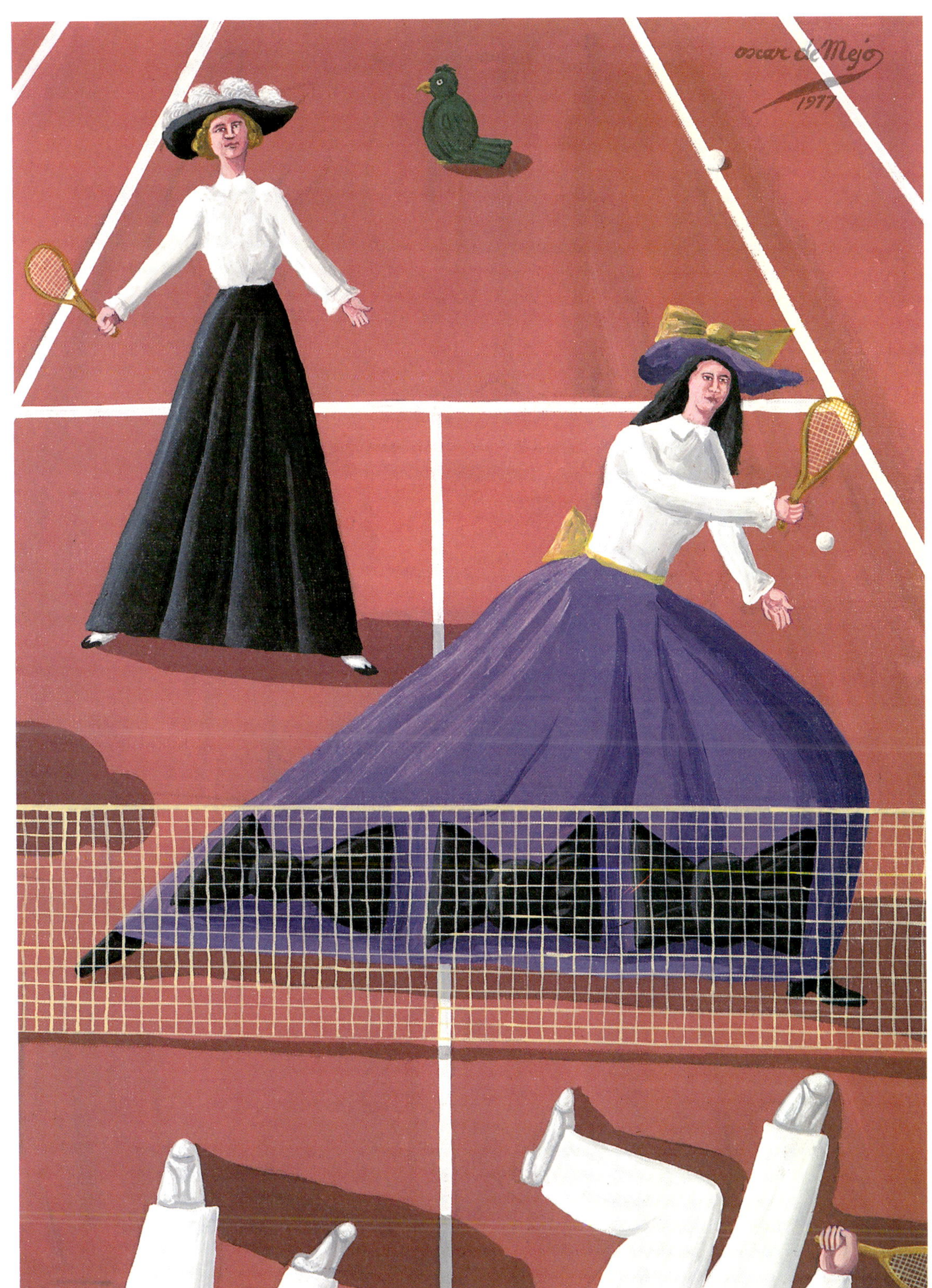

A *Romantic Foursome* [c. 1880]. 1977.
Canvas, 24×18″. Private collection,
New York

*This painting is called A Romantic Four-
some because the players are all romantically involved. The lady on the left is in
love with the gentleman on the right; the
lady on the right is also crazy about the
gentleman on the right; the man on the left
is in love with both ladies but is undecided
to which one to propose; and the man on
the right loves someone who is not in the
picture. The perspective which I use in
depicting the two players in the foreground
could only be attempted in a moment of
great courage and with inspiration from
the great artist Mantegna.*

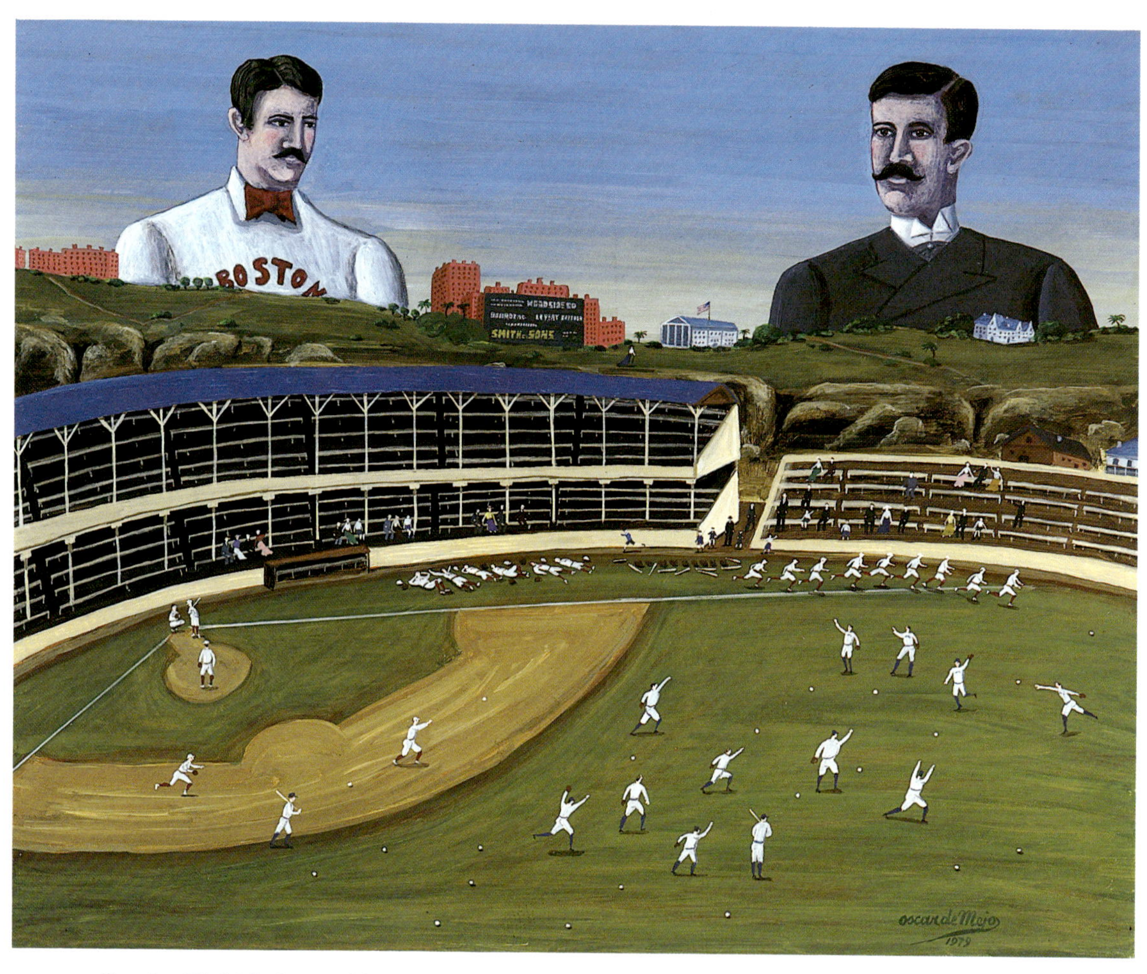

On the Field I [c. 1900]. 1979. Masonite, 24 × 30″. Private collection, New York

On the first day of spring training two great figures of the sport come in spirit to watch the game—Albert Spalding (left) and the first baseball Super Star, Mike "King" Kelly of the Boston Base Ball Club.

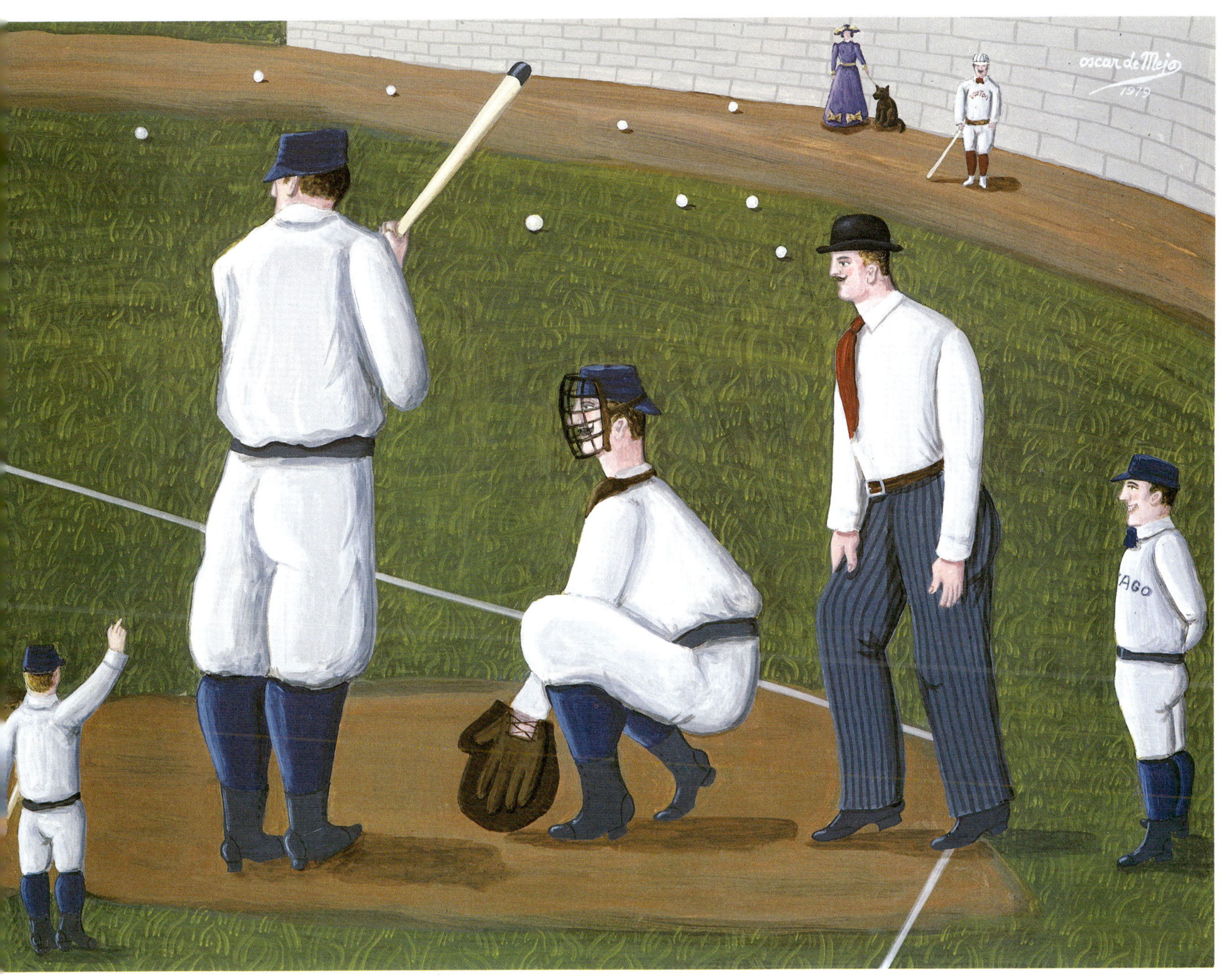

On the Field II [c. 1900]. 1979. Masonite, 18×24″. Private collection, New York

This is a close-up of some players in the
game being played on the preceding page.

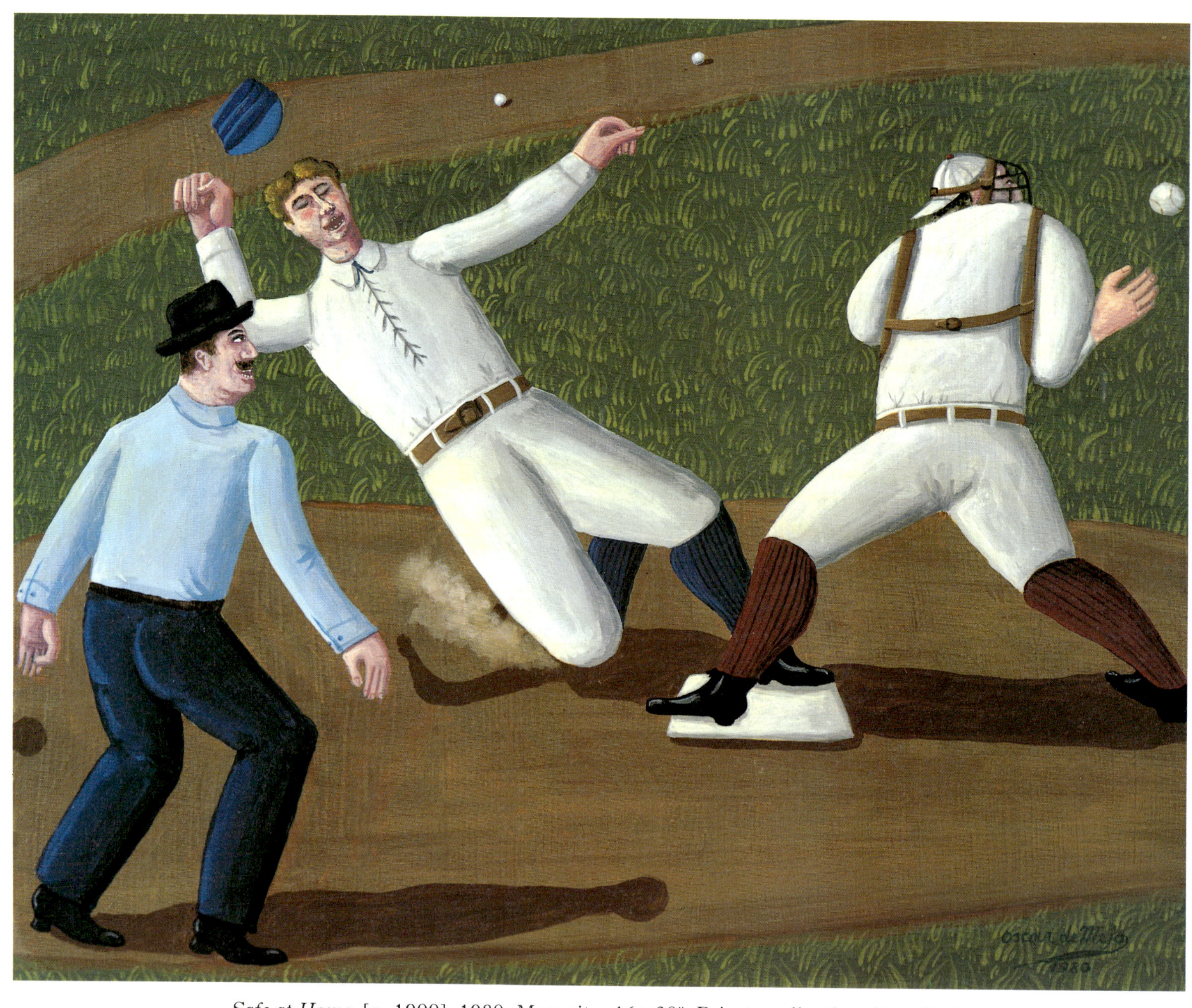

Safe at Home [c. 1900]. 1980. Masonite, 16×20″. Private collection, New York

Sometimes in a baseball game some players
attain the graceful posture of ballet dancers.

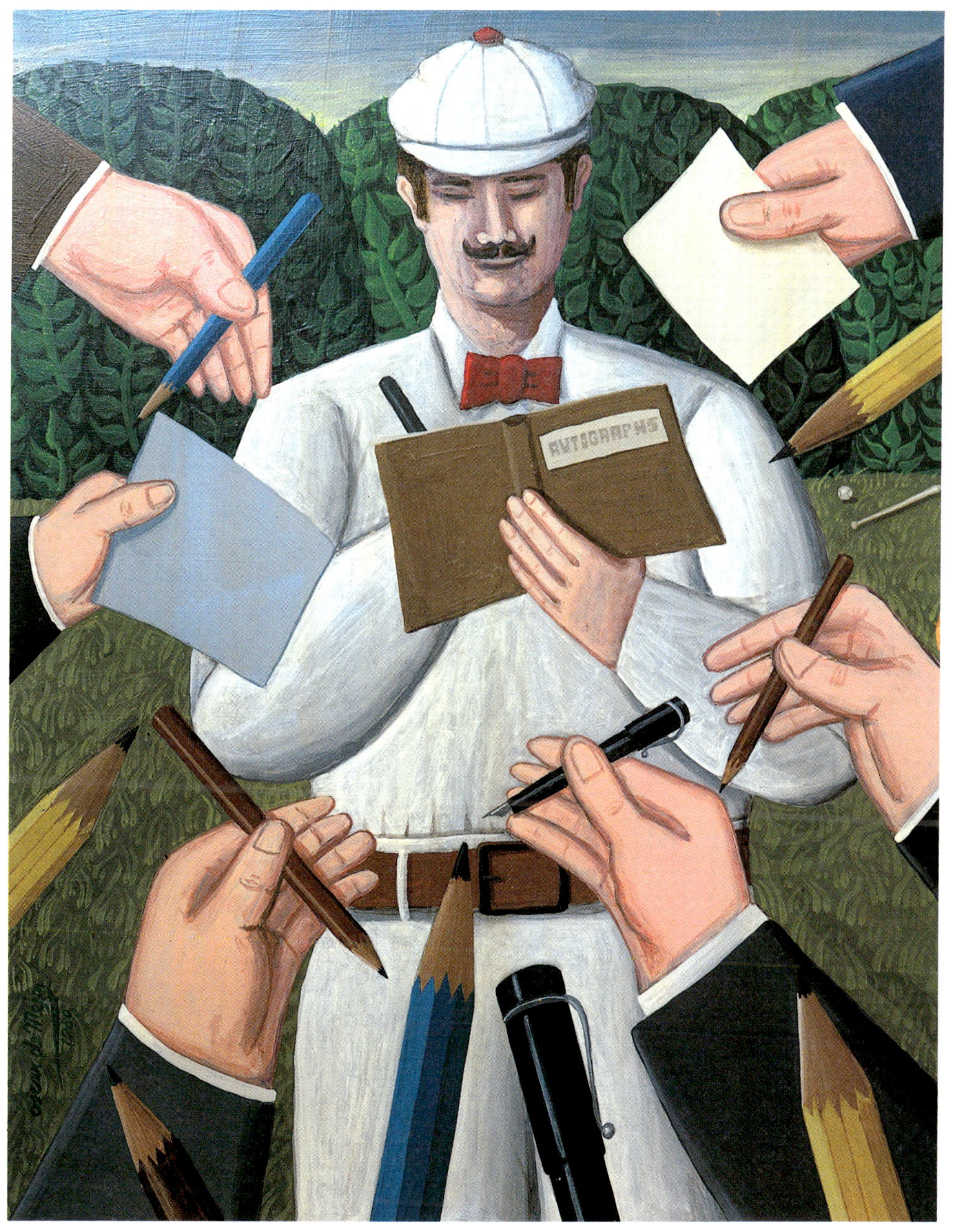

The Autograph [c. 1900]. 1980. Masonite, 20×16″. Private collection

I could make all kinds of convincing arguments to explain why I decided to call this picture The Autograph, *but let's not go into that. The young baseball champion seen here is quite happy to sign his name time and time again. Yes, it's a boring routine, but thanks to it he has at home a fabulous collection of pencils and fountain pens—especially fountain pens.*

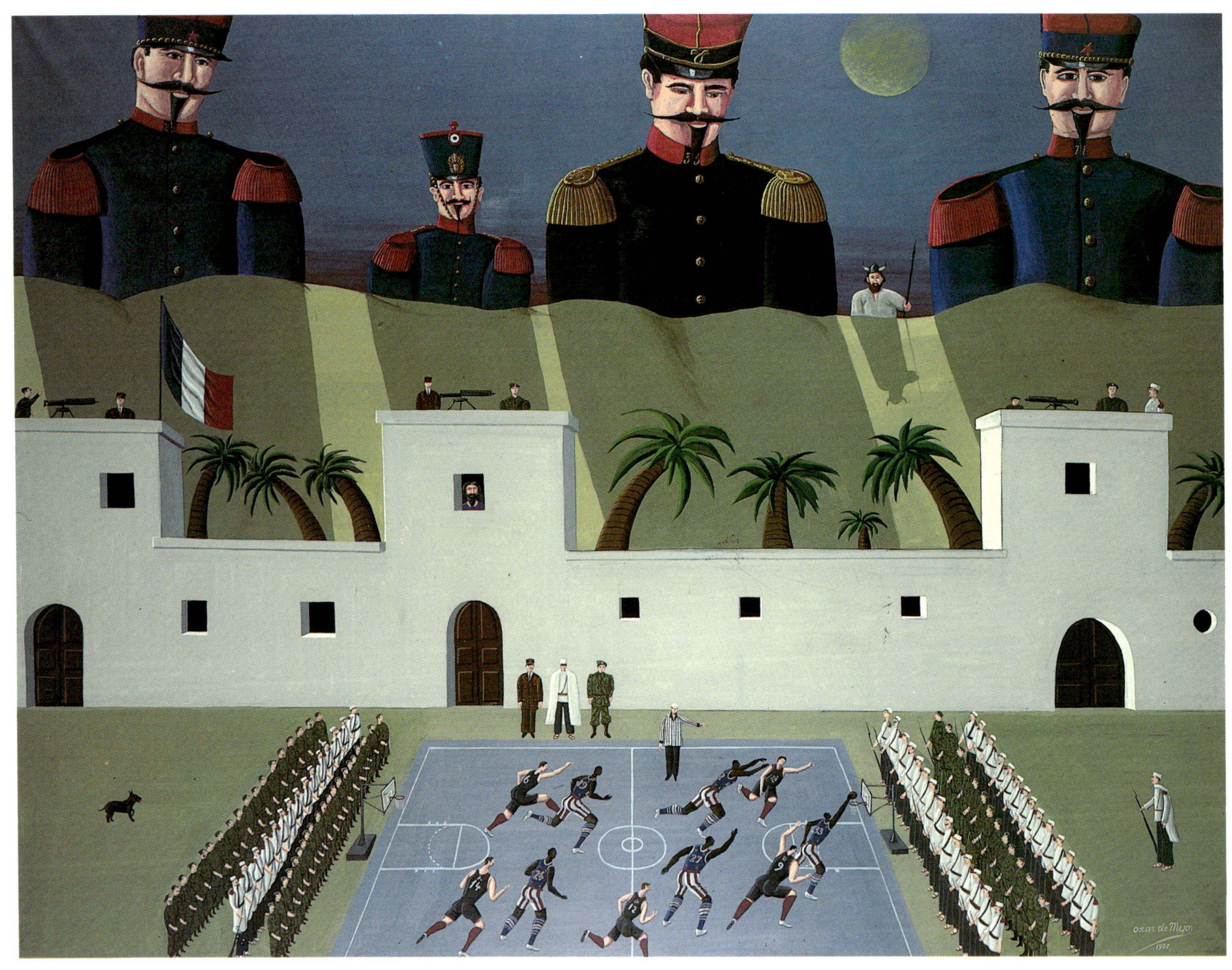

The Globetrotters in Algeria [1957]. 1977. Canvas, 72 × 96″. Metromedia, Los Angeles

Great personages of France are present at
a performance given by the Globetrotters
for the French Foreign Legion.

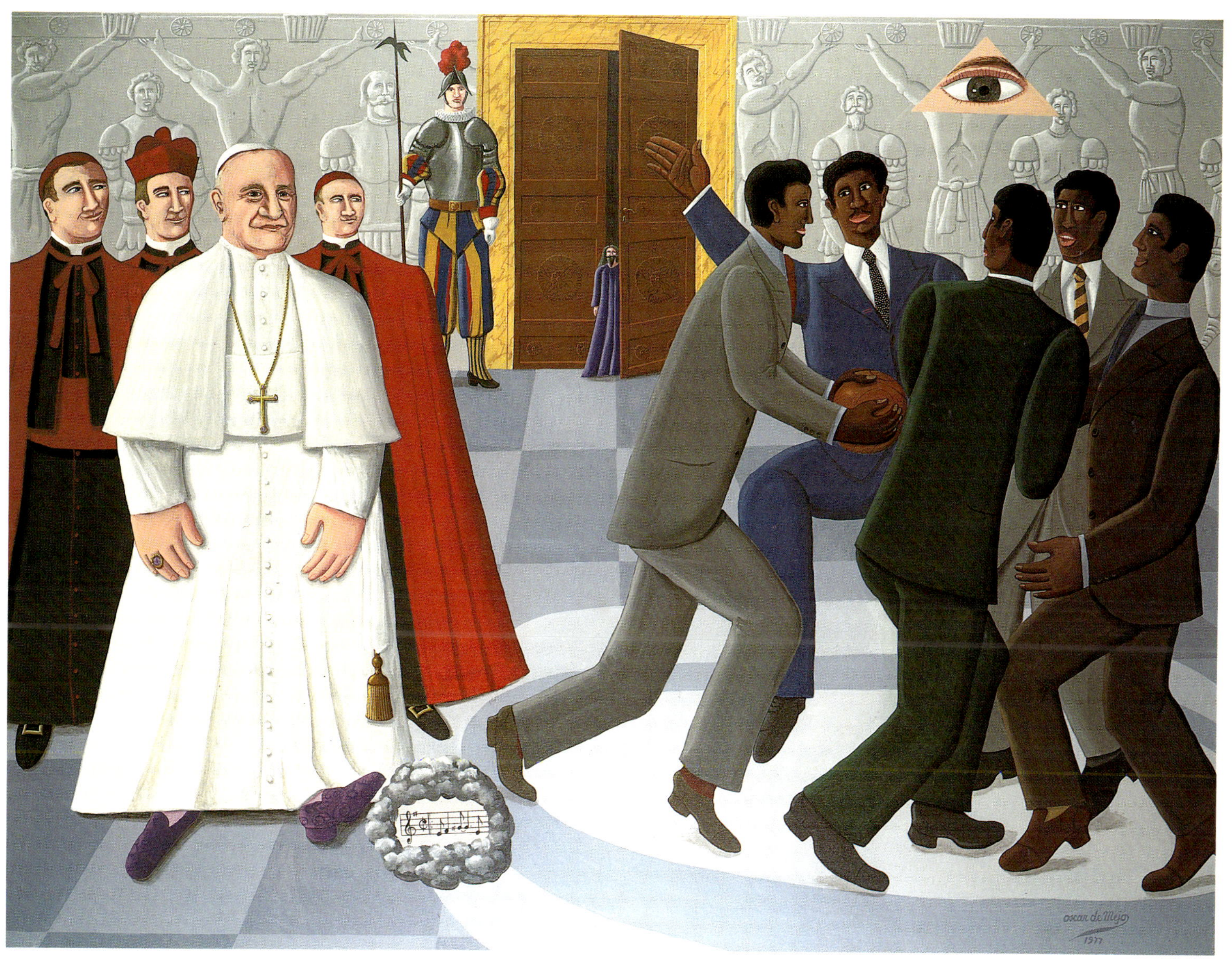

The Globetrotters in the Vatican. 1977. Canvas, 72×96″. Metromedia, Los Angeles

*Invited to the Vatican for an audience with
the Pope, the Harlem Globetrotters give a
demonstration of their opening number.
Pope John XXIII taps his foot to the beat
of "Sweet Georgia Brown" as the Eye of
an astonished God looks on.*

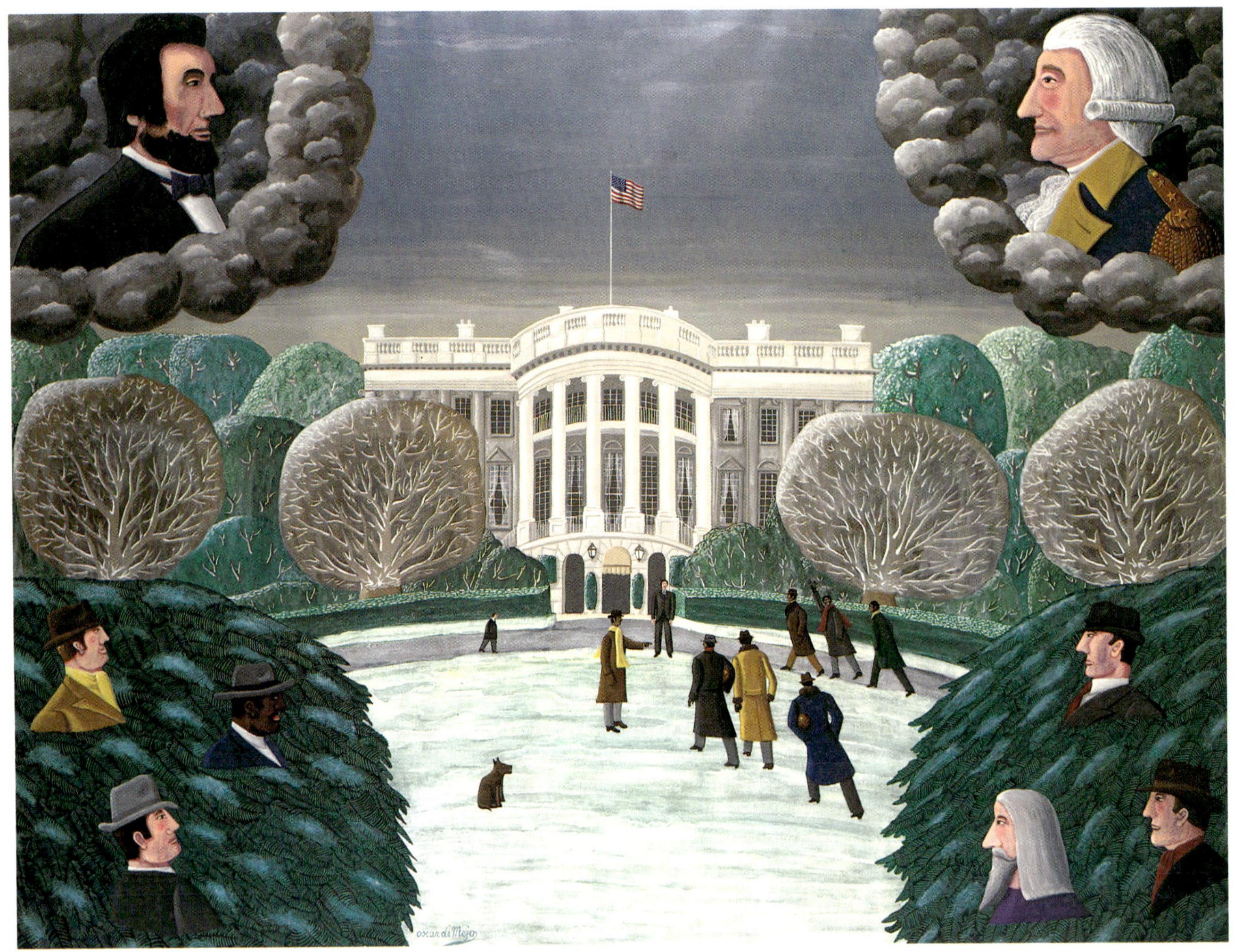

The Globetrotters at the White House. 1977. Canvas, 72 × 96″. Metromedia, Los Angeles

Here the Harlem Globetrotters are about to enter the White House for an informal visit with President Gerald Ford. The atmosphere is cheerful and yet solemn as the athletes think of some of the great presidents of the past. In the trees, security men watch carefully. The old man with a beard is a little spirit who follows the Globetrotters wherever they go.

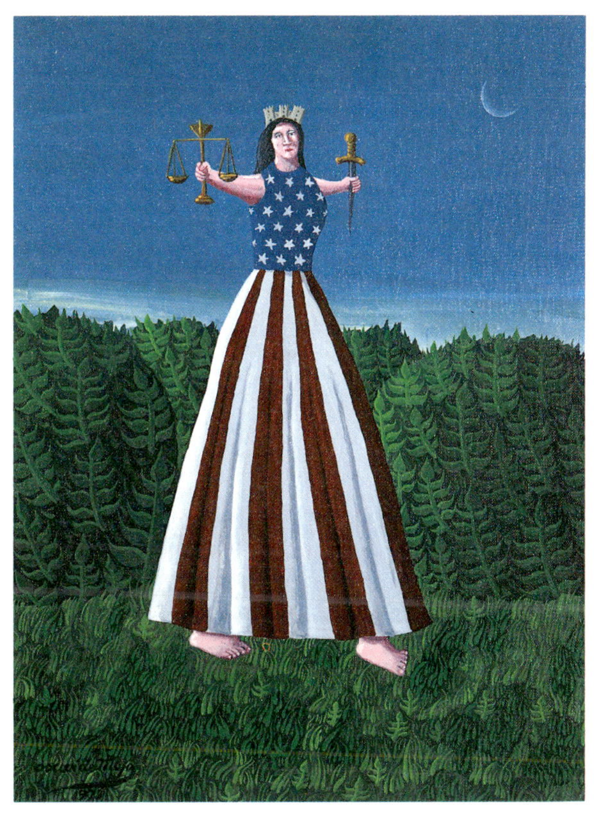

AMERICAN HISTORY

Mother America. 1973. Masonite, 18 ×
14". Private collection, New York

*Mother America is not to be taken lightly.
Her sword vouches for that. But the jus-
tice she dispenses, equal for all, is abso-
lutely accurate: she has a very precise scale
with which to measure it.*

*Paul Revere is warning the countryside of
approaching British soldiers. It is the start
of the Revolutionary War.*

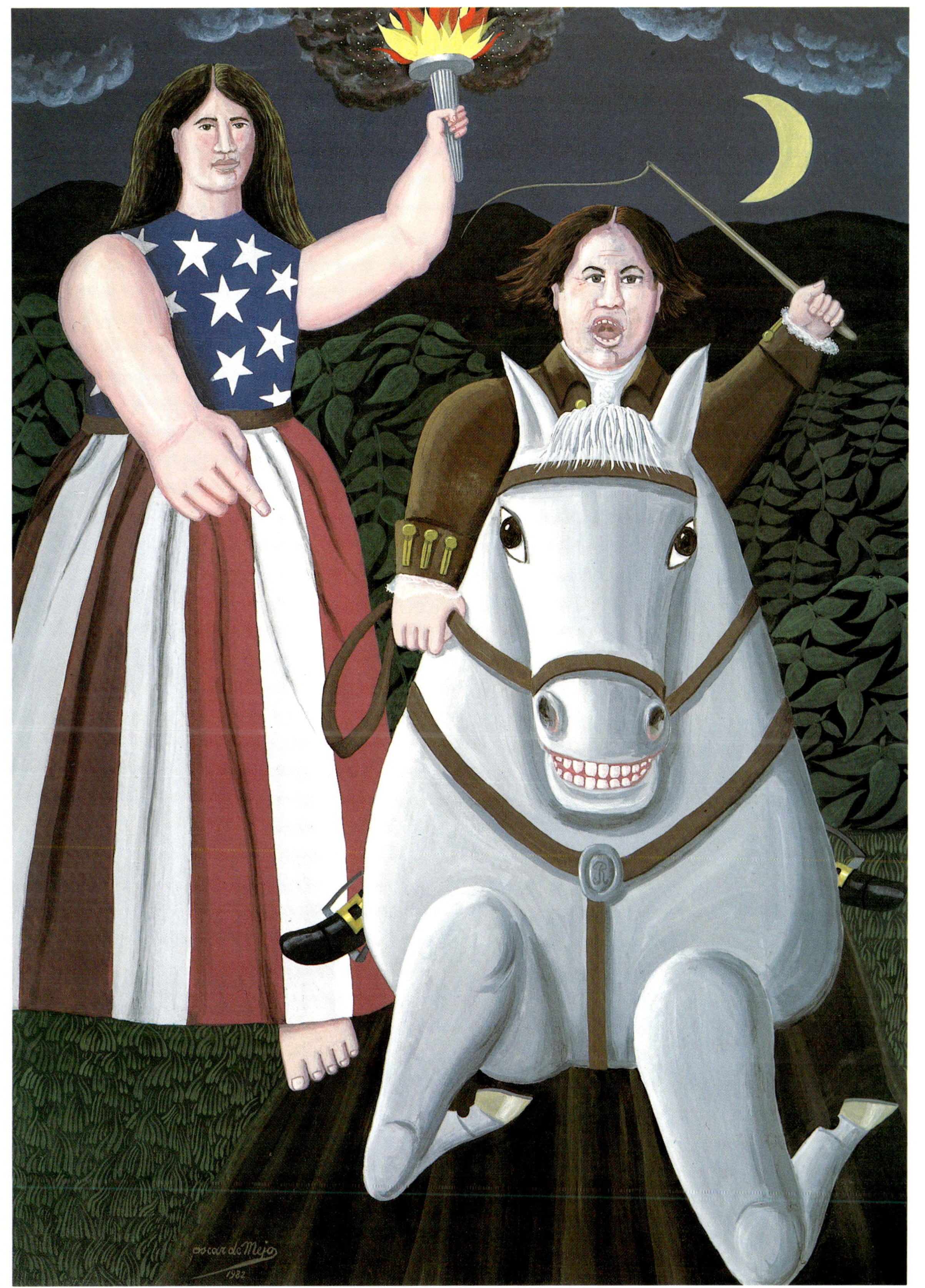

The British Are Coming [1775]. 1982. Canvas, 36×50″. Aberbach Fine Art, New York

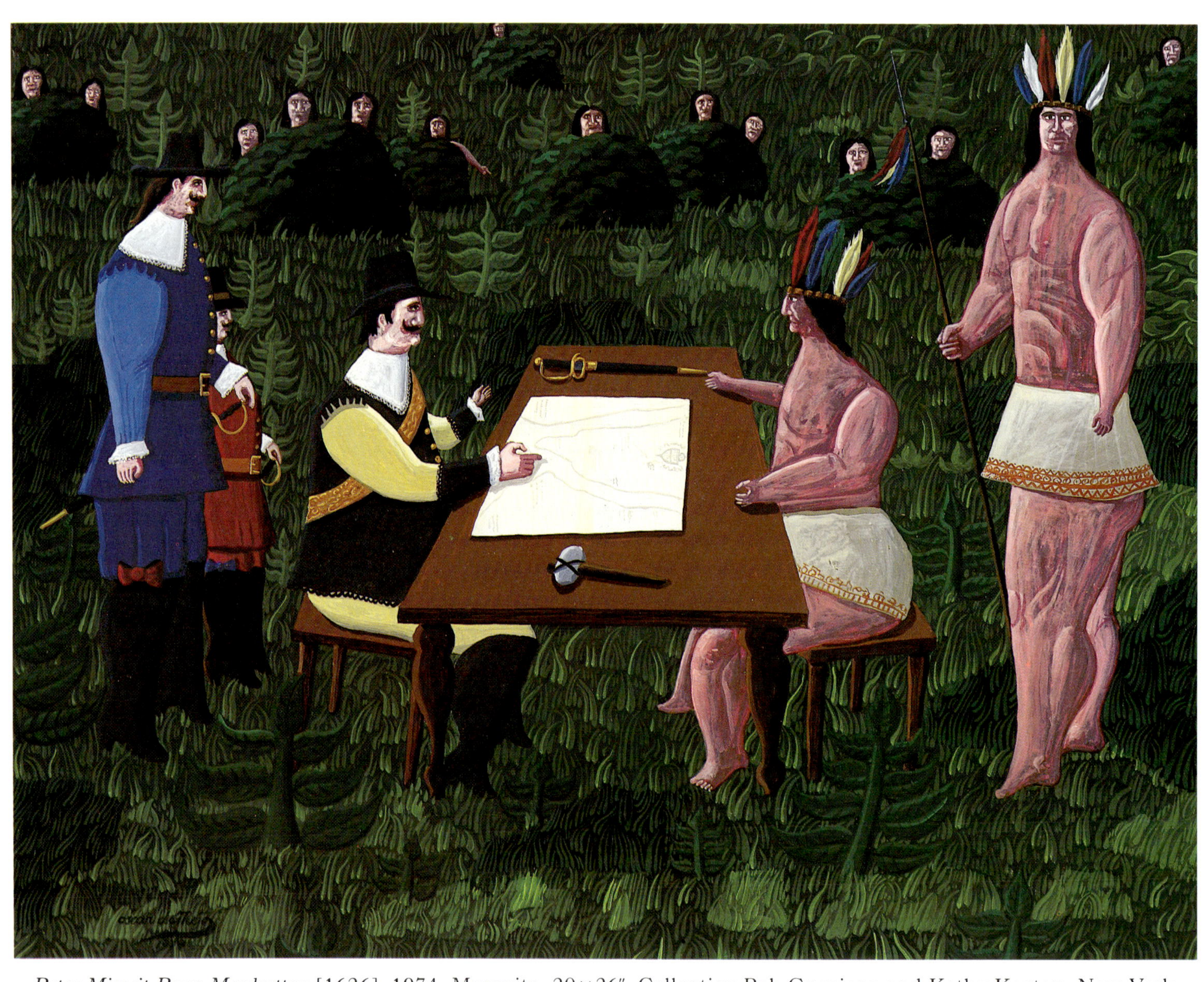

Peter Minuit Buys Manhattan [1626]. 1974. Masonite, 20×26". Collection Bob Guccione and Kathy Keeton, New York

*For 60 guilders (about 24 dollars) a group
of Dutch settlers headed by Peter Minuit
buy Manhattan Island from the Indians
and name it New Amsterdam. When the
British capture it in 1664, they rename it
New York.*

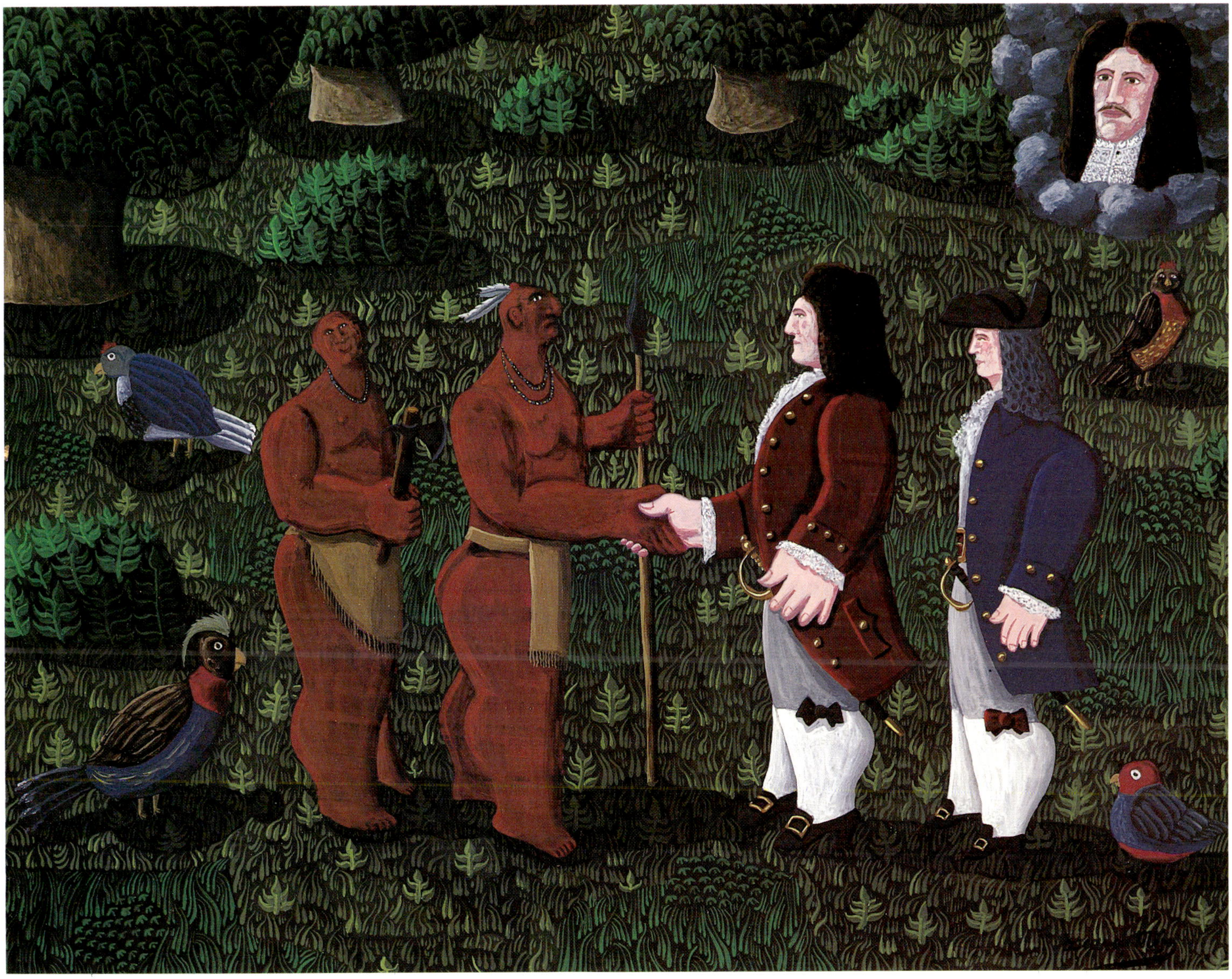

The Founding of Philadelphia [1682]. 1973. Masonite, 20 × 26″. Collection Bob Guccione and Kathy Keeton, New York

In the name of King Charles II (upper right corner) William Penn, the Quaker leader, visits the construction site where the city of Philadelphia will be built. The well-fed Indians receiving him vouch for the opulence and fertility of the territory.

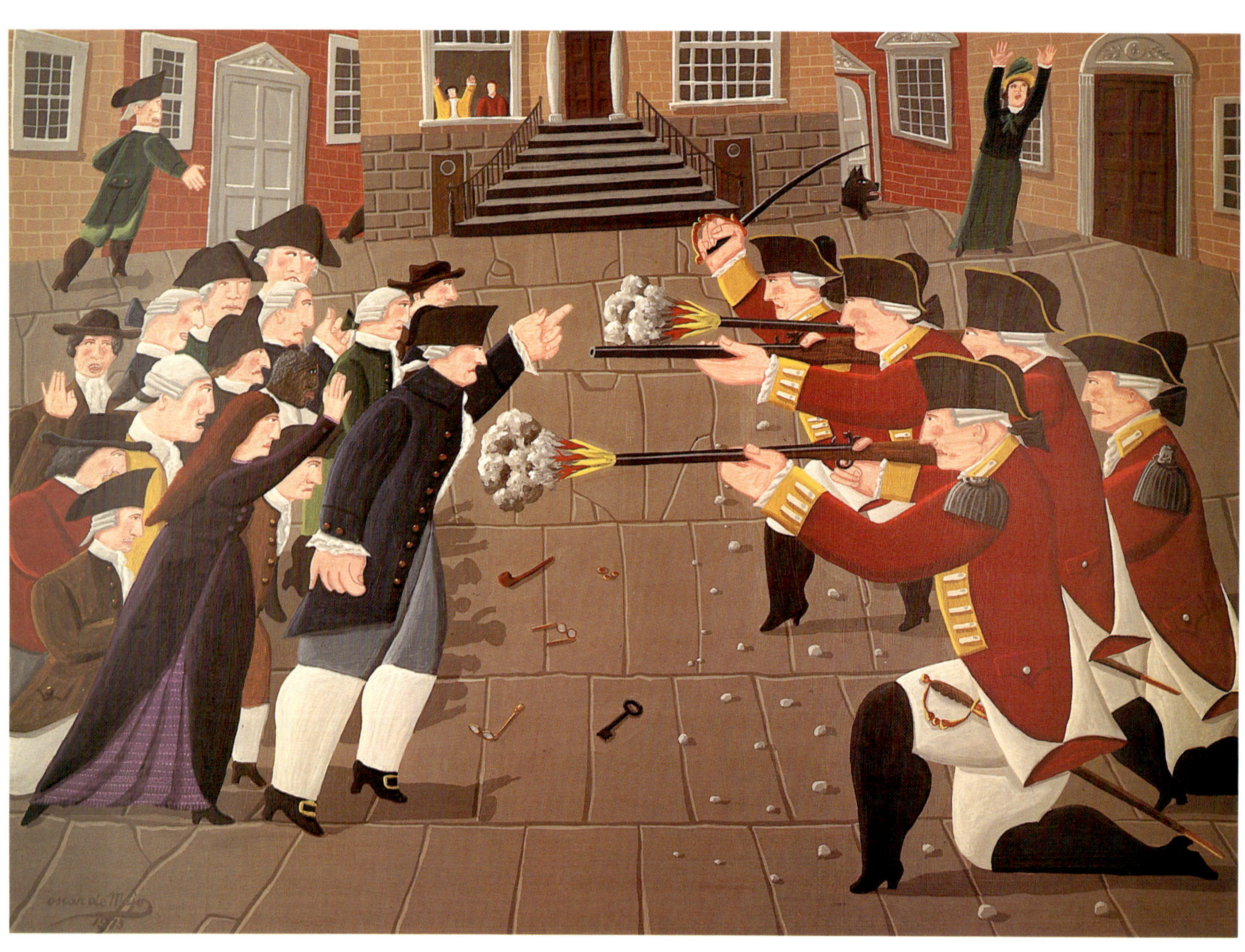

The Boston Massacre [1770]. 1973. Masonite, 26×36″. Collection Paul Foley, New York

On March 5, 1770, a crowd of hotheads
throws stones at a British sentry near the
Custom House. A riot follows. A British
officer, Captain Thomas Preston, tries to
stop his soldiers from firing, but it is too
late. Five Americans are killed, among
them Crispus Attucks, the first black to
die in the Revolutionary War.

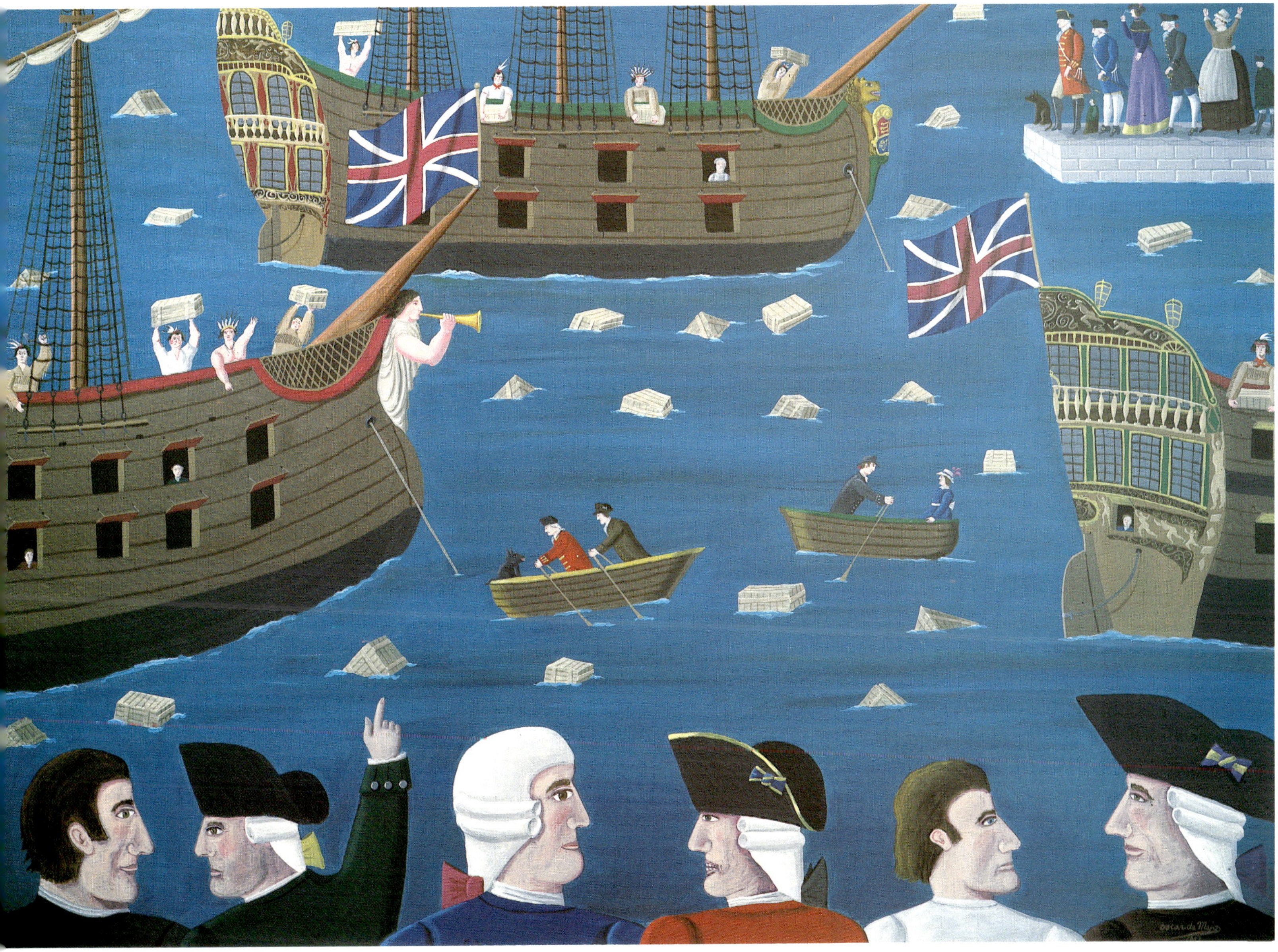

The Boston Tea Party [1773]. 1982. Canvas, 48×68″. Aberbach Fine Art, New York

Admiring bystanders watch as proper
Bostonians, dressed as Indians, dispose
of His Majesty's newly arrived tea.

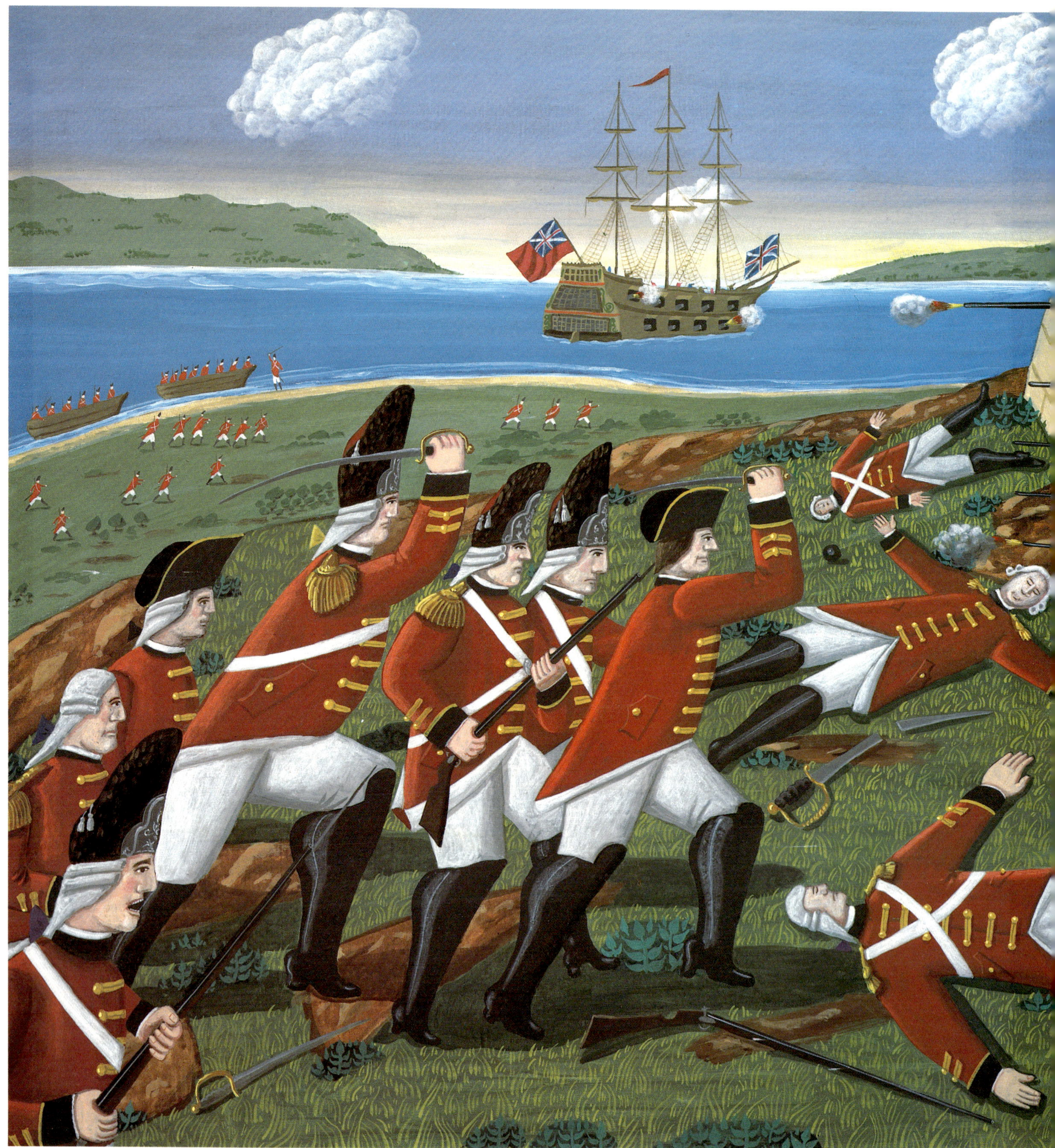

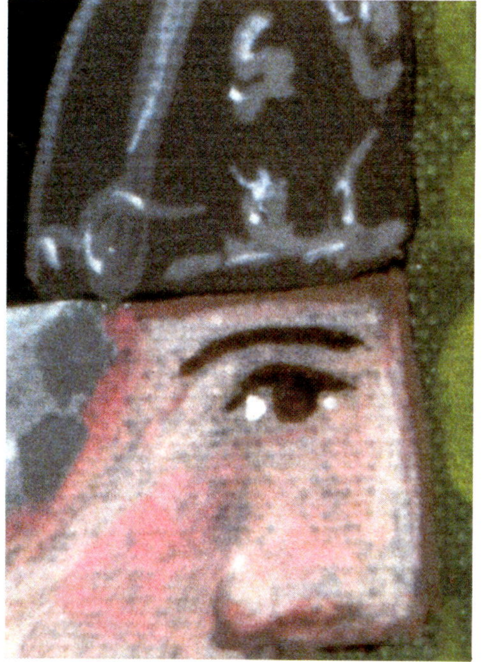

The Battle of Breed's Hill [1775]. 1982.
Canvas, 36×50″. Aberbach Fine Art,
New York

*On June 17, 2,400 British troops attack
the 1,600 Americans entrenched on the
hills near Boston. With great courage, the
Red Coats march in parade formation
against the enemy lines. Israel Putnam,
the American colonel, tells his men not to
shoot "until you see the whites of their
eyes." It is a ferocious encounter. Twice
the British are repulsed before taking the
hill; they count 1054 casualties against
the 100 American dead. This is the fight
often called the Battle of Bunker Hill.*

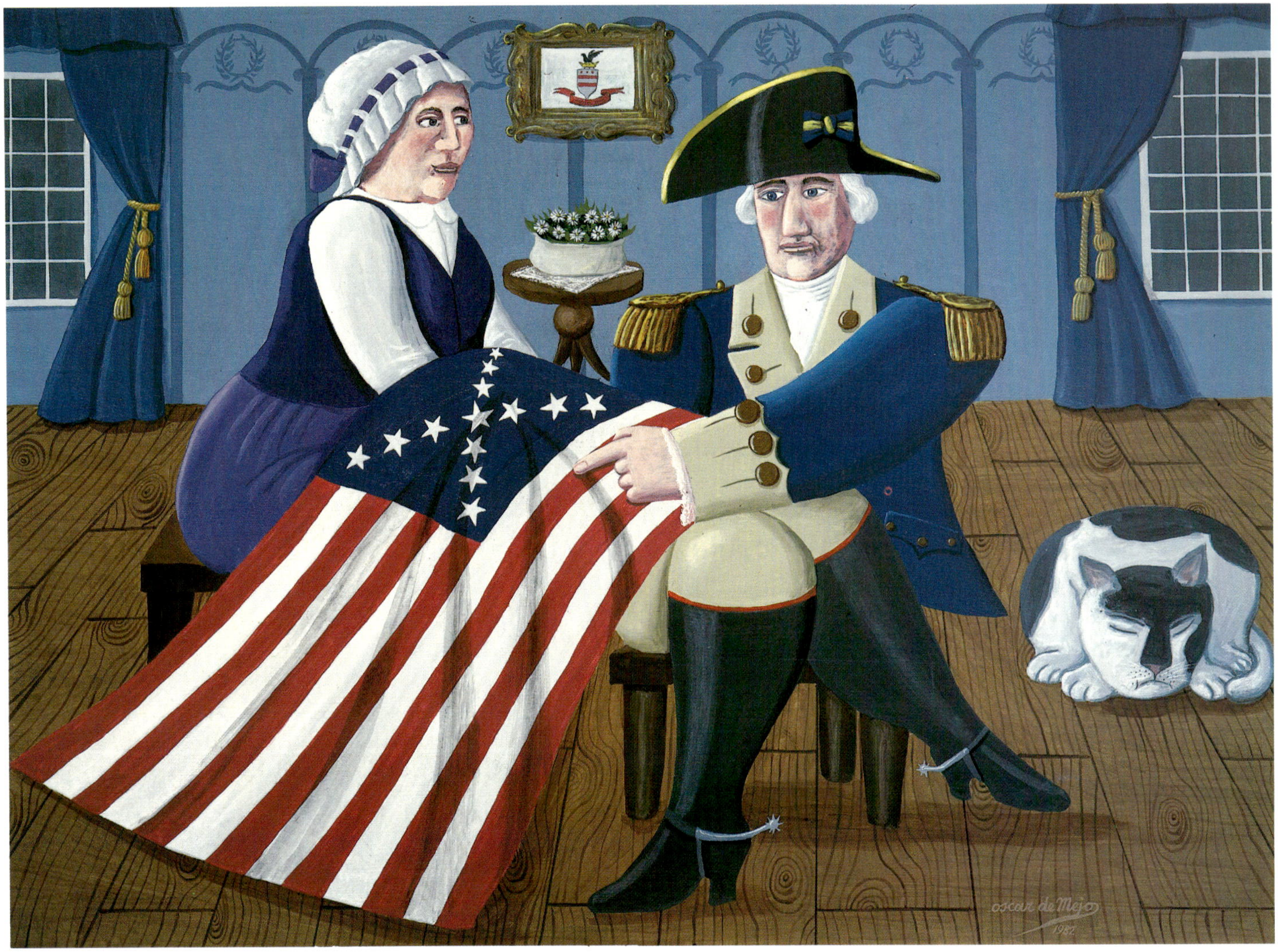

The General and the Seamstress [1776?]. 1982. Canvas, 36×50″. Aberbach Fine Art, New York

This painting deals with the legend of Betsy Ross. General Washington has to choose the flag for his newly created army. "This is the one I want," he says, but then Betsy shows him one more flag, with one star surrounded by twelve stars in a circle. In the background on the wall is the coat of arms of the Washington family, placed there only minutes before the arrival of the General by the wily seamstress.

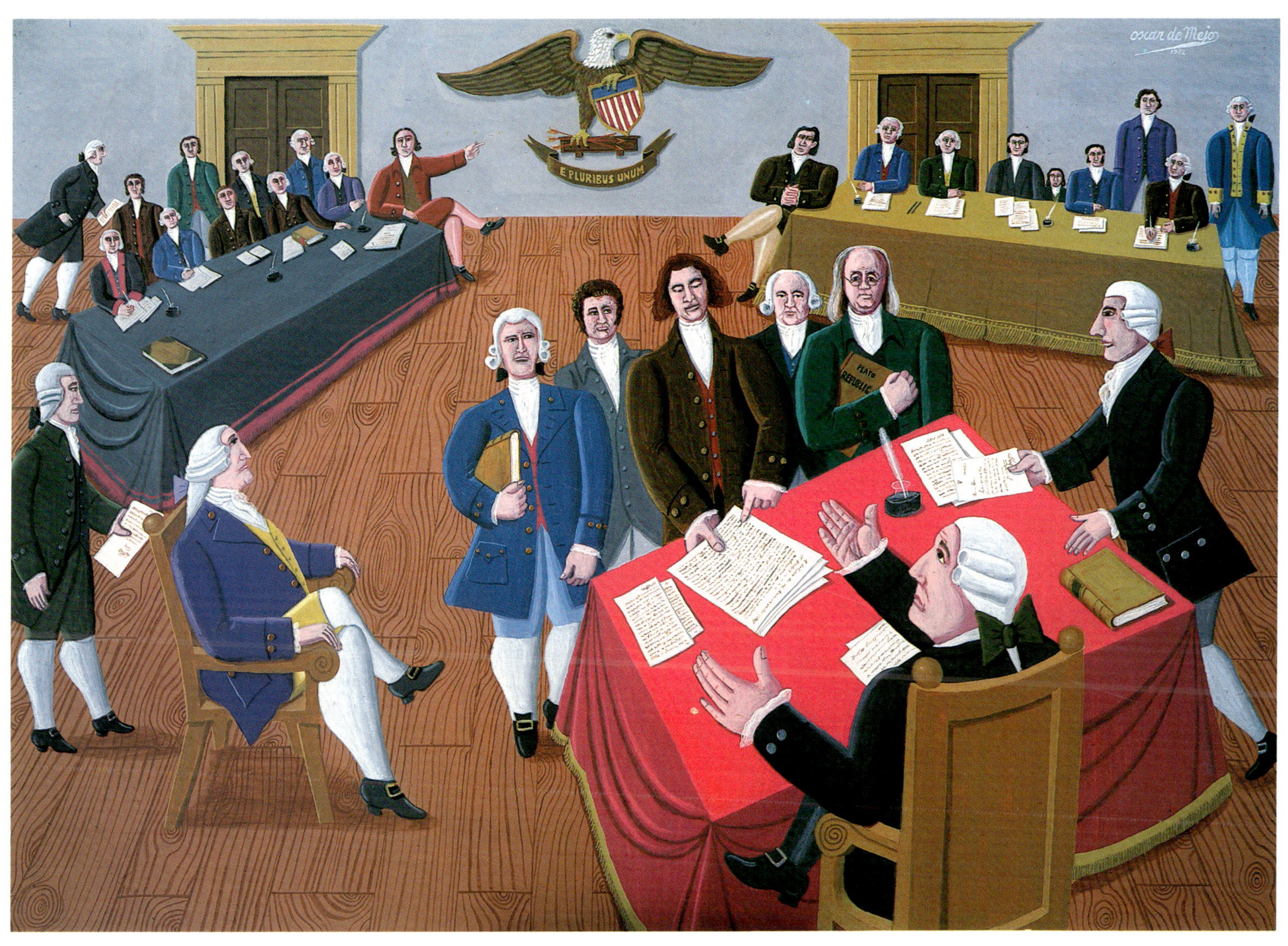

Declaration of Independence [1776]. 1982. Canvas, 48×68″. Aberbach Fine Art, New York

Roger Sherman, Robert Livingston, Thomas Jefferson, John Adams, and Benjamin Franklin present the draft of the Declaration to the Congress in Philadelphia. After a debate and some changes, it is adopted on July 4.

81

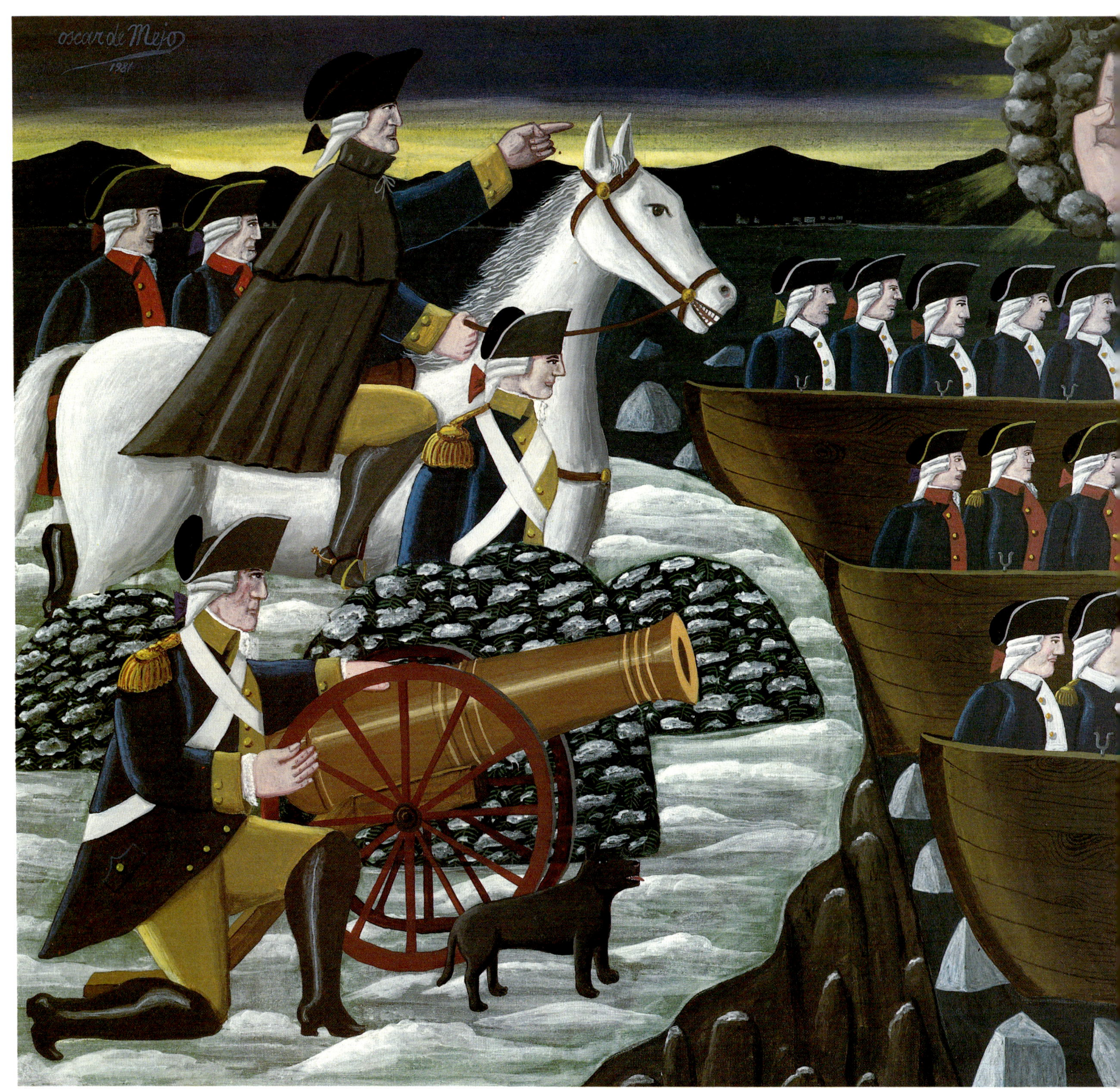

The Crossing of the Delaware [1776]. 1982. Canvas, 36×50″. Aberbach Fine Art, New York

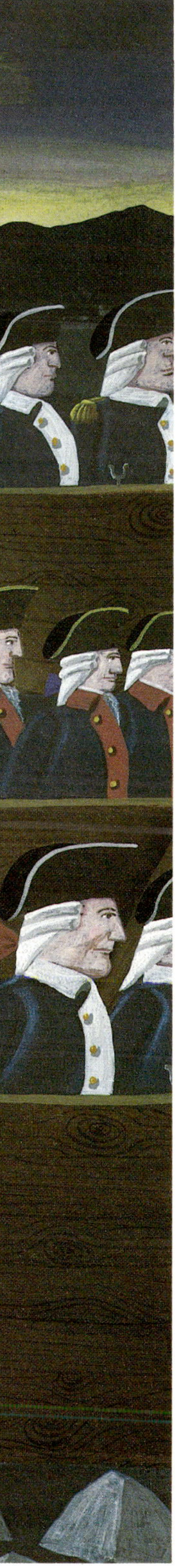

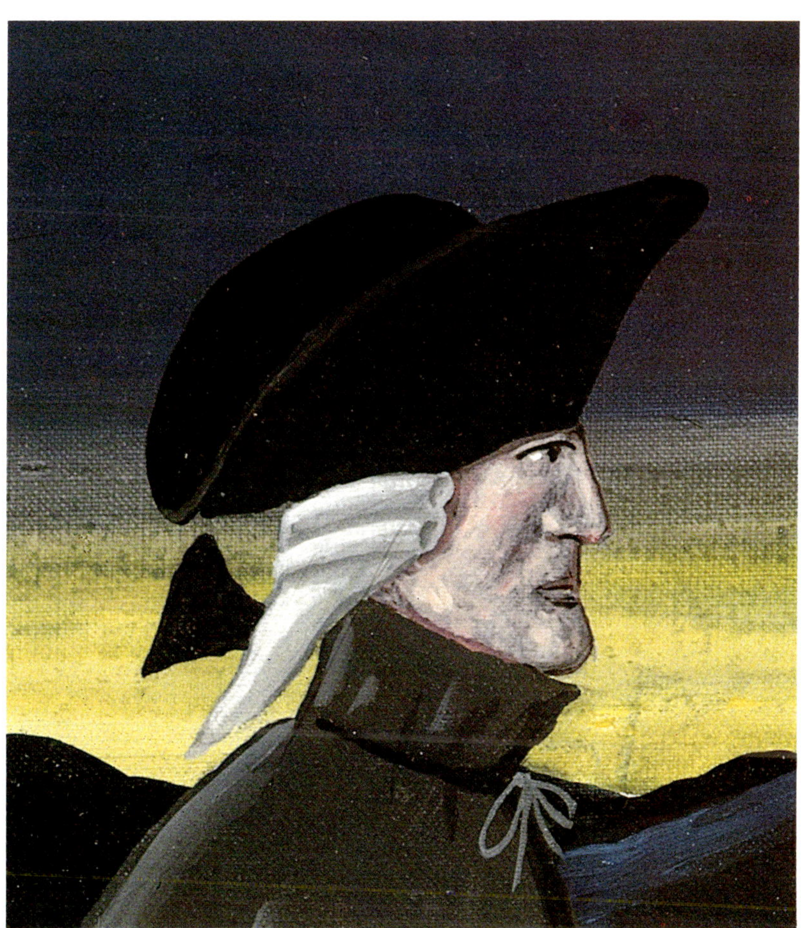

Washington and his soldiers have to cross the Delaware River on their way to Trenton, quite a feat in the coldest of weathers and the partially frozen waters of the river. A blessing from the sky protects the brave men, and the crossing is accomplished.

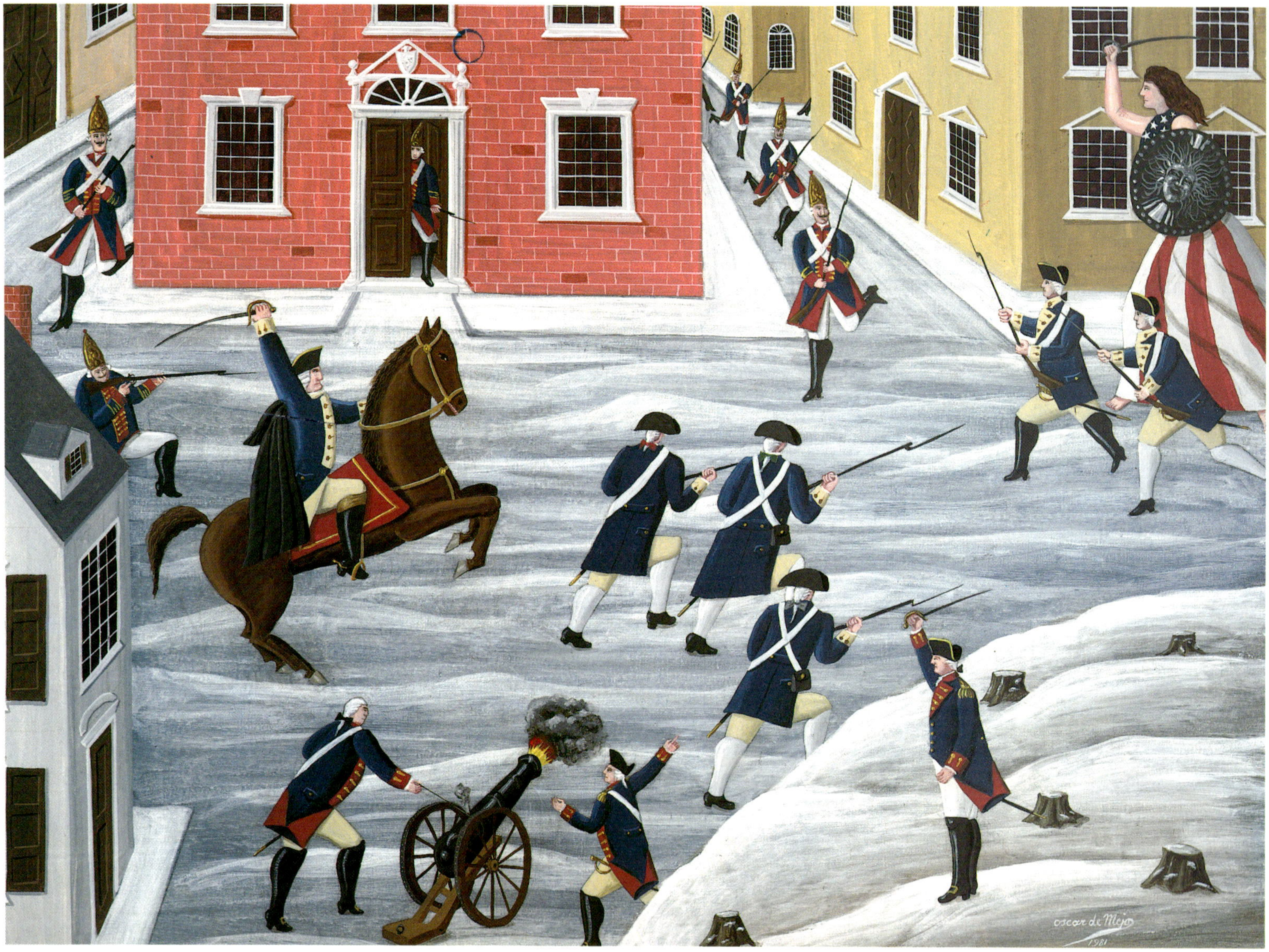

The Battle of Trenton [1776]. 1981. Canvas, 36×50″. Aberbach Fine Art, New York

Washington and his men surprise the sleeping Hessian mercenaries. "Der Feind! Heraus! Heraus!" ("The Enemy! Get out! Get out!") cries the German sentinel while the Americans, bayonets aslant, appear from all sides. The huge lady with sword and shield, symbolically guiding the Americans, represents the new Republic, strong and ready for battle and victory.

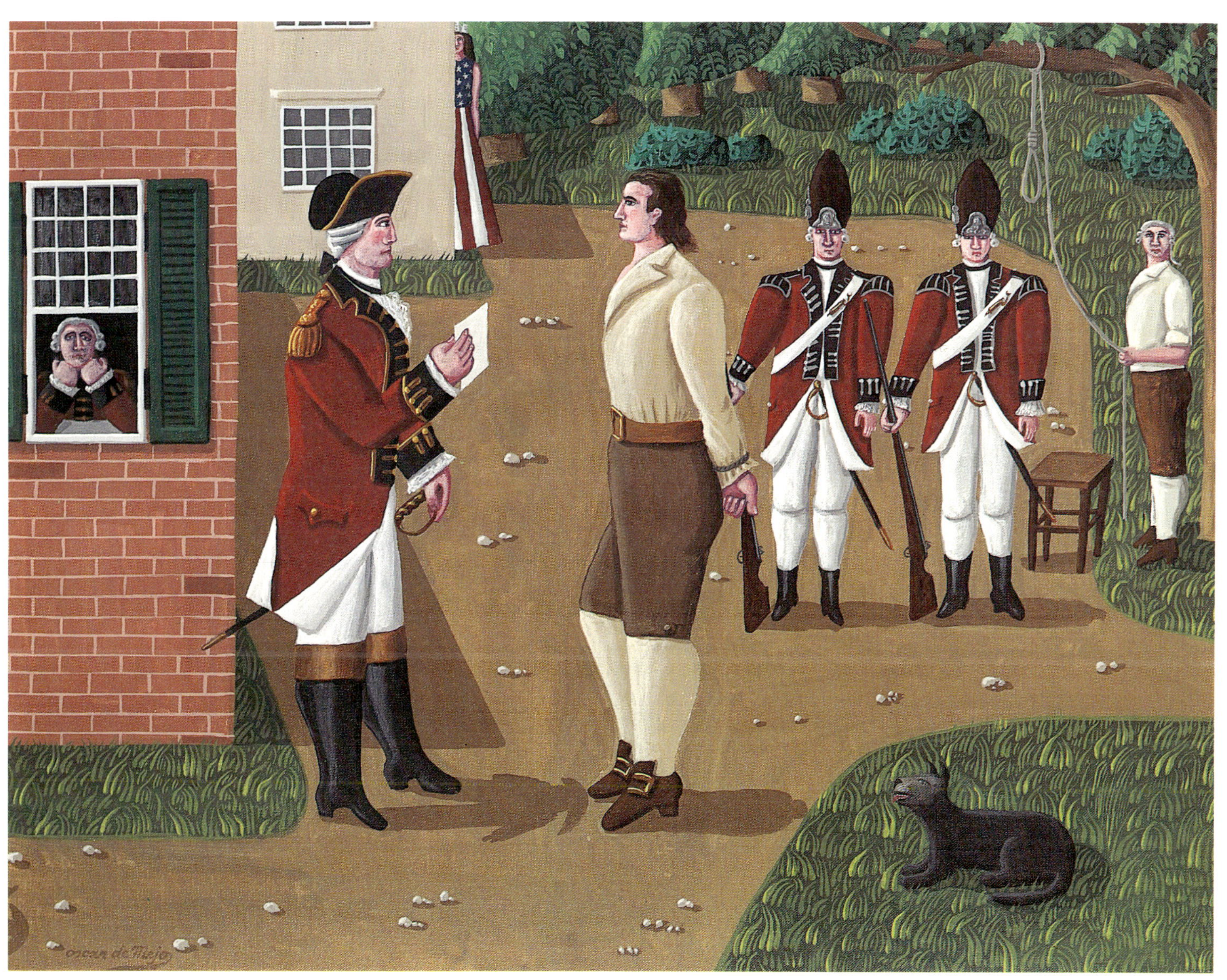

The Bravery of Nathan Hale [1776]. 1975. Masonite, 20 × 26″. Collection Liliane Wilcox, New York

Nathan Hale, a 21-year-old graduate of Yale University, is hanged by the British as a spy. A romantic statement is attributed to him as he faces death: "I only regret that I have but one life to lose for my country!" It is said in Manhattan that the spot of the execution is located where 65th Street and Third Avenue cross. The figure in the window at left is a British officer personally disturbed by the hero's death. The young Republic looks on in dismay from behind a wall (above, center left).

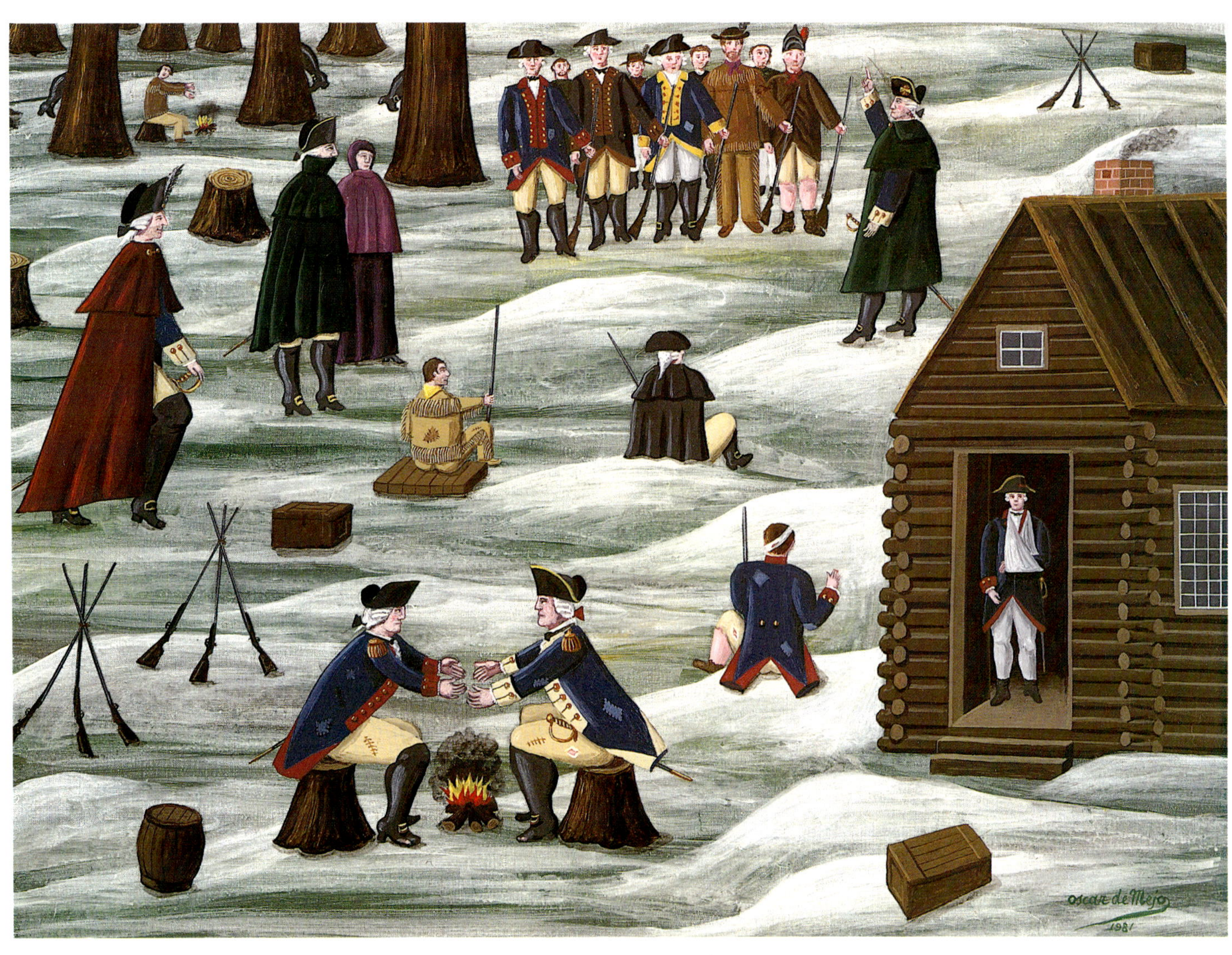

Valley Forge [1777]. 1981. Canvas, 26× 36″. Aberbach Fine Art, New York

Depicted here is the hardship of the newly born American army at the beginning of the Revolution. The tall French officer on the left is America's friend and ally, the Marquis de Lafayette. The two bundled-up figures next to him are Martha and George Washington on an impromptu visit from their Philadelphia home. They watch Baron von Steuben drill the troops.

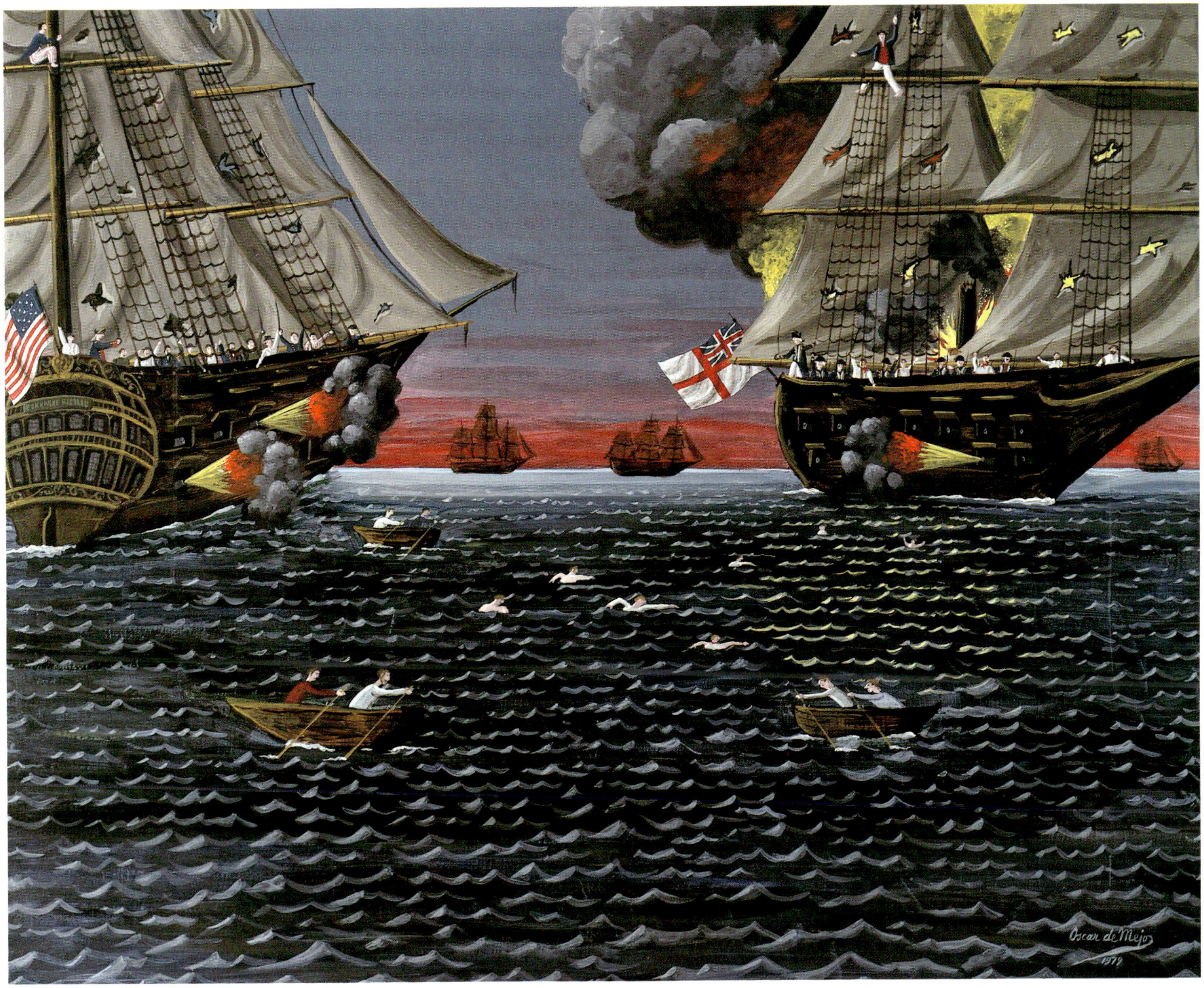

The Bonhomme Richard *Attacks the H.M.S.* Serapis [1779]. 1979. Masonite, 24 × 30″. Aberbach Fine Art, New York

87

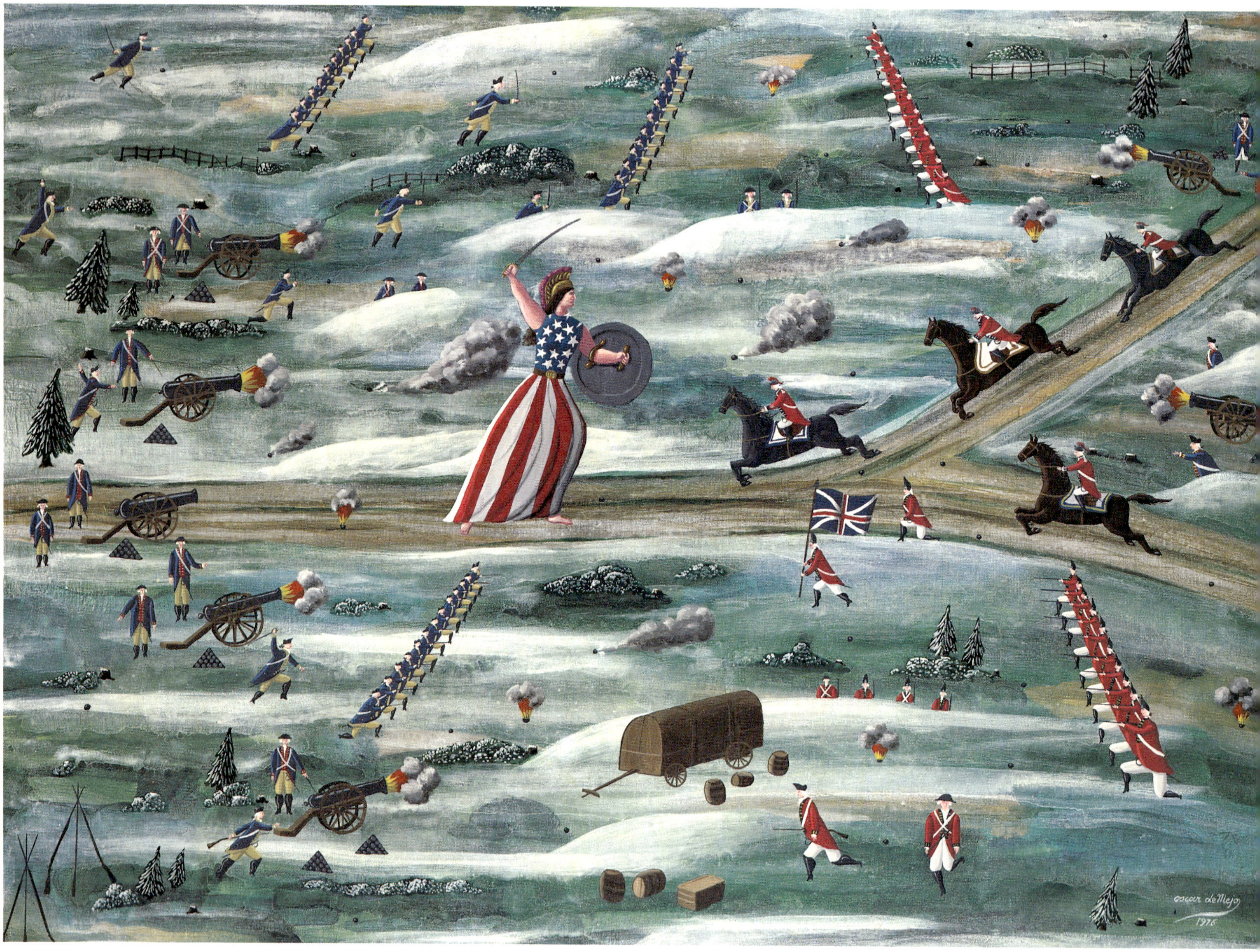

The Battle of Cowpens [1781]. 1981. Canvas, 36×48″. Private collection, New York

*Masterfully planned by the Americans,
this battle sets a trap for the British cavalry led by the daredevil Colonel Banastre
Tarleton. It is a bloody fight but a smash-
ing victory for the Americans, who fight
valiantly. They are led by that great lady,
the new Republic.*

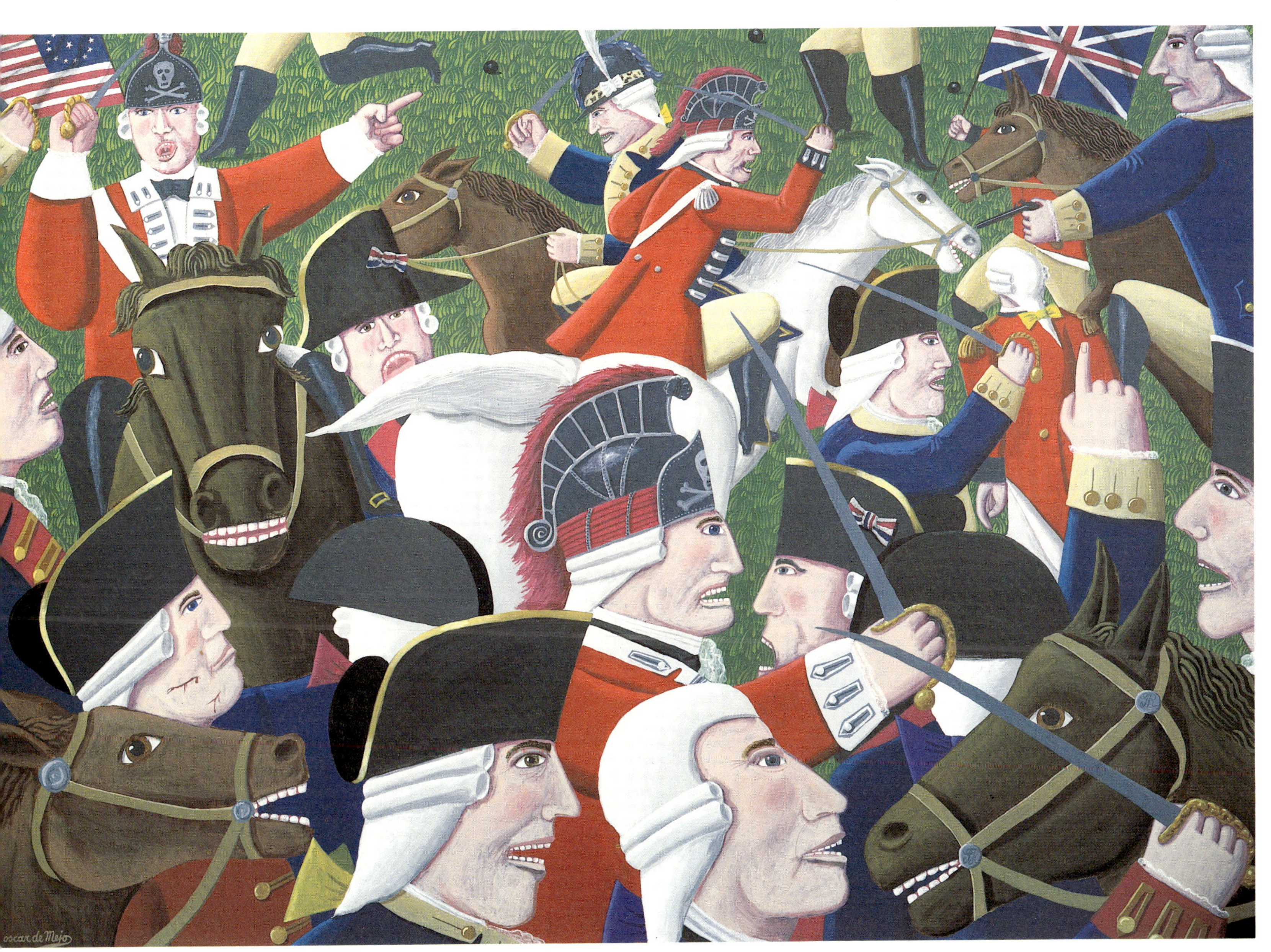

The Battle of Cowpens [1781]. 1982. Canvas, 46×66″. Aberbach Fine Art, New York

Surprised by the American resistance, Banastre Tarleton (upper left corner) orders his dragoons to counterattack, but the outcome of the battle is by now decided.

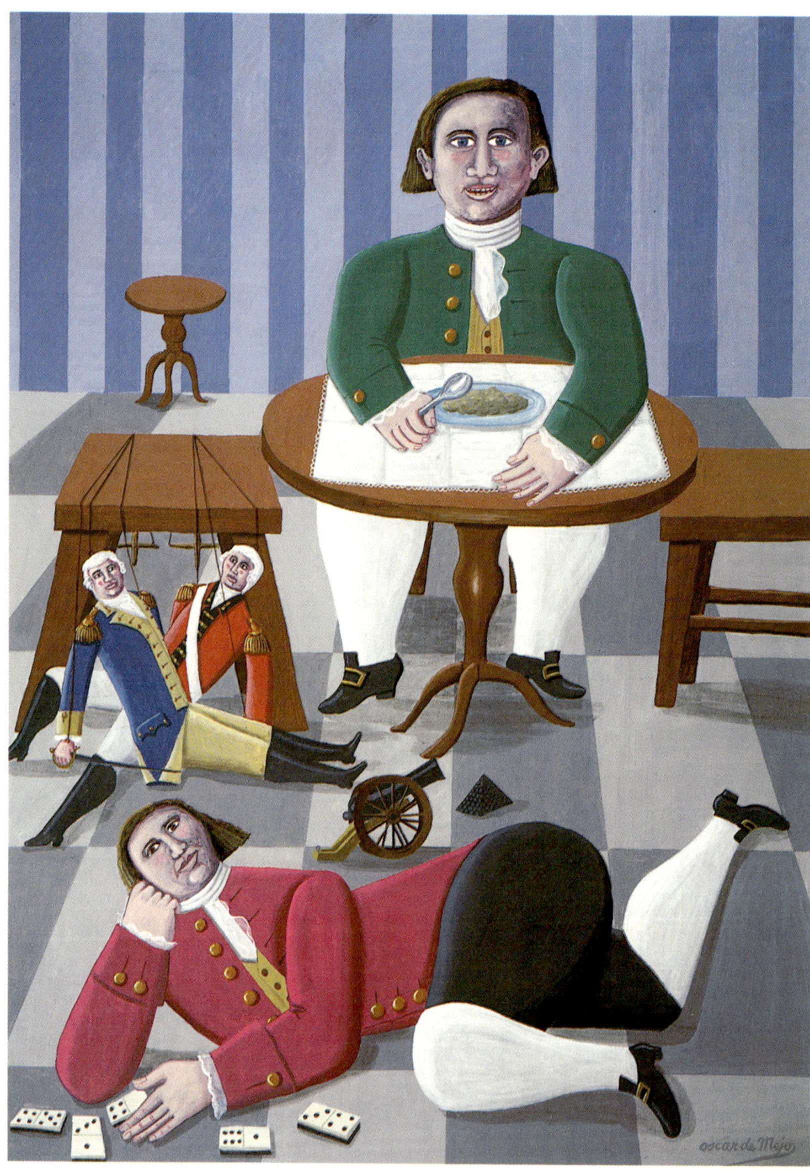

Children of the American Revolution. 1982. Canvas, 36×50″.
Aberbach Fine Art, New York

*James, the younger of the two boys, is
still eating his slightly unpatriotic "por-
ridge," but Allan, the older one, plays with
a genuine American-made set of dominoes.
The children often indulge in a game with
the two marionettes (center left), and the
scene they represent features a duel in
which the blue coat never fails to win.*

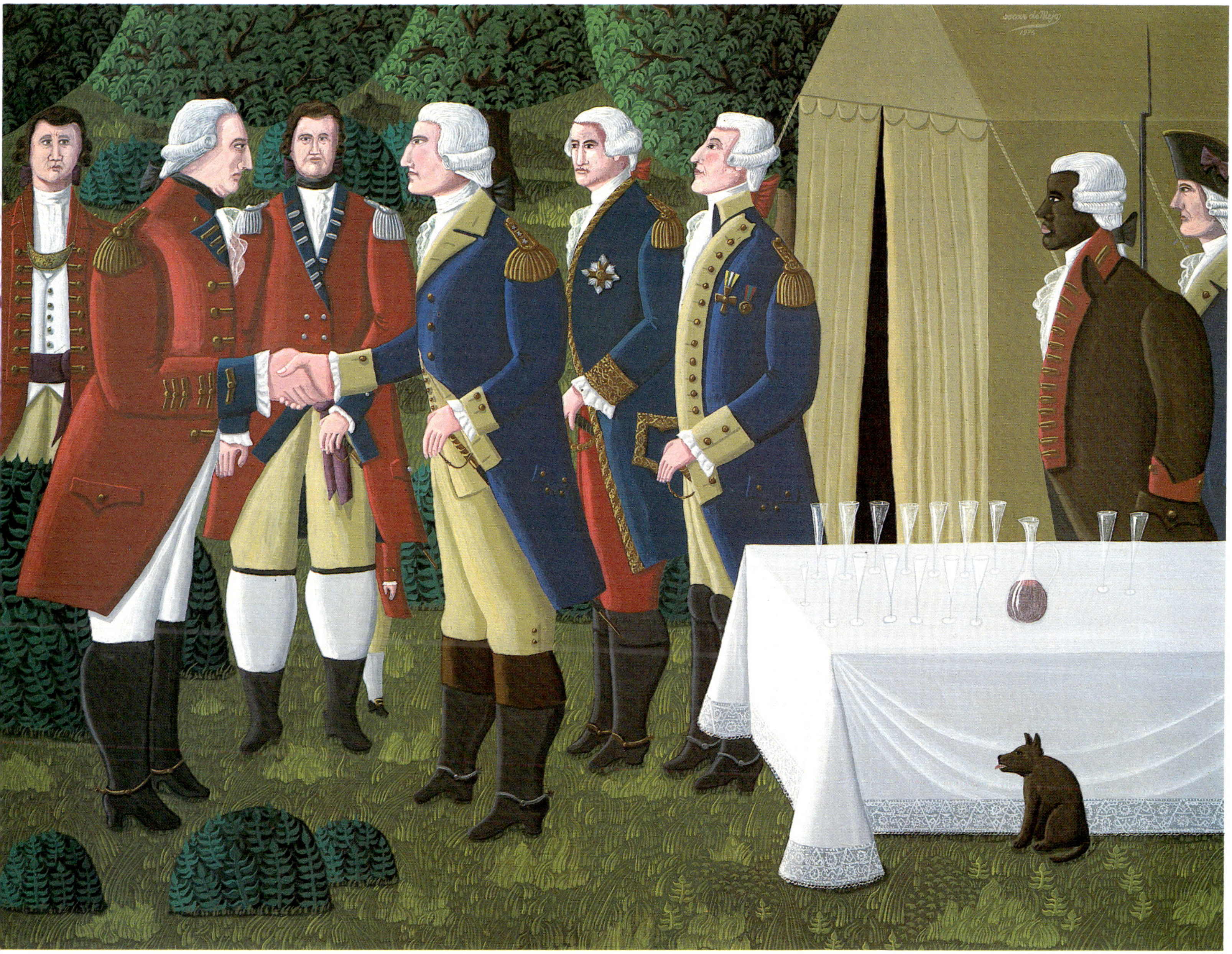

Cornwallis's Surrender [1781]. 1976. Canvas, 38 × 50". Aberbach Fine Art, New York

This is not the actual surrender of the commander of the British forces in America, but rather a friendly, unpublicized meeting of two great adversaries—General Washington and Lord Cornwallis. Escorted by three staff officers, Cornwallis visits Washington's headquarters, where he is met by the general himself and two French officers, Count de Rochambeau and the Marquis de Lafayette. The small glass on the table is meant for the little officer half hidden behind one of Cornwallis's escorts. The dog in the foreground belongs to General Washington's valet (second from right).

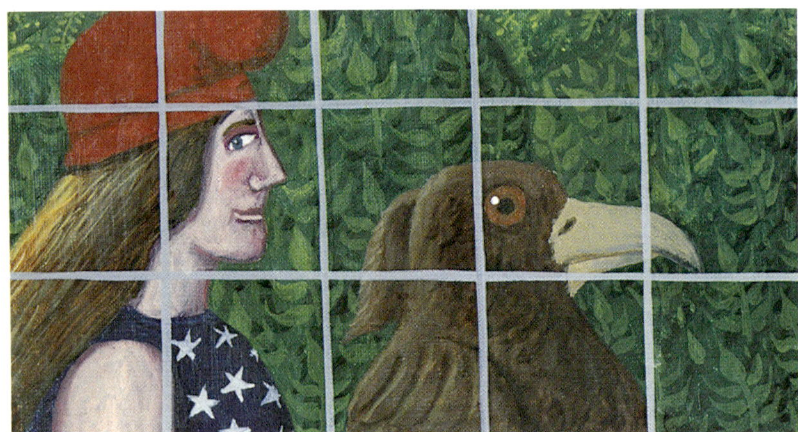

After the final victory is won, George Washington says goodbye to his officers at Manhattan's Fraunces Tavern. It is an informal but moving ceremony, and several of his veteran soldiers actually cry. There are no speeches. Washington simply embraces his friends one by one. Outside the window waiting for him are Miss Liberty and the Great American Eagle.

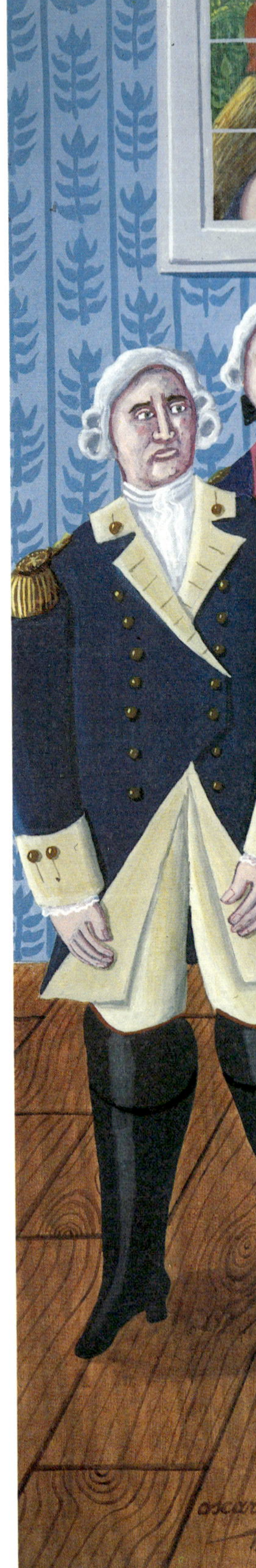

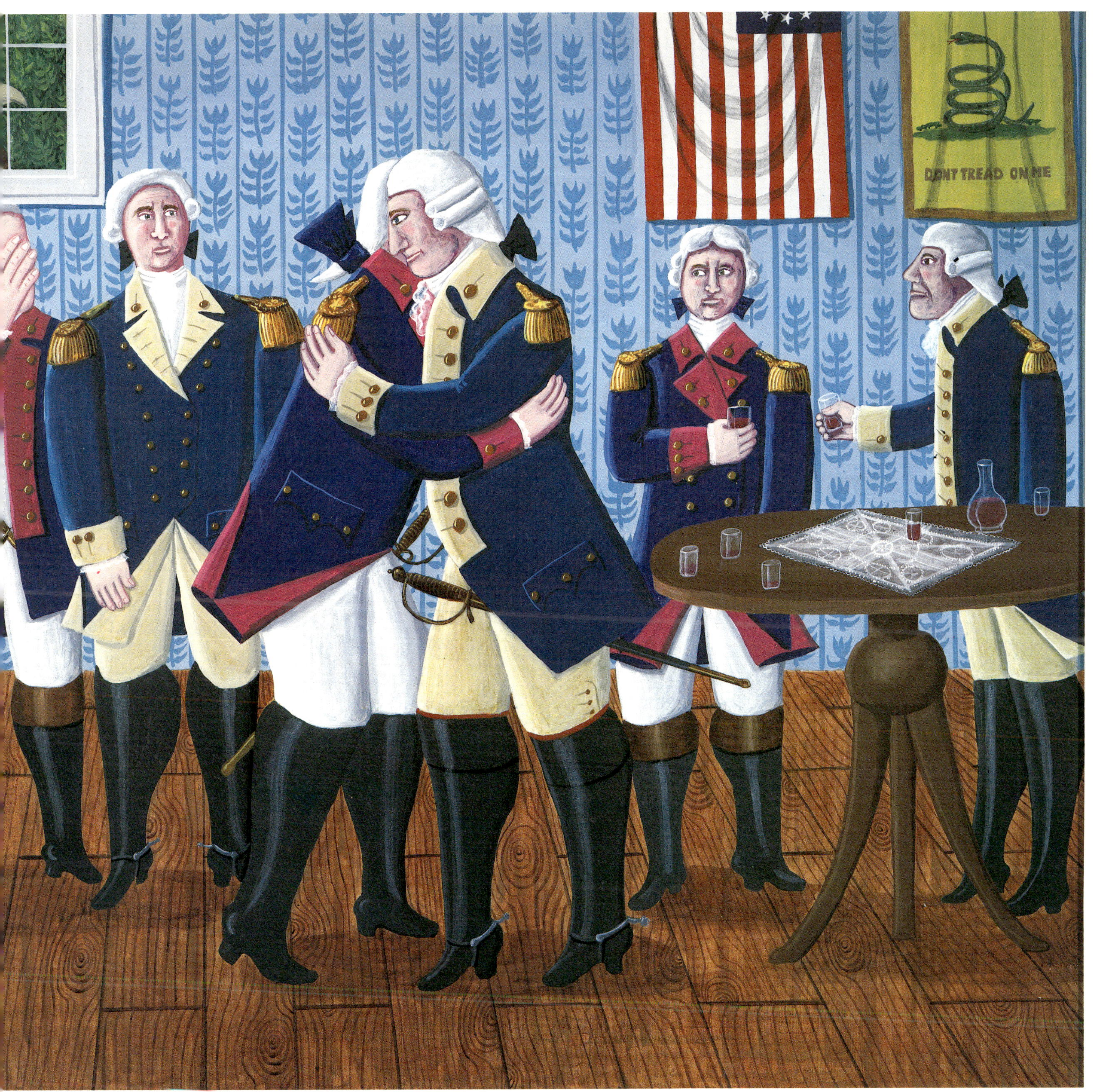

Washington's Farewell [1783]. 1982. Canvas, 36×50″. Aberbach Fine Art, New York

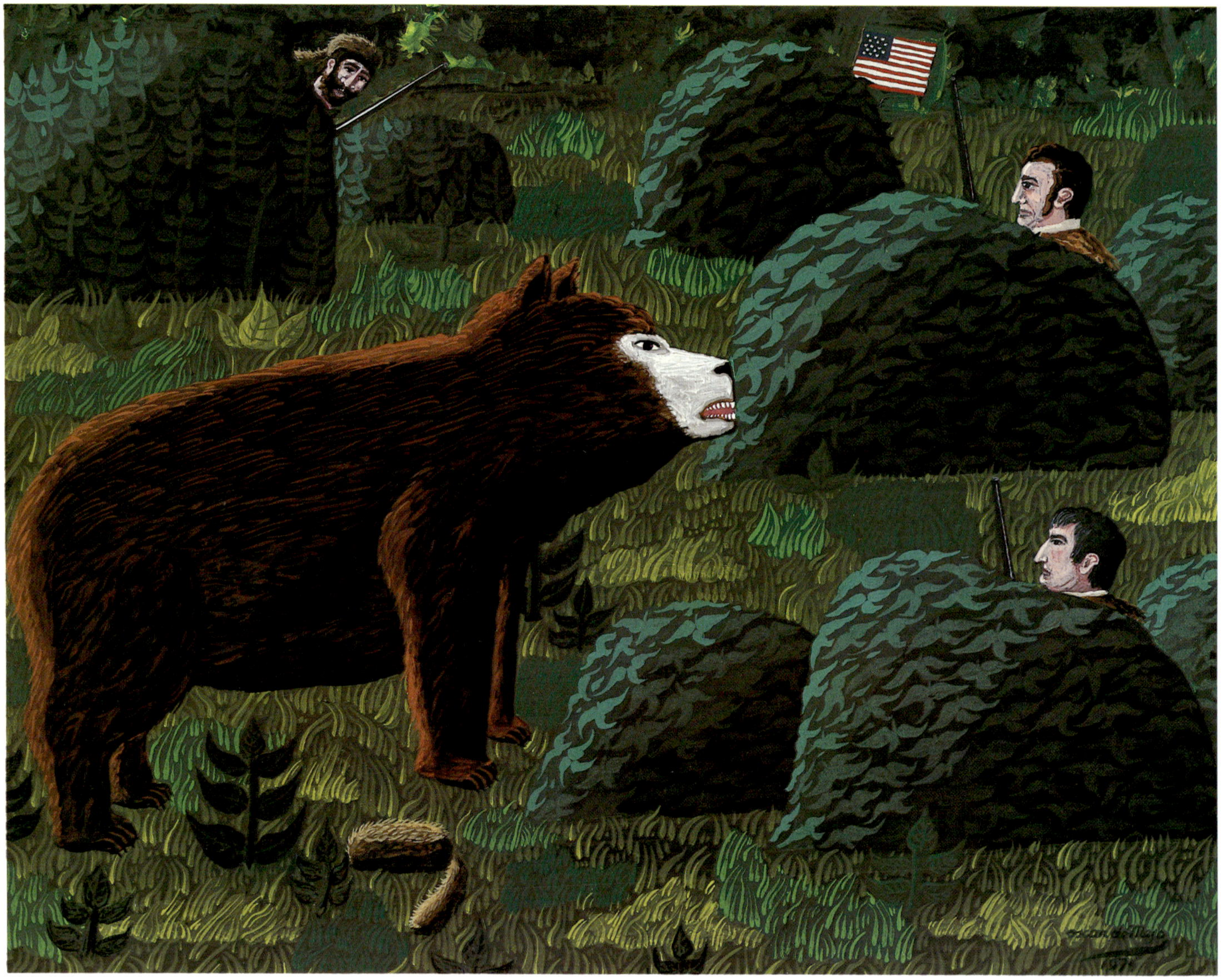

Lewis and Clark [1804]. 1974. Masonite, 20×26″. Collection Bob Guccione and Kathy Keeton, New York

Thomas Jefferson's dream—the exploration of the West—materializes when Meriwether Lewis and William Clark leave St. Louis and follow the Missouri River to expand American markets and develop good relations with the Indians. Despite a memorable encounter with a grizzly bear and minor incidents and mishaps, the expedition is a great success.

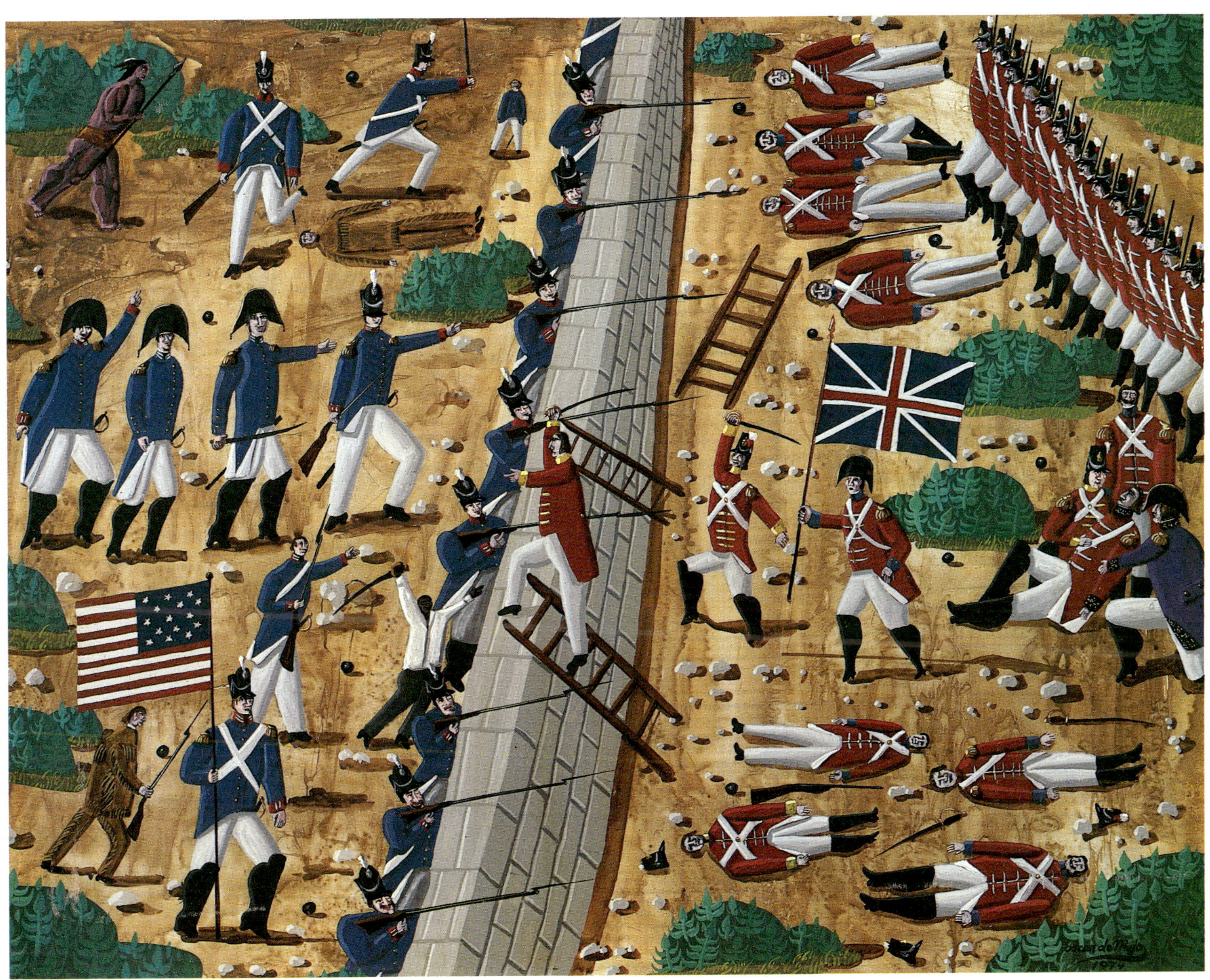

The Battle of New Orleans [1814]. 1974. Masonite, 20 × 26″. Collection Bob Guccione and Kathy Keeton, New York

This is the end of hostilities in the War of 1812 between England and the United States. In two suicidal frontal attacks on New Orleans, held by the Americans, the British lose 2,000 of their troops, including their leader, General Pakenham (center right). Ironically, peace had already been declared before this encounter, but the news has not reached the combatants.

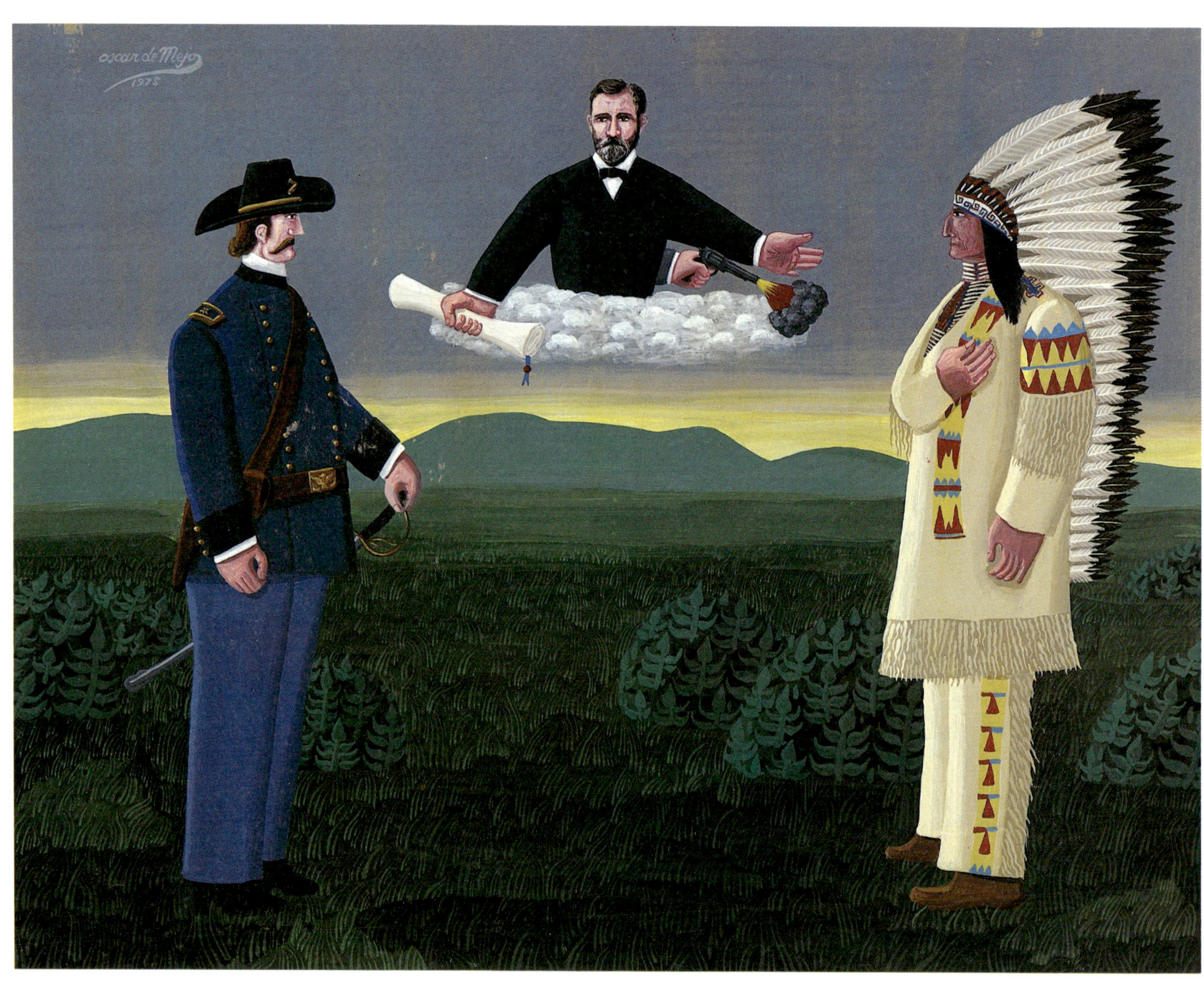

Conquest of the Wild West. 1975. Masonite, 20 × 26″. Collection Bob Guccione and Kathy Keeton, New York

While presidents try to develop good relations with the Indians through written treaties, politicians in Washington often betray the Indians. Then the American cavalry has to fight the enraged Indians.

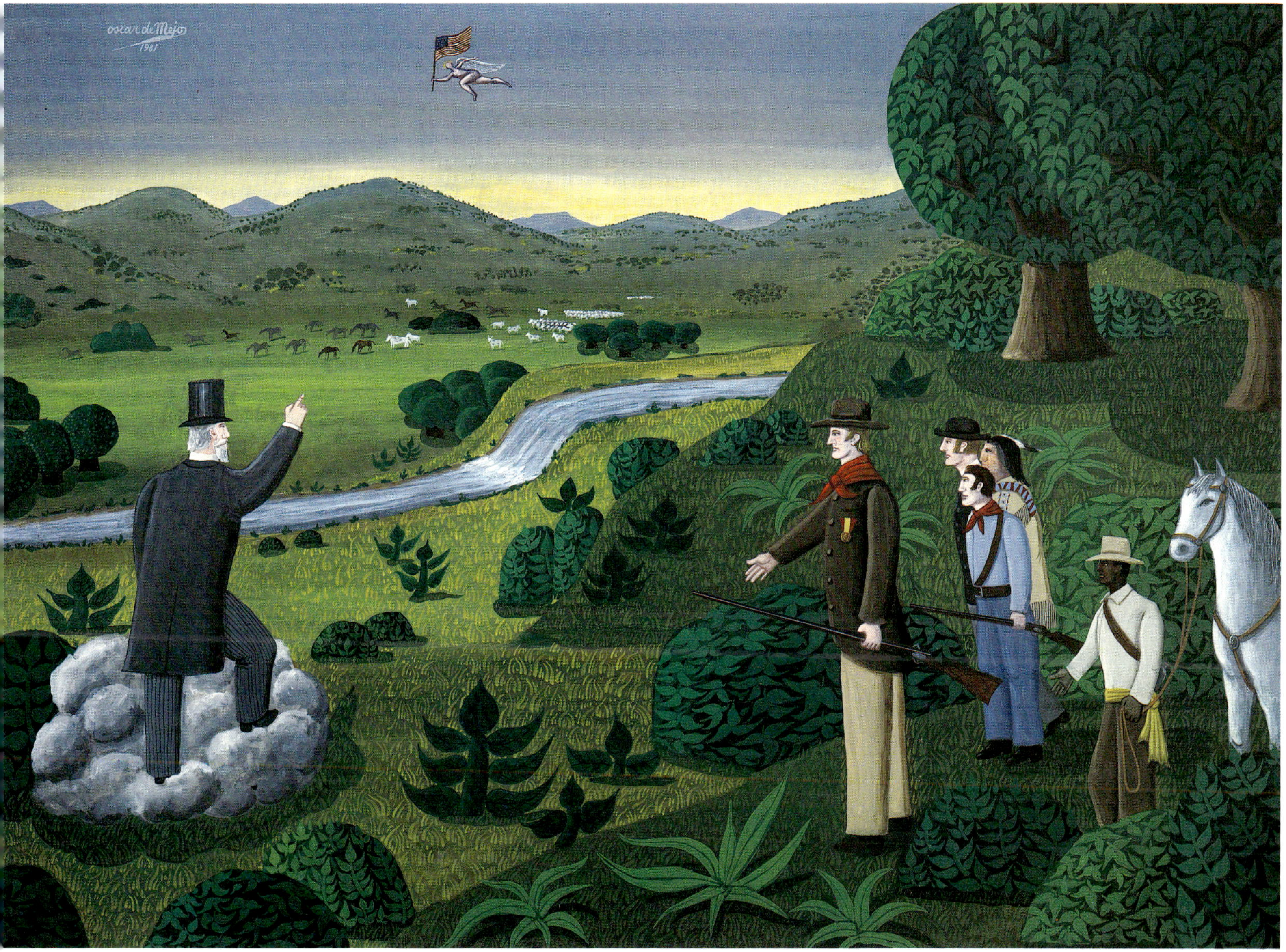

The Father of Texas [1835]. 1981. Canvas, 36 × 50″. Aberbach Fine Art, New York

Stephen F. Austin (with the red scarf on the right) can well be called the Father of Texas for his efforts in the colonization of that state. Acting as "Empresario" for the Government of Mexico and following his father Moses' dream, he looks for and finds an ideal piece of land for his American settlers. From the Great Beyond, Moses approves the choice.

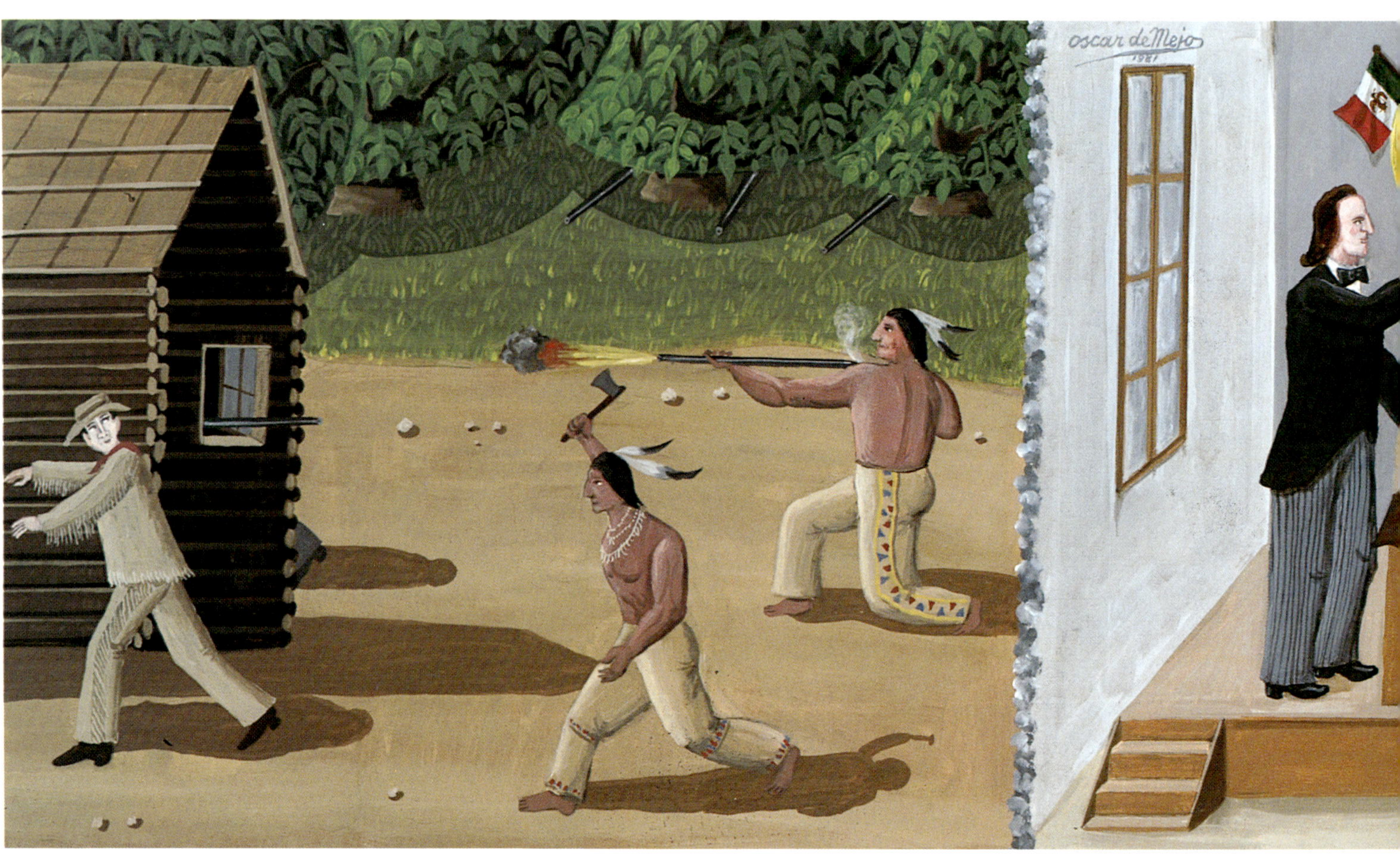

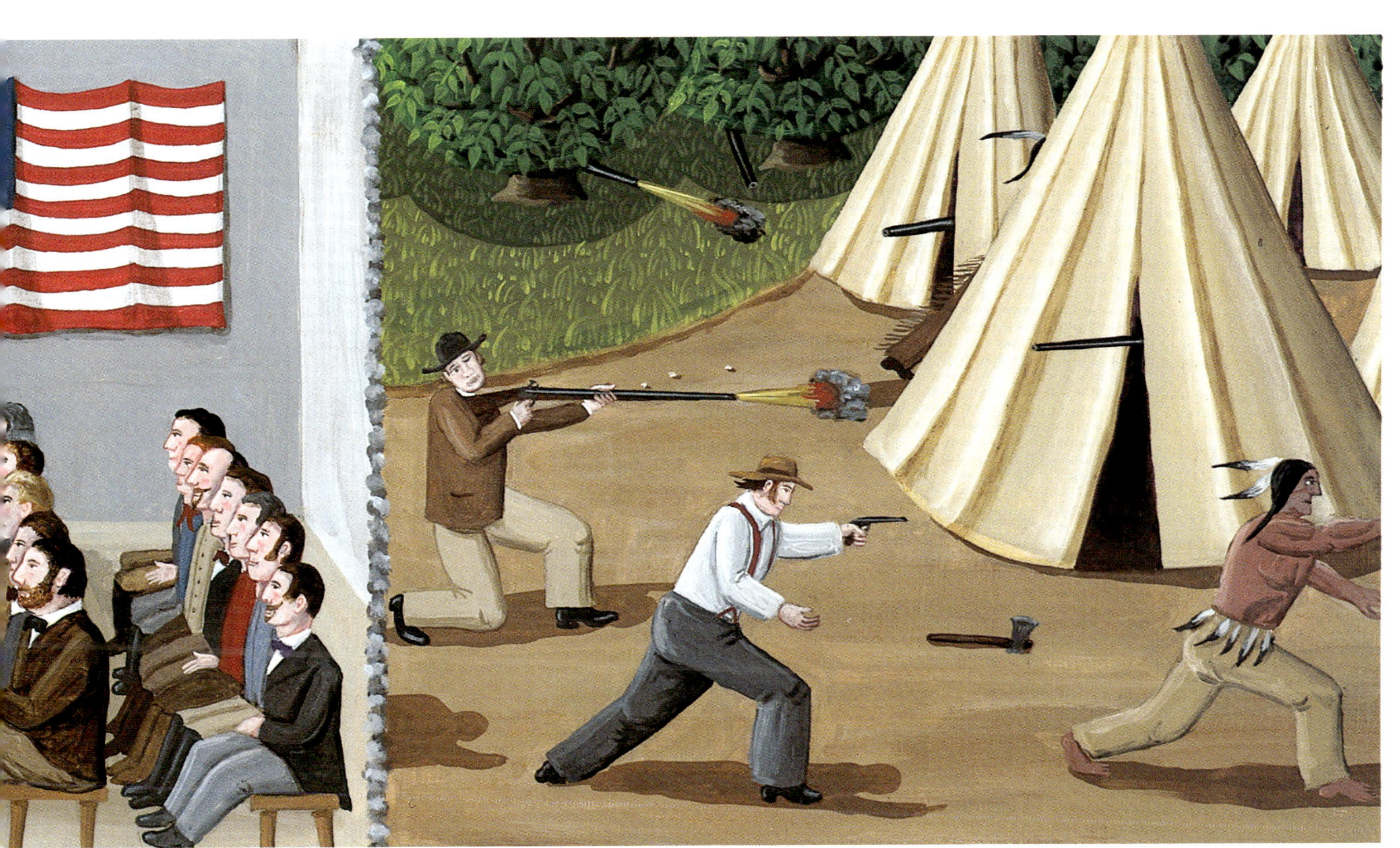

The Birth of the Texas Rangers [1827]. 1981. Canvas, 14×54″. Private collection, New York

When Stephen Austin's settlers started moving into Texas, the welcoming committee of local Indians started robbing and shooting them. Austin gathered his men in a shack known as the Town House and formed them into horse patrols which counterattacked and taught the Indians not to do unto others . . . etc.

Thus, the Texas Rangers were born.

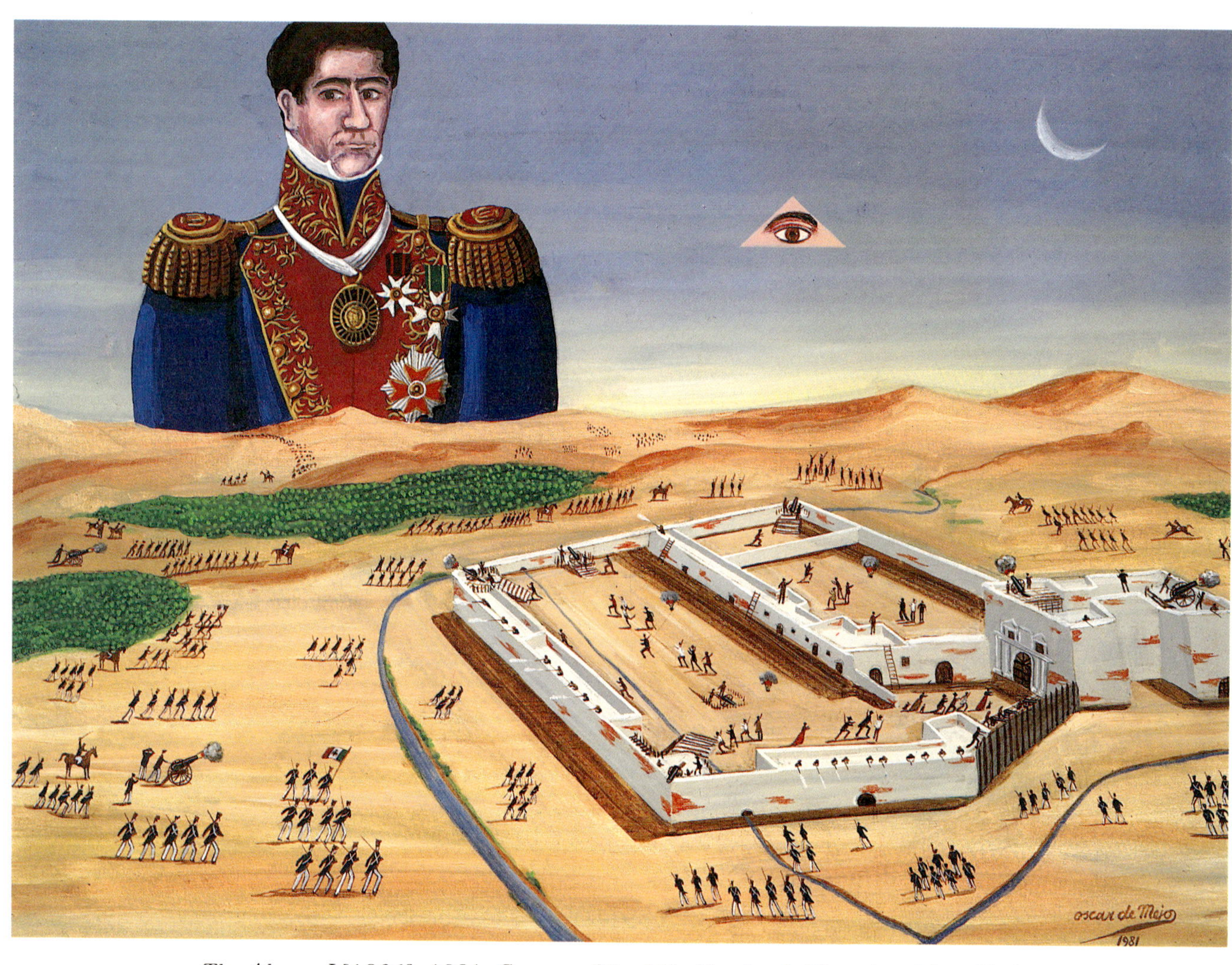

The Alamo I [1836]. 1981. Canvas, 26 × 36″. Aberbach Fine Art, New York

The colonization of Texas by the Americans becomes unpopular in Mexico and General Santa Anna calls up an army of 3,000 men to expel the foreigners. The Texans take measures to meet the threat— 150 of them with some women and children gather in the fortress of the Alamo near San Antonio. Led by General Santa Anna, the Mexicans close in and prepare for the attack.

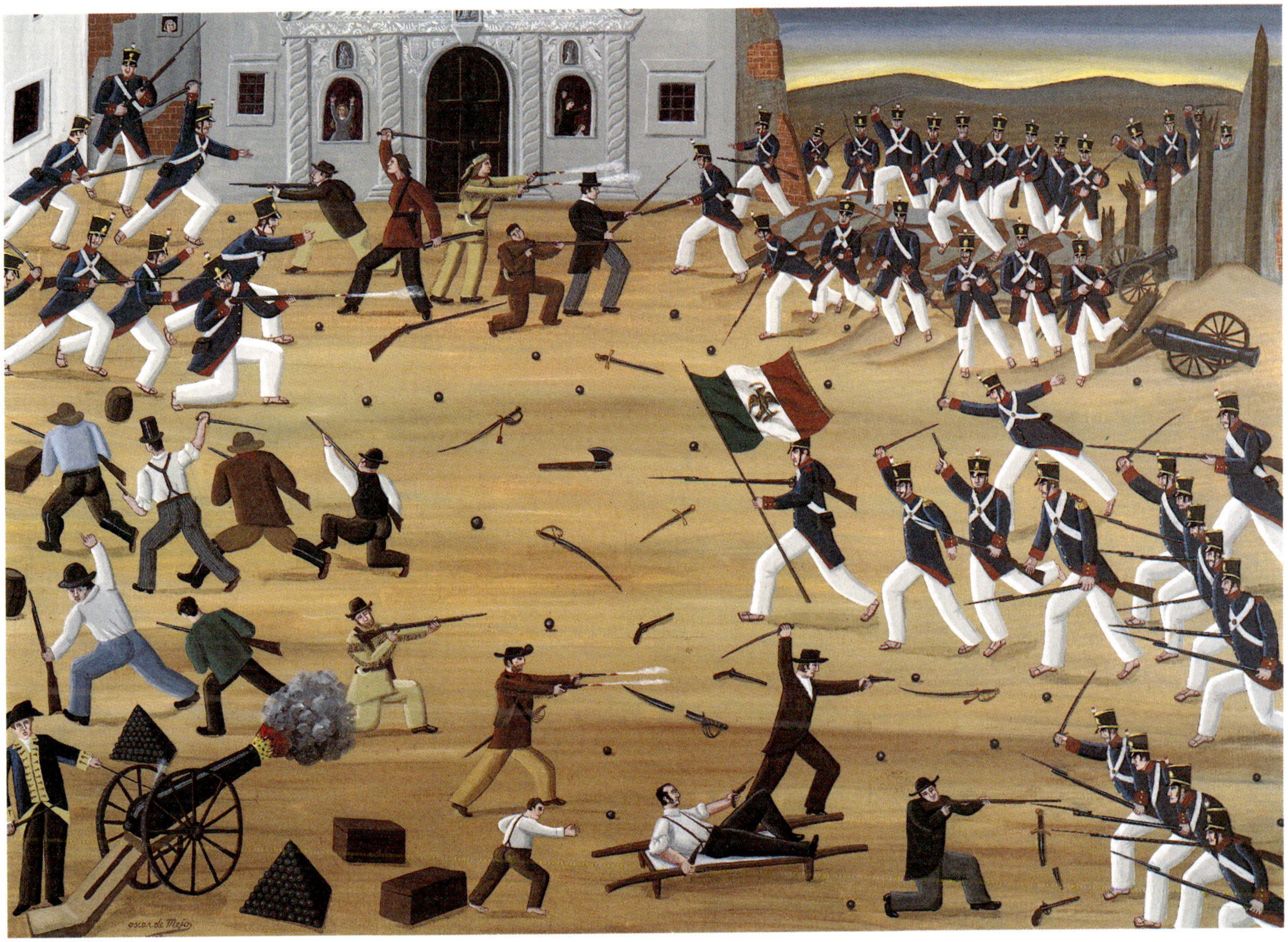

The Alamo II [1836]. 1981. Canvas, 48×68″. Aberbach Fine Art, New York

With the Mexican army band playing the "Degüello," a march indicating total annihilation of the enemy, the soldiers invade the fortress. The Americans put up a desperate fight—among them are Davy Crockett and his Tennessee Mounted Volunteers (above center), artilleryman Almeron Dickerson (lower left corner) wearing an old Revolutionary War uniform, ailing Jim Bowie (center foreground) holding the knife of his invention. Santa Anna orders all the Americans killed.

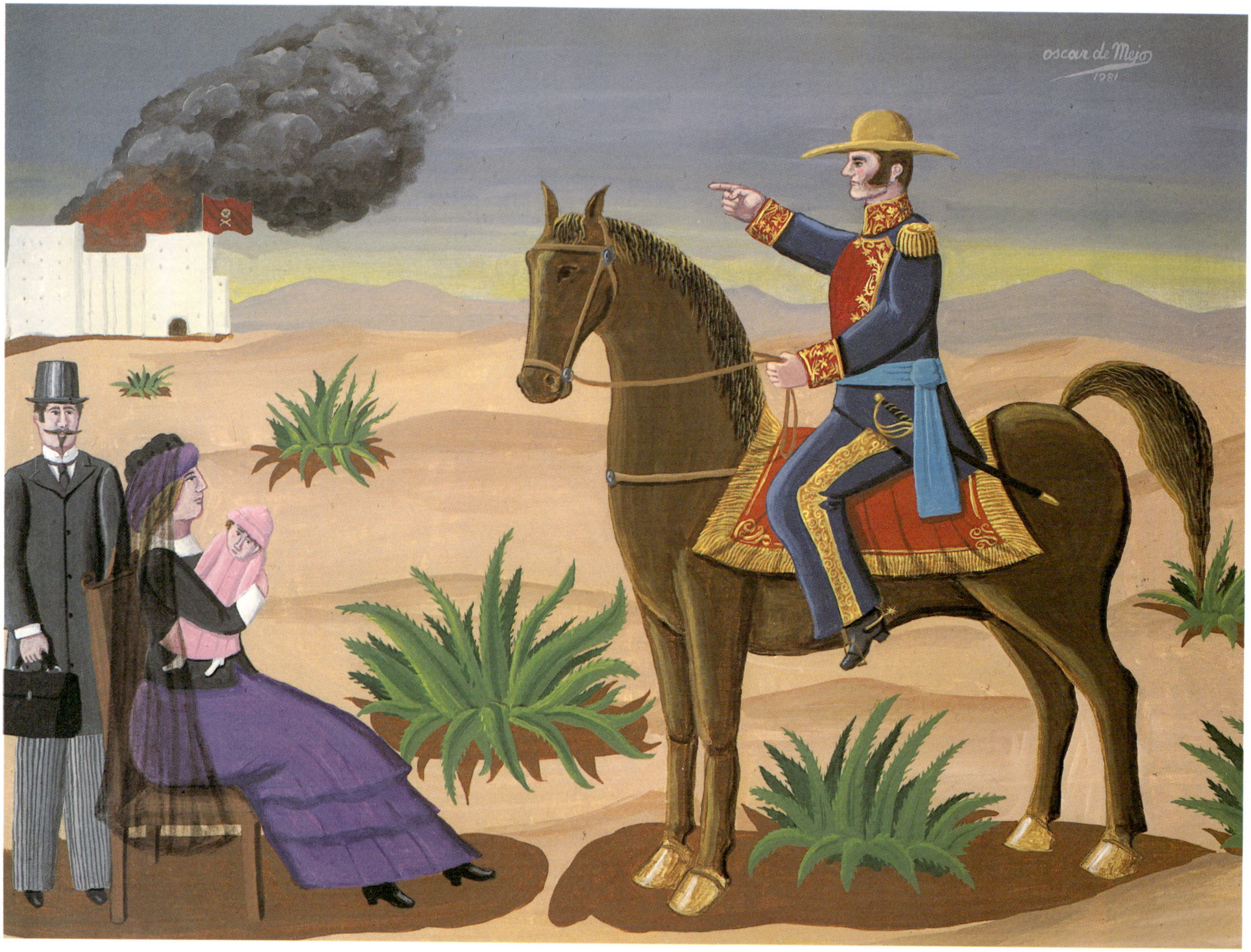

The Alamo III [1836]. 1981. Canvas, 26×36″. Aberbach Fine Art, New York

Wounded Susannah Dickerson, the young widow of an American gunner killed at the Alamo, is brought before General Santa Anna. Pointing at the smoke rising from the fortress (the fallen Americans were burned in a pyre), he tells her to go back home and tell the Texans that death will be the fate of anyone opposing the Mexican Army. Mrs. Dickerson holds her 15-month-old daughter Angelina.

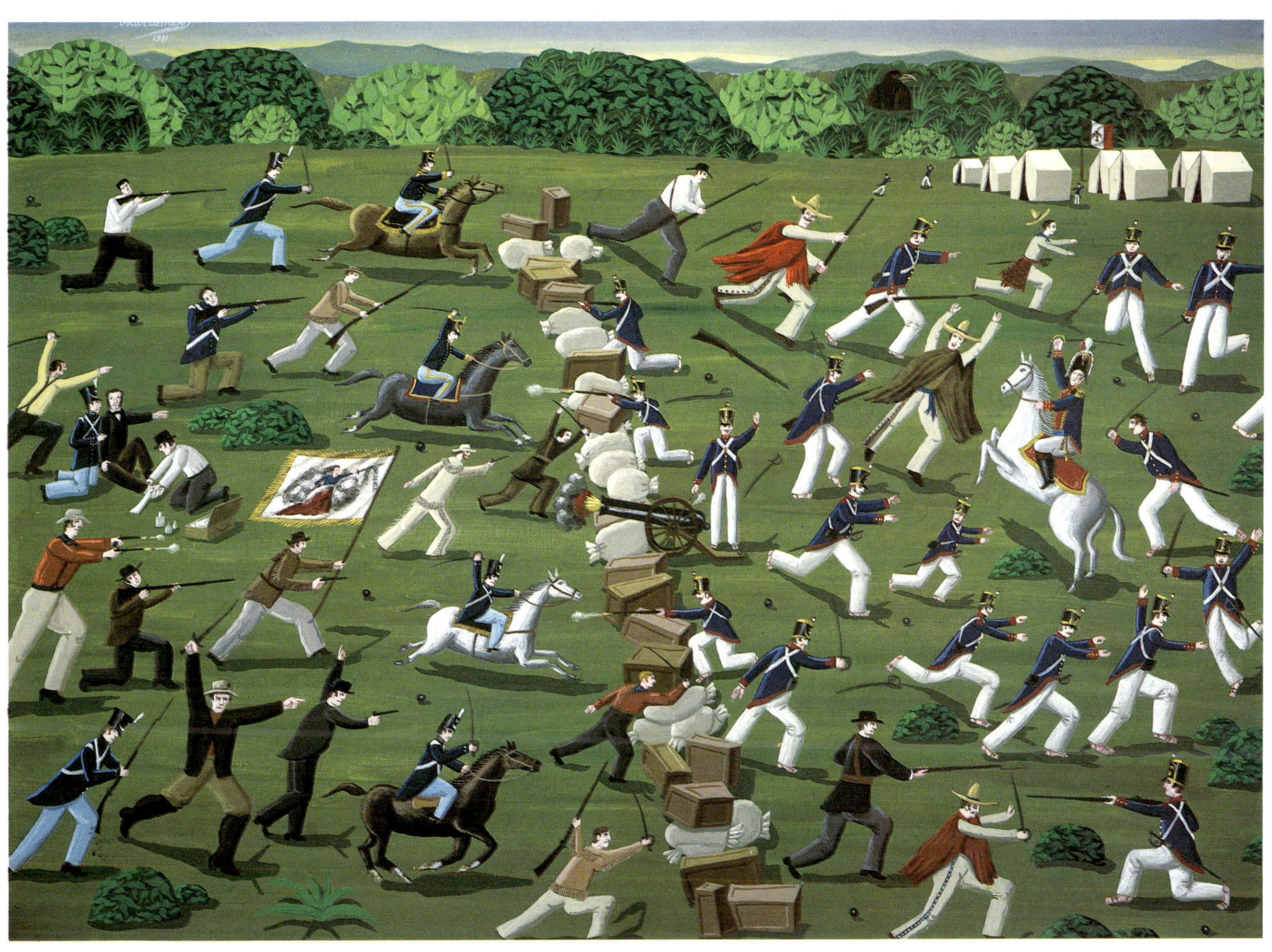

The Battle of San Jacinto [1836]. 1981. Canvas, 36×50″. Aberbach Fine Art, New York

Sometimes history creates a harsh fate for the villain. In a surprise attack at San Jacinto, the Texans shout "Remember the Alamo!" while cutting Santa Anna's army to pieces. Over 600 Mexicans are killed and the rest taken prisoner. Sam Houston (center left) leads the charge and is wounded. General Santa Anna (center right on a white horse) tries to stop the rout of his men, then gives up and flees.

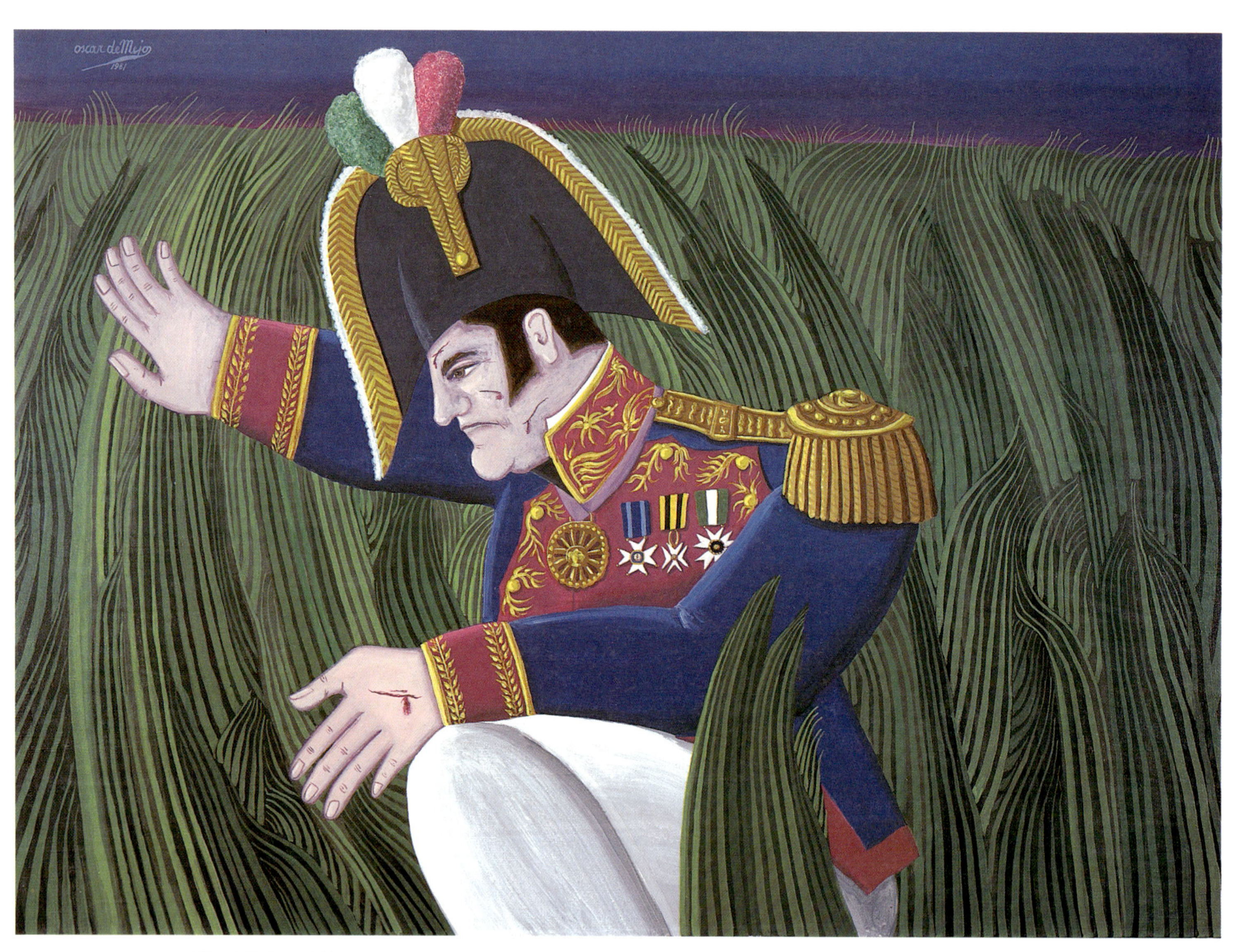

The Night of San Jacinto [1836]. 1981. Canvas, 36×50″. Aberbach Fine Art, New York

After the battle of San Jacinto, in order
to avoid capture by the Texans, defeated
General Santa Anna seeks shelter in the
surrounding swamps.

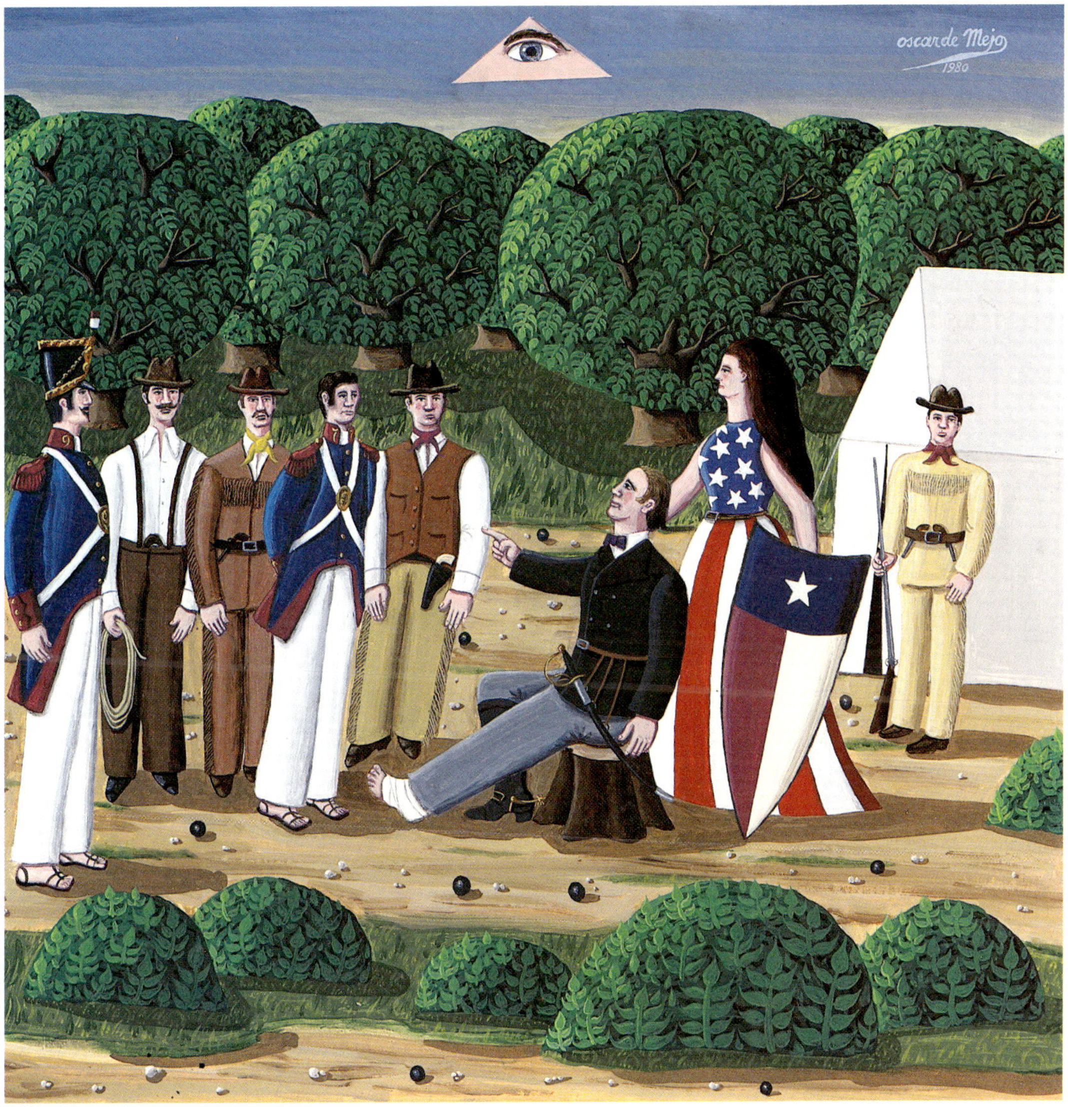

Sam Houston and Santa Anna [1836]. 1980. Masonite, $30 \times 30''$.
Private collection, New York

*Captured General Santa Anna is brought
before Sam Houston, who generously
spares his life. The Eye of God looks on
approvingly as Miss Liberty stands majes-
tically at the side of the victor.*

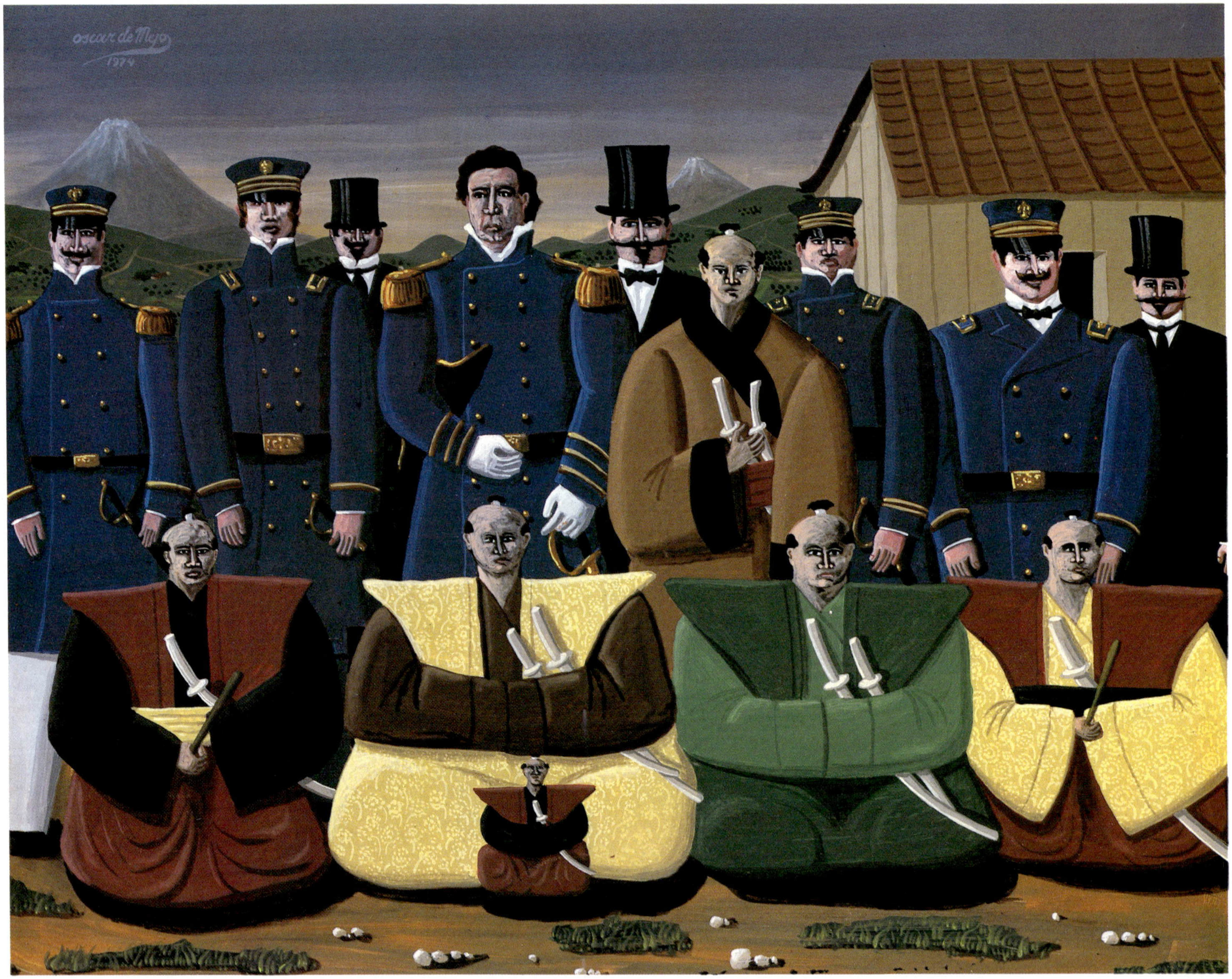

Commodore Perry in Japan [1853]. 1974. Masonite, 20 × 26″. Collection Bob Guccione and Kathy Keeton, New York

Commodore Matthew C. Perry's expedition opens Japan's ports to American commerce. After meeting the Mikado's representatives, the Commodore and his men are feted enthusiastically. The little samurai (center foreground) is not a child but just a little samurai.

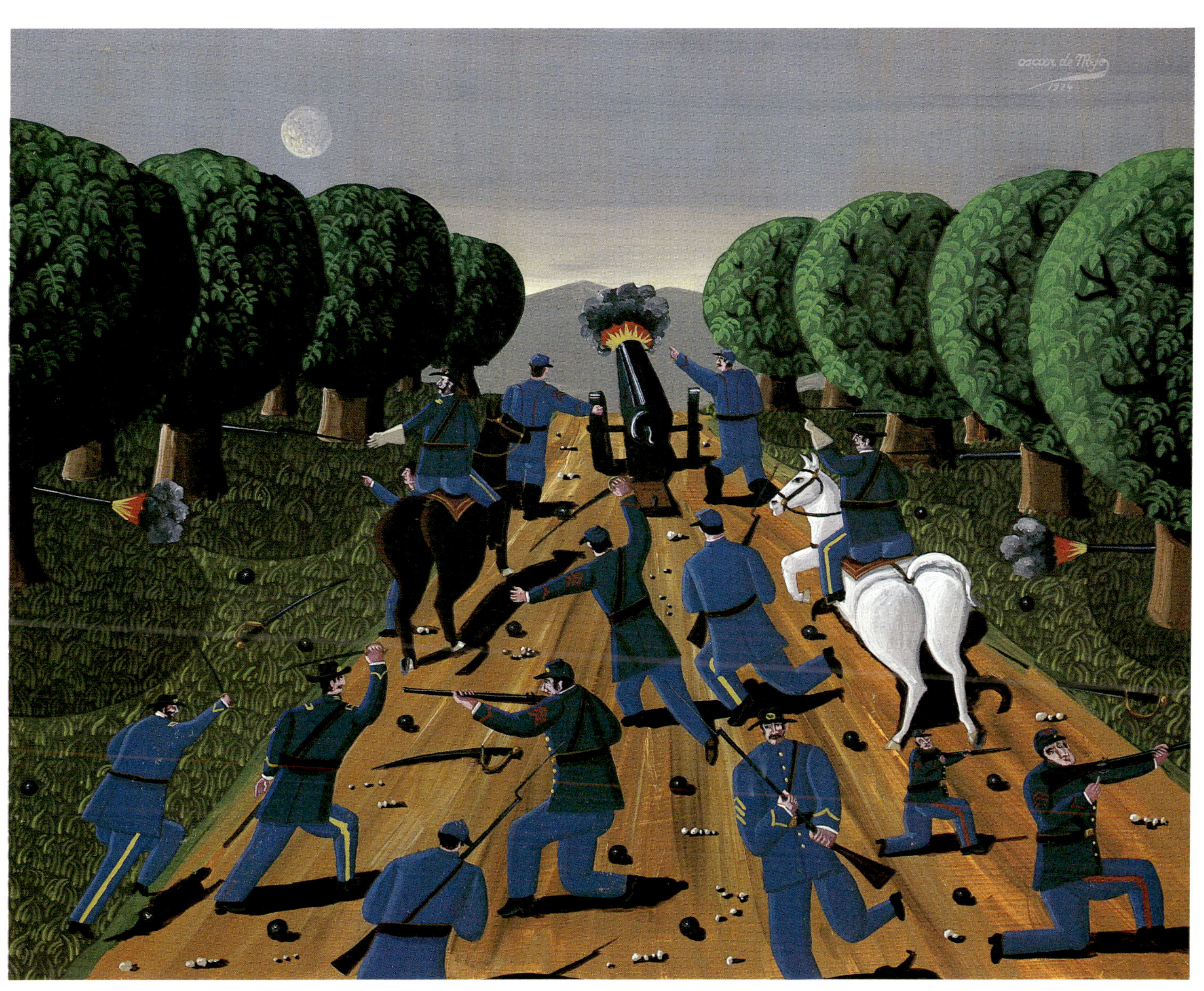

Incident at Bull Run [1861]. 1974. Masonite, 20 × 26″. Collection Bob Guccione and Kathy Keeton, New York

In the first battle of the Civil War, a group of Union soldiers is ambushed by Confederate sharpshooters.

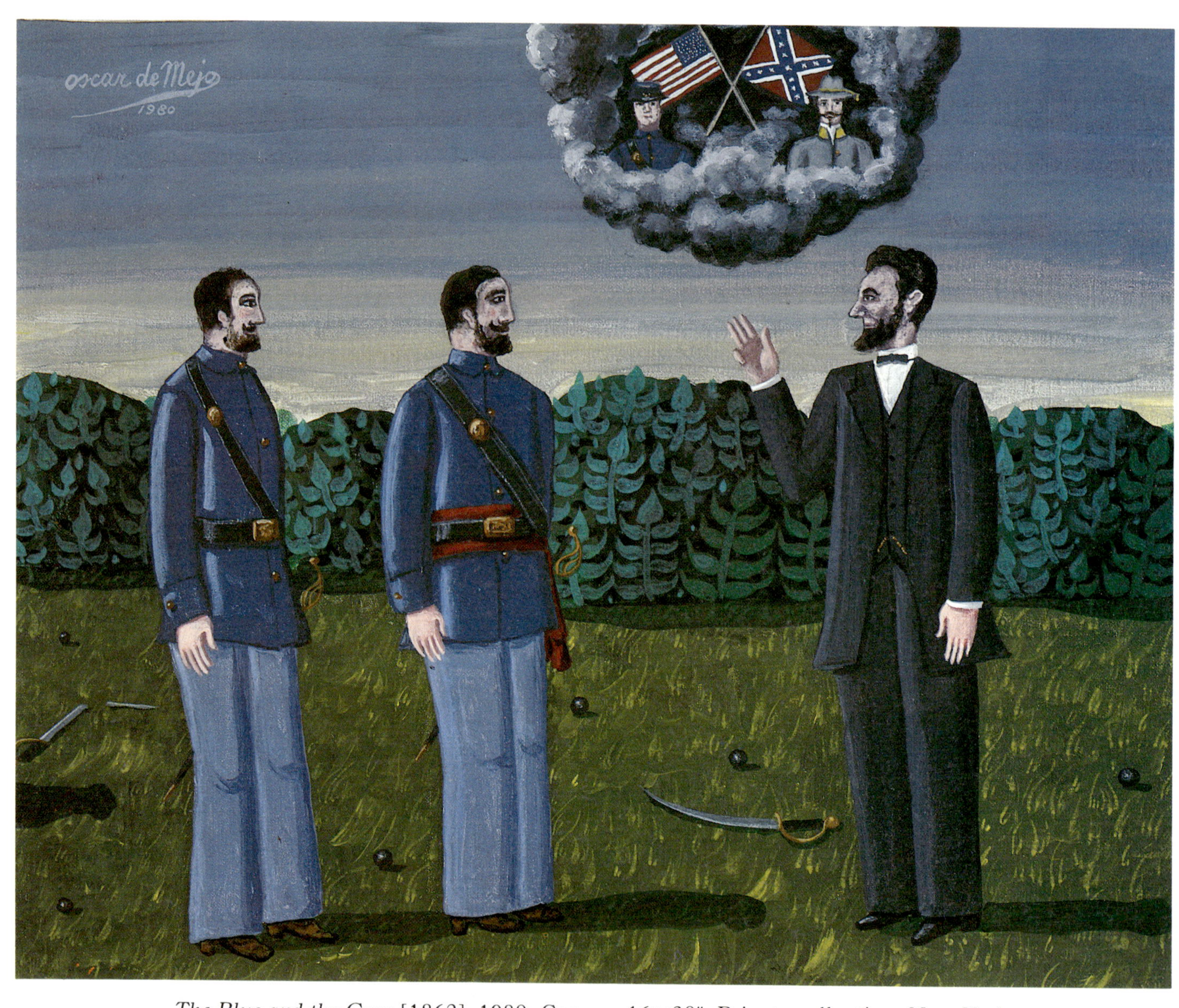

The Blue and the Gray [1862]. 1980. Canvas, 16 × 20″. Private collection, New York

Talking to two Union officers, President Lincoln reminds them that the Confederates they are fighting are after all their brothers. Victory must be won but hate must be banned.

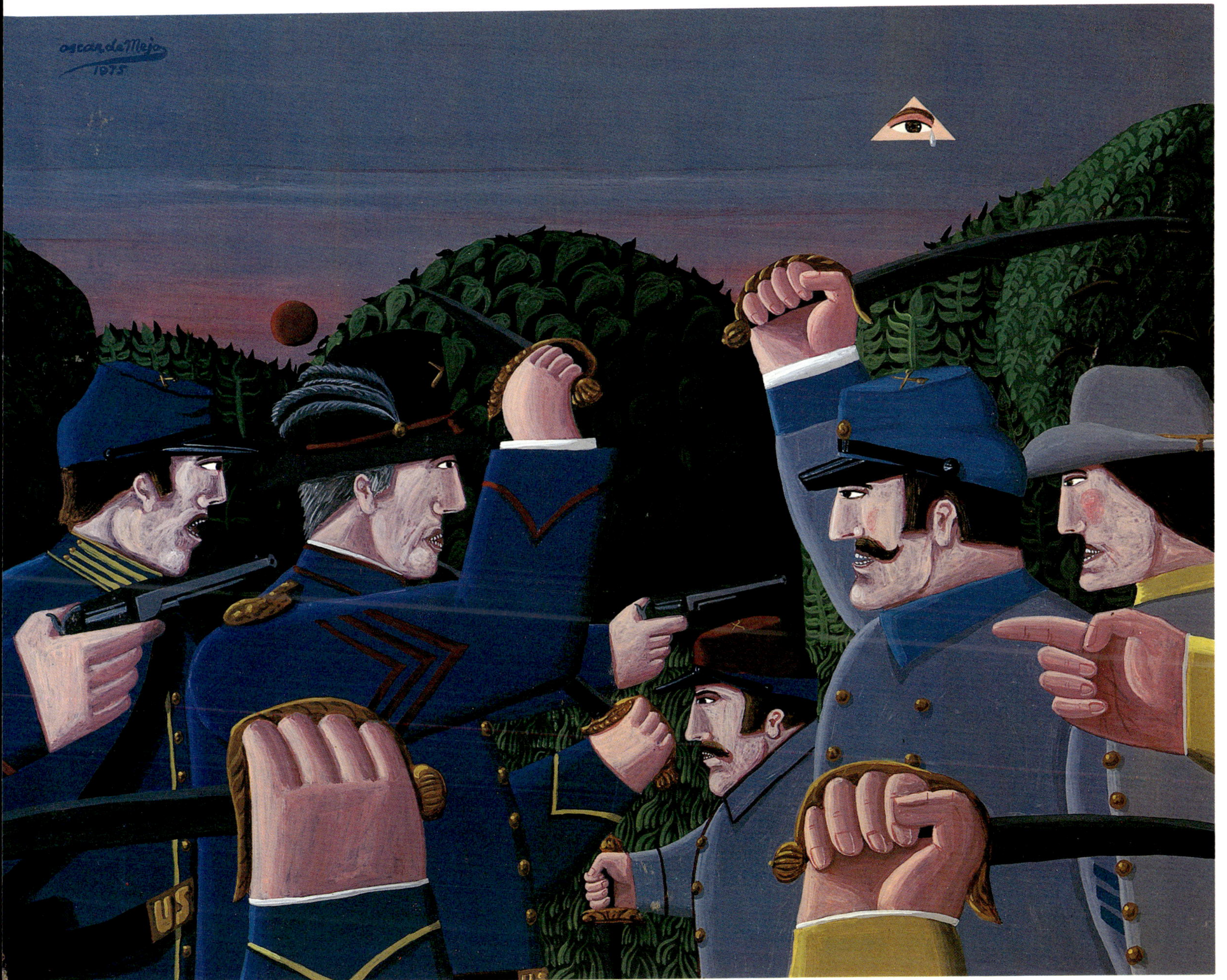

Antietam [1862]. 1975. Masonite, 20 × 26″. Collection Bob Guccione and Kathy Keeton, New York

Unionists led by General McLellan fight
the Confederates led by General Lee in
one of the bloodiest battles of the Civil
War. God, looking down at the slaughter,
cannot help shedding a tear.

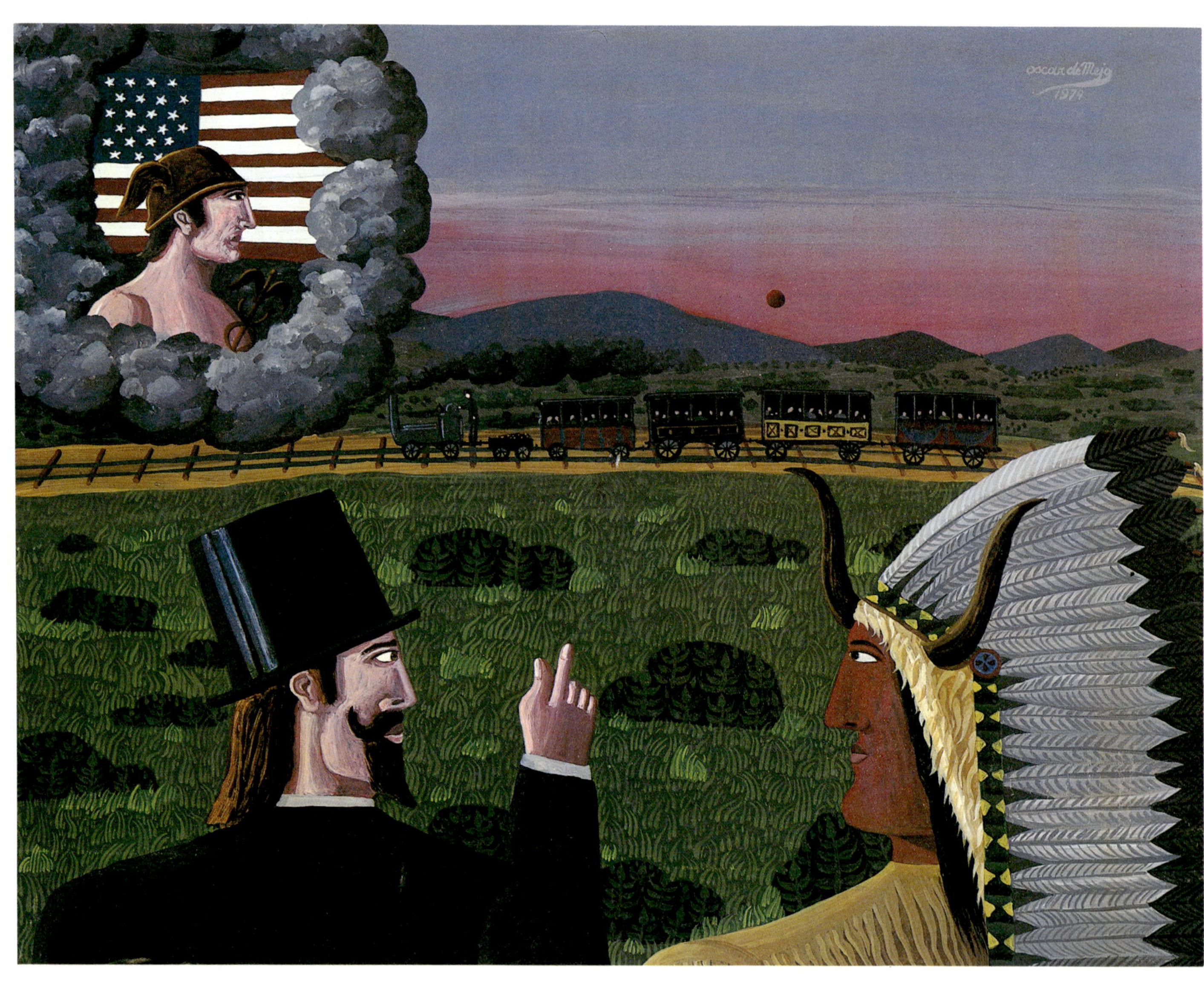

The Iron Horse [c. 1870]. 1974. Masonite, 20×26″. Collection Bob Guccione and Kathy Keeton, New York

An American businessman explains to an Indian chief the advantages of railroad train service. Mercury, the ancient God of Commerce (top left), looks on benignly.

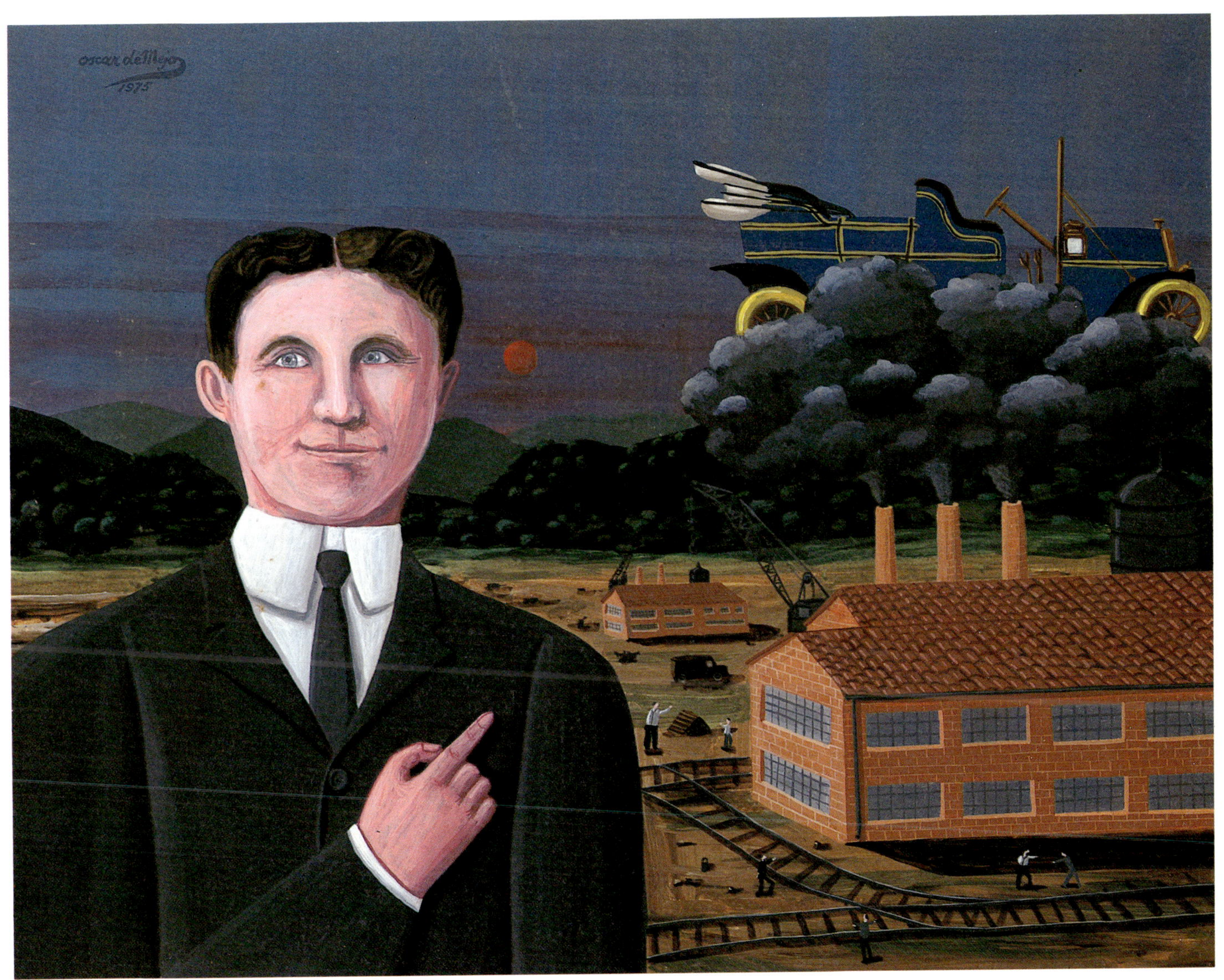

Ford and the Model T Car [1908]. 1975. Masonite, 20 × 26″. Collection Bob Guccione and Kathy Keeton, New York

Young Henry Ford makes history when he invents the Model T. From the hard work in the Dearborn factories emerges the glorious car which will revolutionize world transportation systems.

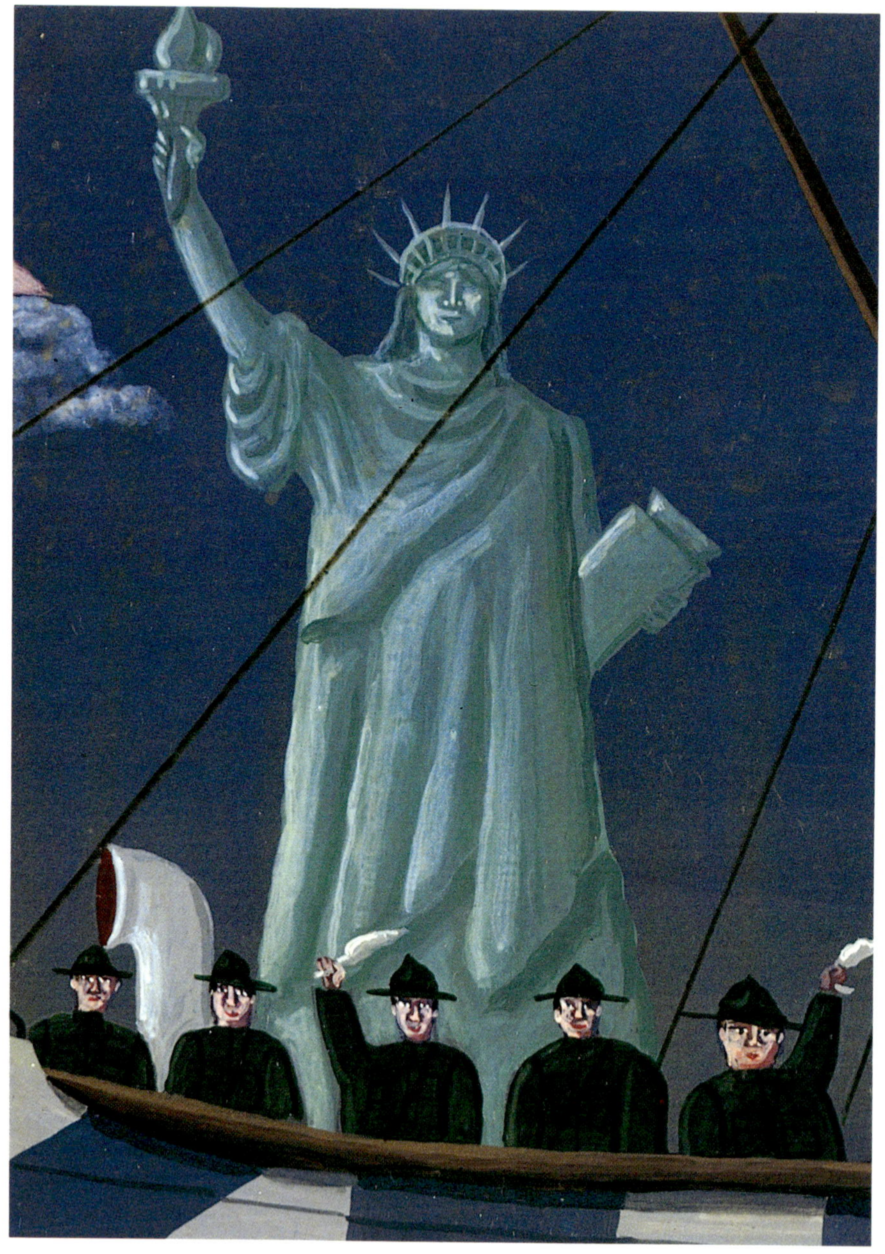

The Statue of Liberty looking at the soldiers leaving the Port of New York says: "Farewell and God bless you!" but God for the time being just says: "Over there!" A great American duty must be performed before God's wish—Peace—can be achieved.

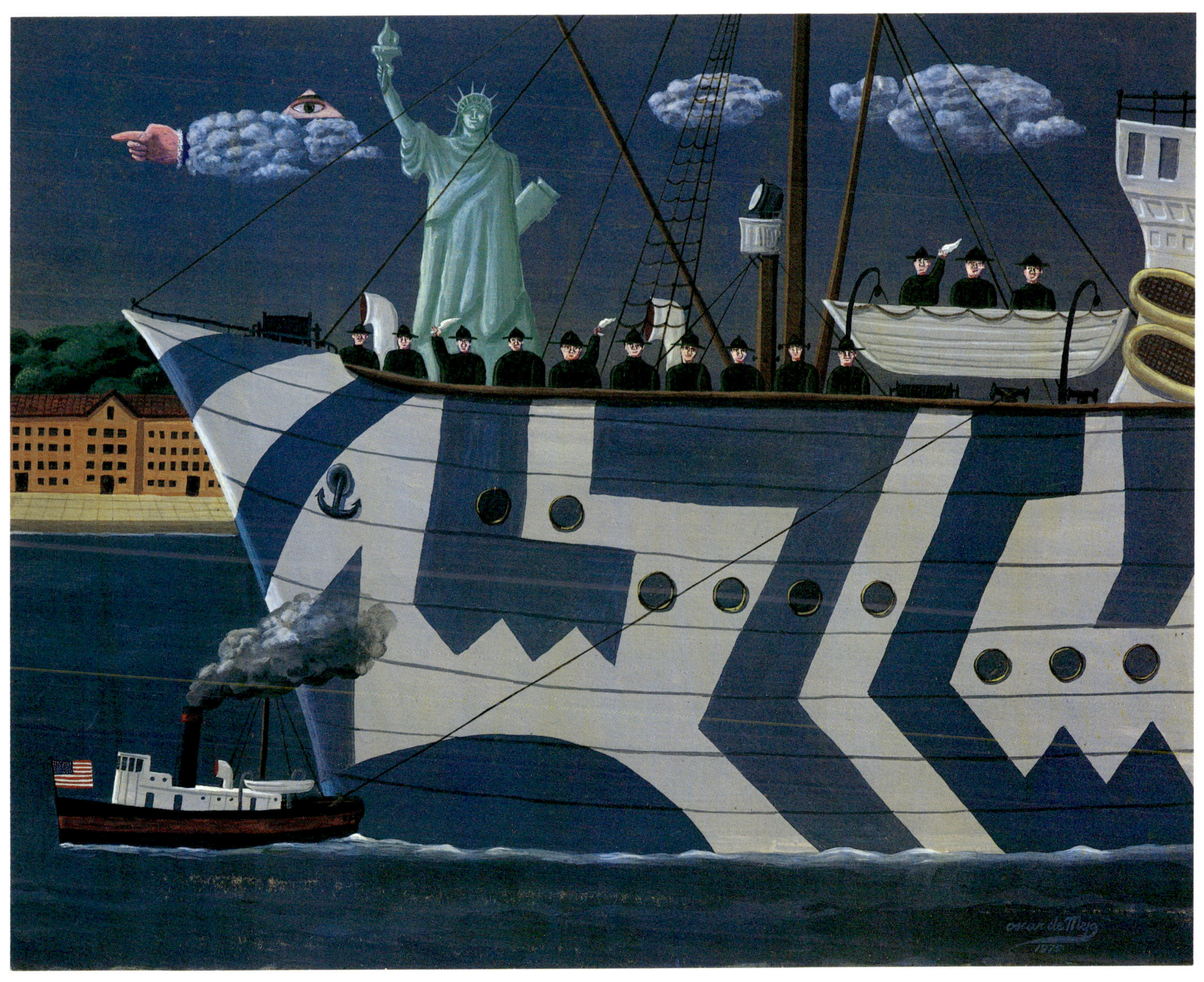

Over There [1917]. 1975. Masonite, 20×26″. Collection Bob Guccione and Kathy Keeton, New York

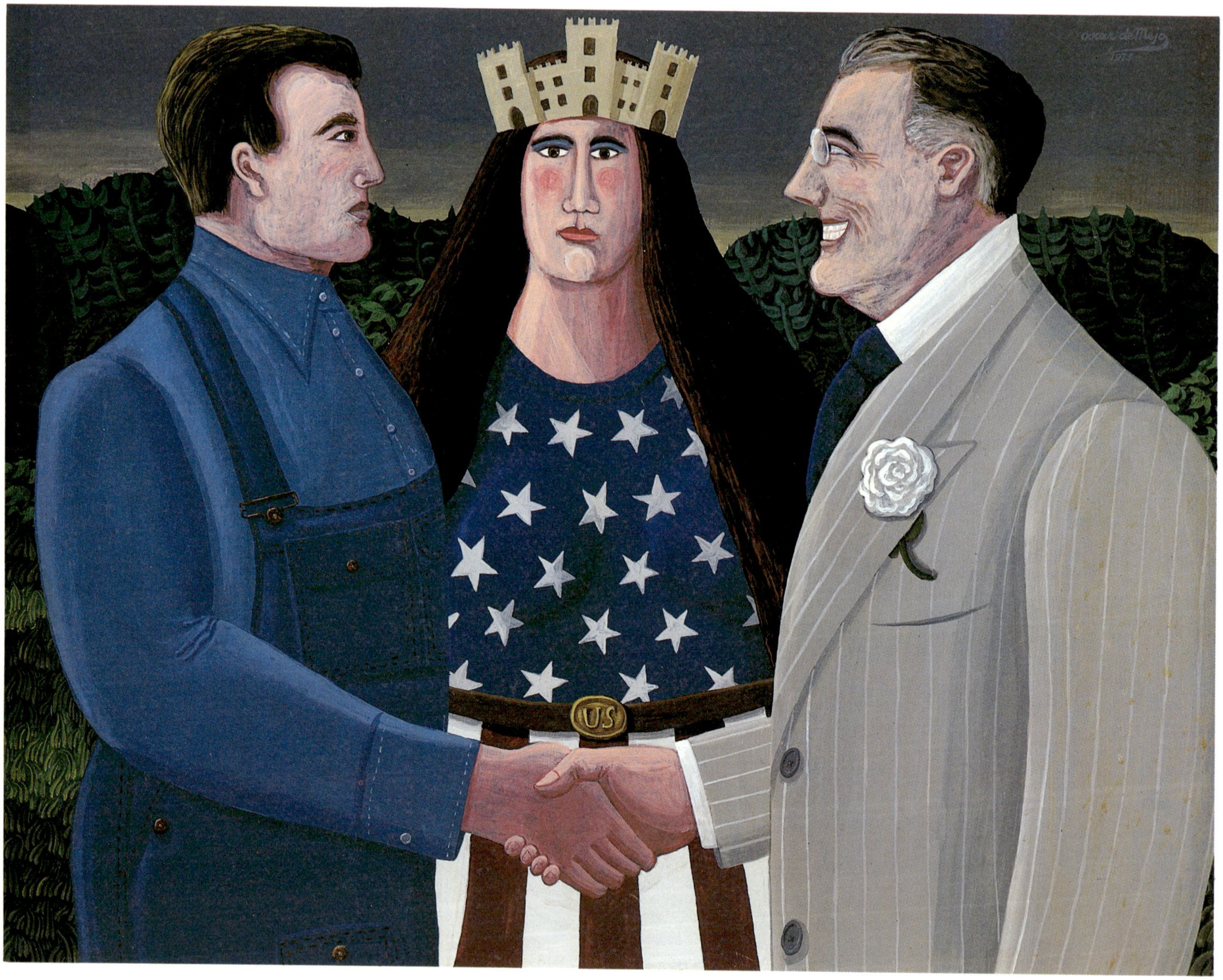

The New Deal [1933]. 1975. Masonite, 20 × 26″. Collection Bob Guccione and Kathy Keeton, New York

America feels strongly that this new President with his engaging smile will get along fine with the workers and will be a blessing for the Nation. Franklin D. Roosevelt is to guide the United States through twelve of the most critical years of its history.

BIOGRAPHICAL OUTLINE

1911	Born August 22 in Trieste, then in the Austro-Hungarian Empire, now Italy
1918–29	Attends elementary and high school in Trieste
1935	Takes law degree at University of Siena
1937	Takes degree in political and social sciences at University of Padua
1938–41	Works for insurance company in Trieste and Rome
1941–43	Works as analyst of film reviews for an Italian film distributor
1944	Marries actress Alida Valli (née Altenburger)
1945	First son, Carlo, born in Rome
1946	Leaves Italy for England
1947	Arrives in New York on January 1, proceeds to Hollywood
1949	Begins career as an artist in Hollywood with show at Taylor Galleries, Beverly Hills
1950	Second son, Lawrence, born in Santa Monica. First show in New York, at Carlebach Gallery
1951–60	Paints steadily. One-man shows at Cowie Galleries, Los Angeles; Santa Barbara Museum of Art; Palace of the Legion of Honor, San Francisco; Sagittarius Gallery, New York; Romi Gallery, Paris; Stendhal Gallery, Milan
1952	Becomes U.S. citizen
1953	Separates from Valli
1960–69	Conducts public relations business; paints in spare time
1967	Is divorced from Valli, marries dancer Dorothy Graham
1970	Goes to Italy with sponsorship of two Italian industrialists
1971	Shows at Levi Gallery in Milan
1972	Participates in various group shows, among them the Biennale of Art Naïf at the Lugano Museum, Switzerland. Show at the Galleria d'Arte dei Bibliofili, Milan. Becomes interested in historical subjects. Returns to U.S.
1973	Series of sixteen paintings on the American Revolution commissioned by Paul Foley, board chairman and president of the Interpublic Group of Companies. Twelve paintings on the history of the Italian Unification commissioned by Mondadori Editore, Italian publishing firm. Awarded the Medal "Ambrogino d'Argento" by the city of Milan

1974   Takes part in show "La Grande Domenica" at the Museo La Rotonda di Via Besana, Milan. "Five Great Moments in American History," series of five paintings, commissioned by Graphic Press New York. Series of eight paintings commissioned by Carlo Amato of Old World Gallery, New York, for Merck Sharp & Dohme, Belgium. Series of twenty-five paintings on the history of America commissioned by New York publisher Bob Guccione

1975   One-man show at Graham Gallery, New York. Series of eight paintings on sports in the American Revolutionary period commissioned by *Sports Illustrated* magazine. Shows American Revolution series at New World Pavilion, Hall of Presidents, in Jamestown, Virginia, April through August; at the Botetourt Gallery, College of William and Mary in Williamsburg, Virginia, September through October; at the Davlyn Gallery, New York, November 15 through December 1. Participates in show "Die Kunst der Naiven," November and December, 1974, at Haus der Kunst, Munich; February and March, 1975, at the Kunsthaus Zürich

1976   Series of fourteen paintings illustrating the story of the Harlem Globetrotters commissioned by Carlo Amato of the Old World Gallery for Metromedia; two lithographs commissioned by George Caspari, New York

1977   Series of paintings on the Kentucky Derby commissioned by *Sports Illustrated* magazine. *The Inauguration of George Washington* shown by Virginia Independence Bicentennial Commission at Yorktown Victory Center, April 1 to October 31. Group show, "Adam and Eve," at Portal Gallery, London

1978   Group show at Musée d'Art Naïf de l'Ile de France

1979   Participates with fifteen paintings in show "Patriotic Folk Art" at Yorktown Victory Center, Virginia, November 1979 through May 1980. Three original lithographs in group show "Into the '80s Collection" at Alex Rosenberg Gallery, New York, December 1979 through January 1980

1980   Four lithographs presented at New York Art Expo by Lublin Graphics. Cards with *The Red House* released in Europe by UNICEF

1981   Group show at Musée de l'Art Naïf, Vicq, France

1982   Group shows "Twentieth Century Images of George Washington" at Fraunces Tavern Museum, New York, February 1 through April 30, and "Le Génie des Naïfs" at Grand Palais des Champs-Elysées, Paris, April 14 through May 2

BIBLIOGRAPHY

Bihalji-Merin, Oto. *Die Malerei der Naiven*. Cologne: Verlag M. DuMont Schauberg, 1975, pp. 243, 244, 265.

———. *Masters of Naïve Art*. New York: McGraw-Hill, 1972, pp. 274, 294.

Blanchard, Roger. *La Chanson Traditionnelle et les Naïfs*. Paris: Art et Industrie, 1975, p. 339.

Blini, Livio, and Walter Carlino. *Naifs Italiani Oggi*. Milan: Edizione Seletecnica, 1974, pp. 31, 264, 265.

Bolaffi, Giulio. "Catalogo Nazionale dei Naifs n. 2." Turin: Giulio Bolaffi Editore, 1974, p. 59.

Catalogue, Haus der Kunst, Munich, for Nov. 1, 1974–Jan. 12, 1975, pp. 62, 551, 556.

Catalogue, Kunsthaus Zürich, for Jan. 30–March 31, 1975, pp. 54, 459, 464.

Comanducci, *Dizionario dei Pittori Italiani*. Milan: Patuzzi Editore, 1972.

De Mejo, Oscar. *Fresh Views of the American Revolution*. Paintings by Oscar de Mejo, notes and comments by Paul Foley. New York: Rizzoli International, 1976.

De Micheli, Mario, and Renzo Margonari. *I Naifs Italiani*. Parma: Passera & Agosta Tota Editori, 1972, pp. 146, 147.

Dizionario degli Artisti Italiani del Secolo. Turin: Giulio Bolaffi Editore, 1979, p. 121.

Fourny, Max. *Album Mondiale de La Peinture Naïve*. Paris: Editions Hervas, 1981, pp. 71, 195.

Graphis Annual 76/77, pp. 516, 517.

———, 77/78, p. 296.

———, 79/80, pp. 139, 140.

Catalogue, Musée International d'Art Naïf Anatole Jakovsky, 1982.

Jakovsky, Anatole. *Peintres Naïfs*. Basel: Basilius Presse, 1975, p. 186.

———. *Les Proverbes Vus par les Peintres Naïfs*. Paris: Art et Industrie, 1973, pp. 172, 173.

Margonari, Renzo. "Naifs?" *La Nazionale-Parma*, 1973, pp. 116–18, 172–74.

———. *Antologia dei Naifs Italiani*. Como: Casalino Editore, 1979, pp. 113–15.

Pauwels, Louis. *L'Arche de Noé et les Naïfs*. Paris: Art et Industrie, 1977, pp. 214, 215.

Renard, Hélène. *Le Rêve et les Naïfs*. Paris: Max Fourny, 1981, pp. 144, 145.

Rodman, Selden. *The Eye of Man*. New York: Devin Adair, 1955, p. 11.

Wiesmer, Herbert. *Naive Malerei Heute*. Pfarrkirchen, Germany: W. Laumer, 1981, pp. 205, 206, 217.

INDEX OF ILLUSTRATIONS

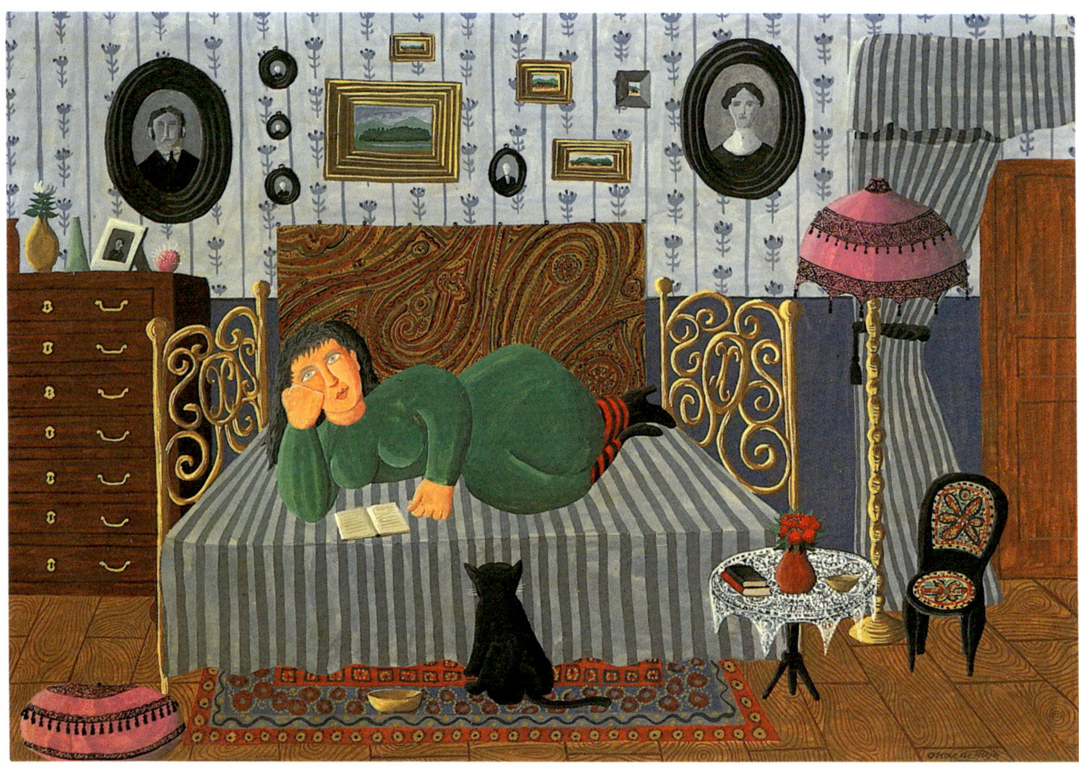

The Brass Bed. 1950. Tempera on wood, 10 × 14″. Collection Gwyneth Alexander, Philadelphia

PHOTOCREDITS

Eeva-Inkeri: 3, 7, 10, 11, 14, 18, 19, 31, 34, 35, 39–41, 44–46, 50, 53–55, 58–60, 62, 63, 67–71, 74–76, 85, 88, 89, 91, 94–96, 105–114; Roy Elkind: 73, 77–83, 87, 90, 92–93, 97, 103, 104; Bruce C. Jones: 84, 86, 100–102; Sylvia Sarner: 6, 37, 38, 42, 47, 51, 61, 64–66; Manu Sassoonian: 48, 49; *Sports Illustrated*: 56, 57